THE WEEKEND GARDENER

MONTAGU DON

First published in Great Britain 1995
Bloomsbury Publishing Plc,
2 Soho Square, London W1V 6HB

Text copyright © 1995 Montagu Don
Design copyright © 1995 Bloomsbury
Publishing Plc

The moral right of the author has been
asserted

A CIP catalogue record for this book is
available from the British Library

ISBN 0 7475 2012 7

10 9 8 7 6 5 4 3 2 1

Printed by Oriental Press Ltd

Designed by Bradbury and Williams
Edited by Caroline Taggart

PICTURE SOURCES

Heather Angel: *title spread*, 11, 18, 22, 38,
41, 42, 46, 62, 67, 69, 74, 75, 88, 91, 95
(Nigel Philips), 96, 98, 102, 110, 111, 116,
117, 120, 138, 141, 144, 145, 160, 162, 166
bottom, 168, 172, 174, 175, 176, 178, 182;
Aquila Photographics: 27 (S.C. Harrison),
132 (Anthony Cooper), 155 (S.C. Harrison);
Ardea London: 121, 148 (Ake Lindau), 163,
171 (Richard Vaughan), 184, 185 (A.P.
Paterson); Collections: 127 (Michael Allen);
The Garden Picture Library: 52 (Brian
Carter, *all three pictures*), 135 (J.S. Sira);
Garden/Wildlife Matters: 73, 107, 113; John
Glover Photography: 13, 19, 28, 32, 39, 45,
47, 48, 49, 51, 56, 60, 61, 70, 71, 77, 83,
86, 89, 93, 97, 99, 101, 103, 108, 114, 119,
125, 126, 130, 131, 133, 134, 137 *left*, 143
left, 146, 149, 157, 158, 166 *top and centre*,
173, 183; Holt Studios International: 33
(Nigel Catlin), 109 (Nigel Catlin), 140 (Bob
Gibbons), 159 (Nigel Catlin); Andrew
Lawson Photography: 122/3, 169; S.& O.
Mathews Photography: 40, 81; John Price
Studios: *half title*, 7, 16, 17, 31, 37, 82, 105,
115, 137 *right*, 143 *right*, 150, 153, 181.

Illustrations by Kevin Hart

ACKNOWLEDGEMENTS

This book was written whilst I was travelling
a great deal and involved in many other
projects. Only extreme tolerance from all at
Bloomsbury have allowed me to get away with
such a complicated schedule. I owe a special
debt to Roy Williams and Caroline Taggart,
who designed and edited the book respec-
tively and who tolerated my hopelessly erratic
and chaotic schedule with constant good
humour and invaluable advice.

But greatest gratitude must go to my wife
Sarah and my children, who put up with a
husband and father away for half the time and
locked away in his study for the other half,
obsessed by 'that bloody book'. I hope it was
worth it.

CONTENTS

INTRODUCTION

When I was in the middle of this book I met a friend that I had not seen for some while and in the course of catching up with each other's activities I described, at some length, what I was writing. 'Oh,' he said succinctly, 'so you are writing a book about gardening for nice, clever people who are crap at gardening.' Exactly.

To put it slightly more politely, this book is intended for people who have a garden, who like gardens but do not do much gardening and are perhaps not even sure if they want to do any gardening. It is for people who make difficult and sophisticated choices about what they eat, about the clothes they buy, about films, books and a thousand other aspects of their lives, but who when it comes to gardens feel ignorant and inadequate.

I realise that for most people gardening is an intimidating business. For gardeners gardening is nearly always specific: even when you potter you do so purposefully, tying a branch in here, pulling a weed there. But most people are not gardeners, including the majority of those with gardens. Learning to garden is rather like learning a new language: too much talk of the heights of expression it can reach simply adds to the bewilderment and frustration if you are still struggling in the foothills of vocabulary and grammar. Yet a diet of pure grammar is indigestible – as so many dreary gardening books and television programmes attest.

I hope that this book will fire you to garden and convince you that there are few areas of human activity that can be as creative or as pleasurable, but with all the enthusiasm in the world, I can-

not make more time for you. That, and money, are always the big limitations on what you can achieve. However, *The Weekend Gardener* should enable you to use what time you do have efficiently and in the best possible way.

I am a self-taught gardener and have always done many other things than just garden. Like everybody else, I have very limited time to spare. So although my advice might not prove to be ideal for you, at least you know that it is born of the hands-on experience of someone living in the real world.

The book is really a calendar. One of the big problems of trying to be specific about what or what not to do in the garden at any given point in the calendar is that the weather in Britain can vary so dramatically from year to year and county to county, let alone between the Shetland and Scilly Isles.

I have tried to counter this by breaking each month into two weekends. I have not prescribed which weekends they are within the month, although there is a general assumption that the first weekend is in the first half of the month and the second one in the second half. But it does not matter. If you find a job assigned to a particular month, do not be too literal about it. Unless I say that you should *not* do something at a particular time, the best time to do anything in the garden is when you are in a position to do it properly. Plants survive and prosper in the weirdest situations after the most unorthodox treatment. This book is intended to inspire and guide you, not to lay down the law.

Do the work when you have time to do it. The difference between two weekends in March might be enormous. Outside my window as I write (in early March) it is the most gorgeous spring day imaginable. This time last

week there were 15cm (6in) of snow on the ground. Heavy frosts are forecast for the end of the week. There is no way that we can tie the weather to fit a neat pattern.

However, if you can find the time to spend two lots of two hours a month in the garden and you use this book to suit your own particular ends, then I believe that you can make a very beautiful garden.

I am not saying that you will not have to work at it. Anyone who promises you a lovely garden without any effort is a charlatan. As far as I am concerned, one of the great pleasures of gardening is that it includes strenuous physical activity outside in the fresh air. Even the sweatiest garden job is relaxing and a great release from the stresses of modern life. Get stuck in and you will be amazed at how much you can achieve in a very short time. Once the garden is made, the work diminishes enormously. Regular weeding, pruning and general care will keep it ticking over for years.

If you have the opportunity, twenty minutes a day, three days a week, is much better than one session of two hours a fortnight. Not all the jobs outlined in this book need as much as two hours, some need much more. Use your common sense.

In the end gardening has to be fun or it becomes just another domestic chore, like washing up or making the bed. Find an aspect of gardening that makes you happy – independent of what it looks like – and you will be hooked for life. And that is a promise.

Don't be intimidated by your garden. Learn a few basics, give it whatever time you can, and you will soon learn to love it.

PLANNING

Gardens are not immutable forces of nature. They are entirely man-made artefacts which, if not blank canvases, are at least very adaptable.

Which is why planning really means design, inasmuch that to get the most out of a garden, whatever its position or size, you must take the time to think what you want.

In the next few pages I shall outline some design ideas, but the principles of planning the garden remain the same whatever you decide to do.

GETTING TO KNOW YOUR GARDEN

The first stage of the planning process is to take stock of what is already there. This is straightforward enough, but must be done systematically and accurately if it is to be of any use. Really look at the garden, and at the other gardens around yours. Take stock of the differences and the similarities. The design similarities are probably banal – a lawn, path, some shrubs and tired climbers, perhaps a mass of flowers that you could not possibly name. No matter. Be critical. Make a mental note of what you like and don't like and do not worry about names. All that will come later. Notice the effect of the various parts of your garden, from the shadow cast in the evening by a new fence around an utterly bare new plot to the shade of a mature tree in a garden hundreds of years old. See it all with bright, seeing eyes.

Get a compass and find out the garden's orientation. One of the first things a gardener wants to know from a garden is where the sun rises and sets. This, more than any other single factor,

will influence what you plant and how your garden grows.

When you have had a good look, do something about it. Measure it. This is an incredibly good way of becoming acquainted with an object. I remember hearing that Henry Moore went through a phase of guessing the size of the heads of people he met and then measuring them to see how accurate his guess had been. The landscape architect Sir Geoffrey Jellicoe travelled through Italy as a student visiting gardens, each one of which he paced out, measured exactly and then drew. He said that this meant that he literally trod every inch of every garden and became intimate with it. You should pore over your garden like lovers relishing every inch of each other's bodies. Become intimate with it.

Commit that intimacy to paper. Use squared paper, preferably A3. Draw the garden at a scale of 1:100. This is made much easier by metrification because you simply draw 1cm for every metre measured.

It is obviously best to measure as accurately as you can, using a long tape measure. But Sir Geoffrey Jellicoe produced immensely detailed plans of large and complicated gardens using his shoe as a measurement of a foot and a pace as a yard.

The art of surveying a garden is to keep everything firmly fixed to known relatives like buildings, paths or fences. Otherwise you can measure everything accurately and still have the garden swimming around the paper hopelessly adrift from reality.

Start with the house and mark in all the pertinent factors, including doors, windows, manhole covers, vents, and

importance of access. Then use the house as a base point and measure out at 90° from each of the points you have marked until you hit a relevant object, be it a bush, tree, path, lawn or whatever. This relates the horticultural object to the house. Now measure the bush tree or whatever it is. If it is a tree, remember to measure its canopy too – i.e. the shape and diameter of its branches. When you have measured everything relevant that falls in 90° lines from the house, your next step is to triangulate objects to get their accurate relative position. This is easy. All it means is that you cross reference each measurement back to another already established position set at an angle to it. In practice you can often use the same triangulation point for most other measurements.

In a small garden this is no problem, as there are enough points like fences, buildings or steps within easy measuring distance. But in a larger garden you

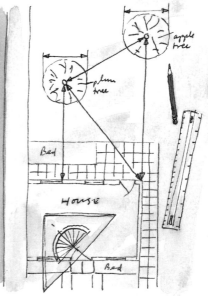

Draw a plan of your garden, marking in all the major features. This will enable you to establish the relative positions of each object accurately.

will have to stick canes in the ground as useful triangulation points. These are best put at 90° from the corner of the house (something you can very easily establish by eye).

A hint: unless you have a very small, undeveloped garden to measure, transfer measurements to the final plan in instalments, while they are still fresh in your mind. Otherwise you end up with a scrumpled up, scruffy piece of paper covered in marks that you have no memory of ever making.

It is always surprising to see the garden committed to an accurate plan, particularly if you do not have a high vantage point from which to look down on the real thing. The eye makes all kinds of concessions to reality that are ruthlessly exposed in a plan. An area that feels big can be measured to be pokey and a tree that is always though to be 'at the end of the garden' can have a canopy that almost reaches to the house.

Clearly mark where north is on the plan so that you can relate how much sunlight each part of the garden will receive.

THE DESIGN STAGE

The next step is the creative one. Tape the measured plan to a board and then overlay it with tracing paper. (If you are not familiar with using tracing paper, do not skimp on the quality – get a pad of heavy sheets. They are deliciously opulent in feel and somehow add import to the whole proceedings.) Take a pencil and rubber and start working out ideas on the tracing paper. The existing garden showing through gives you a framework and keeps a sense of proportion.

As you draw ideas, go outside and try and visualise them. Use string or planks or cardboard boxes to act as hedges, paths, or plants. The ability to visualise accurately is a faculty that I believe can be developed through usage. There are fancy computer programs that will take your plan and make an elevation from it but the best bit of software in the world is clumsy compared to the mind's ability to conjure images.

West-facing:
The next best position. Receives warm sunshine from mid-afternoon until dusk. The windiest position.

North-facing:
Total shade. Unless you are exposed to north winds, it can be very sheltered.

South-facing:
The most sunshine. From mid-morning till mid-afternoon.

East-facing:
Only receives cold, morning sun. Total shade from midday on. Very bad for tender plants.

We all have that ability.

The first things to establish are the practical logistics of the garden. Ignore aesthetics for the moment and deal with the mundane imperatives. How do you get to the back door? How do you move from the back door to the end of the garden? Where will you sit? How much sun does it get and is it sunny at a time of day when you are likely to be sitting there? Where will the compost heap be? How will you get there? Will you have to cross the lawn regularly, and if so would it be better to have a path bisecting it? If you do not want this, might it be best to make it impos-sible to cross the lawn by putting in a hedge or border to block the route? And so on.

A beautiful garden is useless if it is impractical. But you can make the practicalities suit your life with all its idiosyncrasies and foibles. If you change, the garden can easily be changed with you. To be meaningful, the garden must reflect you and the things that make you different from other people, not conform to a set of patterns and rules. Don't be boring!

When you have decided what you want to do you must transfer your design to the ground. I call this process Stringing Out and find it incredibly satisfying. Get hold of a bundle of canes and a decent sized ball of thick twine. Saw the canes into 60cm (2ft) lengths. You will need a cane for every corner on your plan.

Stick a cane wherever your plan indicates a corner or bend of any kind and stretch the twine between the canes, making sure that it is kept taut. Keep referring to the plan, measuring everything off it.

As you put the canes in and as the string is drawn from stick to stick, the future garden comes alive.

If possible, look at it from an upstairs window. It is as though you had laid some tracing paper over the garden itself and superimposed your plan.

Now it is important to do nothing for at least a week. Live with what you have done. You are bound to discover problems that need adjusting. Paths will be too narrow or an area for which you had great ideas will prove to be absurdly limited. Fiddle with the canes and strings until it feels right. Let this take as long as it needs: trust your instincts.

Then, when you are ready, the gardening can begin.

FORMAL GARDEN DESIGN

Until well into the eighteenth century in this country, Nature was seen as a threatening, untamed place inherently hostile to man. Houses and gardens were a refuge, imposing order upon a chaotic, untamed wilderness. Therefore gardens became as formal and strictly controlled as man could make them. Retreats of elegance and beauty were carved out of the surrounding landscape.

It is tempting to see the modern urban world as a similar kind of wild, barbarian threat prowling around our households and an ordered, formal garden as a counterbalance to that. The formal garden becomes a kind of oasis of measured calm in a frantic world.

Formality has many aesthetic virtues. It brings rhythm and balance to the garden. It imposes a structure within which plants can perform unfettered. And because it relies so much on design and shape it tends to look good the year round rather than giving one blazing performance in high summer.

The practical advantages are there, too. The formal garden can be extremely easy to maintain, relying on a few simple tidying operations every month and some trimming and pruning once a year. Tough and reliable plants can be used to achieve the required effect, so that you are not dependent upon great horticultural skill or learning. You can see how the historical lessons of the formal garden can be very attractive to the modern weekend gardener.

So what are these lessons?

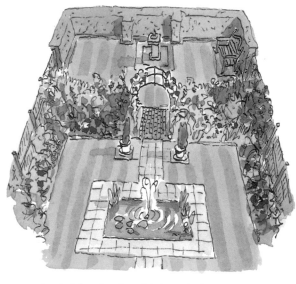

A typical formal garden, with the emphasis on symmetry.

STRUCTURE AND FORM

The formal garden is invariably subdivided into small rectangular or square units. These might be borders or just areas of grass bounded by hedges or lines of trees.

Symmetry is very important. Wherever possible this symmetry is dictated by the house, so a path will run in a straight line from a door flanked by equal spaces.

Structure and form are as important as colour. Many wonderful formal gardens are almost entirely green. Far from being boring, this can have an incredibly complex and subtle make-up,

GETTING PLANTS INTO SHAPE

AN IMPORTANT FEATURE IS THE CLIPPING AND PRUNING OF PLANTS. THIS IS CONSISTENT WITH THE DESIRE TO TAME NATURE, BUT HAS EVOLVED INTO A CREATIVE FORM IN ITS OWN RIGHT. IT INCLUDES THE TRIMMING OF HEDGES, TOPIARY, ESPALIERED FRUIT TREES, TREES PLEACHED AND CLIPPED INTO STANDARDS, BOX BALLS AND CONES, MOWN GRASS, AND CLIMBING PLANTS TRAINED UP TRELLISES, PERGOLAS AND PYRAMIDS.

using grass, hedging, leaves and trees to build your picture.

The garden should be viewable in plan. In simplest terms this means a viewpoint from an upstairs window, although in the seventeenth and early eighteenth century most drawing rooms – from which the garden would have been viewed – were on the first floor, looking down on the garden. In modern terms this may also mean creating some sort of viewpoint within the garden so that you can look down on it.

The garden is always conceived as a whole, even though it may be subdivided into small sections. Every part must relate in some way to every other part. The most obvious relationship is visual, with paths leading from section to section and sections with different planting schemes or orientations sharing a similar size or backdrop. The connection may be thematic or it may simply be that the same kind of hedging surrounds each area. It whatever way it is expressed, there is unity in design.

If you starting a garden from scratch and know that you do not have the time or money – or perhaps inclination – to get too involved with the problems of planting and maintenance, and yet want to have a garden to enjoy, there is much to be said for laying out the framework with hedges and trees and filling the spaces between them with grass. This can be cut once a week and the hedges trimmed once a year. If you go away for weeks at a time the worst that can happen is that the grass will be a little longer than usual. In winter it will look much the same as in high summer. You will have walks and places to sit and be able to match the garden mature without any pressing gardening duties.

If at a later date you decide you need flowers and wish to expand you gardening horticultural horizons, all you have to do is dig up the grass where you want to make borders, by which time the hedges will have grown sufficiently to provide shelter and a visual background.

FEATURES AND FOCAL POINTS

Views and vistas are vital to formal gardening, even in the smallest back yard. Paths are the easiest way to achieve this, but they must lead to a focal point. In the larger garden, gates or a doorway are the ideal end point of a path, inviting you to go through and yet keeping the uninvited world at bay. Or you can fit in a doorway against the wall that leads nowhere – other than in the imagination. Just because a garden is formal it does not mean that it cannot be quirky and playful. The formality is in the framework, not the contents.

In a very small garden a pot set in a niche created by flanking shrubs can be enough to focus the eye. So might a seat at the end of a path, drawing you down to it with a view back along the same route once you reach there.

Water has always played an important role in formal gardening. Its flat surface constantly reflecting shifting images is exactly the right marriage of rigidity and change that this type of gardening embodies. Ponds need to be restricted to symmetrical, geometric shapes. Long thin canals work ex-

tremely well, as do raised ponds. The edges must always be bounded by a hard surface and the planting within the pond kept simple, even austere. Let the water do the work rather than cluttering it up. Fountains inevitably look good (if kept simple) and even tiny trickles of water caught in a small container attached to a wall will make all the difference to the atmosphere.

The final components of the formal garden that always look good are sculptures, pots or any non-plant objects that you can contemplate or be surprised by. The idea is to make it a place where humans and nature can live in controlled harmony – which is perhaps the perfect definition of gardening.

Part of the 'colour garden' at Crathes Castle, near Aberdeen, showing clipped yew hedges arranged formally around a square pond.

COTTAGE GARDENING

Cottage gardens evoke a loose, informal, blowzy style of gardening, with roses scrambling around the windows and the garden path flanked by pinks, sweet William, snapdragons, hollyhocks, delphiniums, lupins, phlox and all the flowers that we think of as typically English. It is a style that has become identified with charm, innocence and a sense of abandonment.

But cottage gardens evolved out of harsh necessity. Only poor people lived in a cottage. The gardens were small and very often in front of the house. The cottagers had no money, little space and even less leisure time. They had to grow vegetables to live and used every spare inch of available ground to do so. Because they were human beings rather than mere beasts of burden, they needed colour and beauty as well, so they slipped the odd flower in amongst the veg. The result was a utilitarian jumble with a heavy stress on fruit and veg and the only grass being on narrow paths to get at the crops. What we now call 'cottage gardening' is a romanticised version of gardening born of hardship.

Having got that bit of social history out of the way, it is a perfectly good idea to use that background in a modern setting.

One of the features of cottage gardens is that they grew organically. They were never planned or designed. It seems to me that this is the most useful inheritance from this tradition for the modern gardener. If you can abandon all the clutter of Design with a capital 'D' and let the garden grow up around

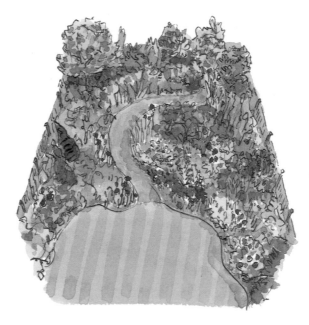

A modern cottage garden, densely planted to save on maintenance.

you organically, then you will save a lot of angst and tap into a much looser, freer form of creativity. You plant according to the dictates of surrounding plants and your own intuition, mixing shrubs, flowers, herbs, fruit and vegetables in an entirely unstructured way. This takes confidence and courage, but the results are both truly modern and much more like old-fashioned cottage gardening. It is also absolutely in line with contemporary organic theory. By planting the garden as a happy jumble you are avoiding the concentration of pests and diseases that monoculture encourages (see pages 112-113 on 'Companion Planting').

The biggest single influence on old-fashioned cottage gardens was geology. The soil dictated what people grew just as it influenced the type of house they lived in. So in chalk areas they lived in flint and brick cottages and grew lime-loving plants such as beech, peonies, clematis, pinks and potentilla, whereas in areas of peat they would often have stone or brick-built cottages with gardens filled with plants like heathers, camellias, lupins, lilies and trilliums.

On top of this there was the consideration of the type of soil – if it was clay you would have a very different garden than if it was a light, sandy loam.

In other words the garden does not fight circumstances. It goes with whatever flow happens to dominate. All formal gardening and most modern gardening has tended away from this, to an imposition of a 'style' chosen by the gardener and thrust upon the garden. Cottage gardening is far more intuitive and responsive to nature.

A MODERN COTTAGE GARDEN

The first essential of cottage gardening is the intensity of planting. Space is at a premium, so the majority of the garden is cultivated. This might seem to go against the underlying principle of a book like this – that one wants maximum effect for minimum effort – but once the garden is created and planted it will largely look after itself. A labour-saving way of establishing large borders which does away with the need for serious digging is to spray the existing vegetation with a glysophate weed-killer (which kills only green vegetation and does not harm the soil) and cover the ground with a thick – at least 15cm (6in) – layer of organic material. This should ideally be manure or compost, but straw or hay will do in the long run. One plants through this layer, digging only when you plant something. The mulch will stop the weeds growing and earthworms will gradually incorporate the layer into the soil. Very soon the plants will grow and create ground cover.

The second rule of cottage gardening is attention to individual plants rather than to the overall design. The needs of each plant are met before the needs of the garden are considered. At worst this makes an ugly mess. At best it creates a composition of great natural charm. To do this successfully you have to have a kind of humility: you cannot impose yourself too much on the plants. Help them to do what they do best and stand back to admire. But it is essential to pack every spare inch with plants. As soon as you have 'specimens' surrounded by grass or any open space,

then the charm is lost and a big yawn takes over. Plants should spill over every path, clamber up every wall or fence, drip into every open window. There must be a sense of the plants taking over the garden.

It is a mistake to be too swirly in your layout of the cottage garden. In order to let the plants have full rein and romp as they must it is a good idea to keep paths straight and borders rectangular. The outline is softened by herbage and the eye does not have to be over busy, which would spoil the overall haphazard effect.

As well as the structure made by flowering shrubs, climbers, hedges and perennials, annuals and biennials of all kinds are terribly important for this

style of gardening. They are cheap – dozens costing just the price of a packet of seed – invariably grow fast, have vivid flowers and can be used to fill gaps to maintain the intense level of planting that is necessary.

The cottage garden should not be a historic reconstruction. That might be an interesting academic exercise but it is not creative. Avoid laboriously using old-fashioned plants and poring over idealised Victorian paintings of cottages. Trust your intuition and instincts – let the garden grow and flow around you, cramming it with plants in an unstructured but sensitive muddle.

A cottage-style garden in Dorset. Again, note the way lots of plants are packed into a limited space.

TOOLS

The best and most versatile tool a gardener has are his or her hands. I use mine to plant, weed, thin, pick, tie and stake. They are adaptable, quickly becoming hardened to wear and tear, self-repairing and always, so to speak, to hand. Use them with vigour and relish.

However, there are times when hands are not enough. I love using the right tool for the job and collect old garden hand tools because of the specific application of craftsmanship to function. There is a sensuous harmony and balance between hand and instrument when you use a good tool properly. So choose your tools with care, in the same way that you might choose a hat or a pair of walking shoes. It must feel right.

The first thing every gardener needs is a **spade**.

There are two main types of spade – the digging spade and border spade. The latter is smaller than the former and used for working within the confines of a planted border. The best spades are made of stainless steel. These cost about five times as much as an ordinary cheapo spade and are about ten times better. There is no single better investment for the garden than a stainless steel spade. It is a joy to use, never sticks in heavy soil and should last fifty years.

You will also need a **fork**.

As with spades, there are digging forks and border forks. A border fork is even more useful than a border spade, as it can be used for weeding. Forks come with various degrees of curve to their tines

(the prongs) which can also be rounded or square sectioned. Go by feel. A **manure fork** is useful for turning and forking compost. This has thinner, longer round tines with sharp points.

A **shovel** is invaluable for general work. A builder's shovel with a solid steel handle is cheap, indestructible and good.

As a rule it is better to use wooden handles, preferably made of English ash. A wooden handle is cheap and easy to replace if it breaks, and it feels good to the skin.

There are three types of handle – D, Y & T. These describe the shape of the hilt. T handles are common on the Continent, but tiring for repeated use. I prefer Y types, made from the split shaft. Enjoy making a decision – it is all part of relishing the tools.

You must have a **hoe**. There are various types of hoe – many beautiful – but if you are to have only one it must be a **Dutch hoe**. You push this through the roots of the plant just below the surface of the soil, and it is extremely fast, easy and accurate to use. The secret of a Dutch hoe is to sharpen the blade like a knife and keep it sharp. This makes it easier to use and more efficient – it cuts rather than rips the weeds, minimising any damage to adjacent plants. As with all tools, go for a wooden handle, disdaining any plastic rubbish.

A **swan-necked** hoe is extremely useful for chopping out specific weeds and for drawing drills before sowing in the vegetable garden.

There are various useful **rakes**.

A garden rake with iron 'combs' or

tines is the best tool for preparing a smooth tilth. I find the flat combs less good than round, nail-like ones.

A **spring-tine rake** or wire rake is designed predominantly for raking leaves and scratching the moss and dead material out of lawns. It can also be very useful on soil to make a seedbed.

A **rubber rake** is good for raking

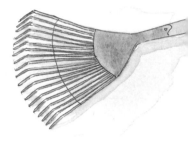

up leaves in a border, as it does not damage the plants it brushes against.

There are various types of **wheelbarrow,** with anything from one to four wheels, but the most useful, and one of the cheapest, is a builder's barrow. This has a single pneumatic tyre, is built to take heavy weights across any slope or terrain and will fit down the narrowest of paths or alleyways.

There are two other containers that fulfil the same function as a barrow, which I would never choose to be without. The first is a **bucket**. Once again, a builder's merchant where they sell strong black buckets is the place to go. I use these as a container for weeds and for ferrying potting compost, fertiliser, water and topsoil. If your garden is anything other than tiny, buy two or three.

The other container is a **trug**. This is a flat wooden basket made from split chestnut and willow. Never buy one made out of plywood – they are travesties of the real thing and killing off an ancient craft. Trugs are perfect for holding hand tools, cut flowers, plants

to be put in the ground, vegetables etc. They look good too.

In your trug, you are likely to want to ferry about string (preferably soft green twine that will not cut into tender growing stems) for tying up; and gloves, which must be long enough to cover your wrist to be of any use. But not secateurs or a knife.

This is because these two invaluable objects should live in your pocket whenever you are in the garden. You should become so accustomed to them that you feel positively undressed without them.

Secateurs are a matter of personal feel if ever a tool was. They come in dozens of shapes and weights but there are only two main varieties, the scissor action and anvil action. I have never seen the point of the latter, although some people swear by them. The former, unsurprisingly, cuts like a scissor, and has a curved, pointed blade so you can snip delicately as well as cut powerfully. The latter cuts down on to a soft metal plate, with a tendency to crush rather than cut. Secateurs must be strong, simple, brightly coloured (or else you are bound to lose them) and very sharp.

A **penknife** is essential for cutting string, taking cuttings and some pruning. It goes without saying that it

must be razor sharp, small and light enough to be no bother to carry in

your pocket. (It also goes without saying that you should always wear trousers with proper pockets for tool carrying.)

Loppers are essentially long secateurs for pruning larger branches. It is important – both for the tool and the plant – to get a clean, easy cut, so secateurs are never enough for every job.

A **pruning saw** is necessary for the same reason. The most useful are short and curved.

Shears are the best hedgecutters and trimmers of small areas. Once again – this is becoming a bit of a refrain – they must be sharp .

Every garden needs at least one **watering can**. These tend to hang around prominently outside, so my logic is that they should be decorative. Sadly the best-looking ones are expensive. You can get cheap and cheerful plastic ones if that is your bent. Either way, the 9 litre (2 gallon) size is best, with a fine 'rose' (the bit that fits over the spout to make a spray) for seedlings and a coarse one for established plants.

Even with the most expensive watering can in the world, a **hosepipe** that reaches to the furthest corner of the garden is important. Cheap ones crack in the frost and sun, expensive ones cost a lot more. I expect over the years the expensive one works out cheaper. Get a system that will enable you to click on and off various sprinklers, tap fittings, extensions etc.

HAND TOOLS

I love **trowels**. They have a weight and curve that is a delight to hold. Or should be. When you buy one, pick it up, get a feel of it – if the delight is less than required, keep looking. Stainless steel trowels are brilliant, but they come in all shapes and sizes.

Hand forks are more tricky. They tend to get used as levering devices and few are strong enough to last that sort of treatment for long. Get the strongest you can find. They are invaluable for hand weeding, which is the most effective weeding there is.

A **short-handled hoe** can be extremely useful when working in a tight space.

GRASS CUTTERS

For a small garden the best mower is the very basic, cheap, cylinder model powered by nothing more sophisticated than your sweat. You push it and it cuts. No engine, no electricity, just perfectly cut grass. If you are fit and well and have less than about 50 sq. m. (500 sq. ft) of grass it is ideal.

Cylinder mowers cut with a scissor action, so the grass has to be dry and reasonably short. They are really only for maintained lawns. A petrol-driven machine will produce a conventional stripy lawn with minimum bother.

Rotary mowers have a single blade that goes round and round and cuts like a knife. They were designed – and are best – for longer grass, but most modern models make a passable job of cutting any length of lawn. I use a Flymo – a rotary mower that floats just above the ground – a great deal. These are

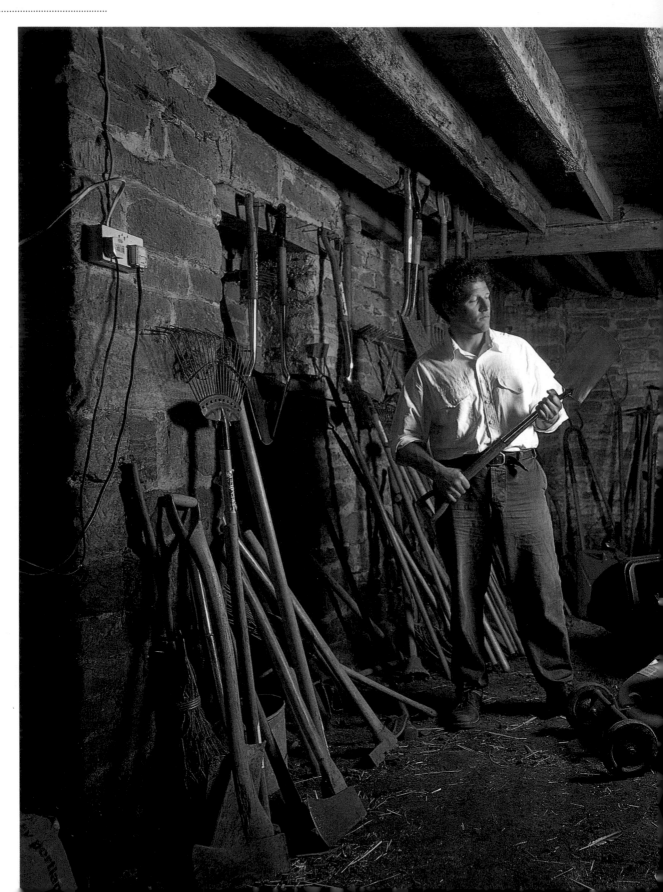

ideal for sloping ground or for any area that is not rectangular.

Whatever you use, there are two crucial factors in your choice of mower: its power – the more the better – and its robustness. So many mowers are hopelessly flimsy. They should be rough, tough machines that start first time and don't fall to bits. Do not be tempted to get something too big: it will just be a nuisance to manoeuvre and cost a lot extra.

Strimmers have revolutionised the upkeep of the larger garden. The same is true of them as of mowers: they have to be robust, light enough to use with comfort and have as powerful a motor as you can afford. If you are using them around trees, be careful not to damage the bark – it is easily done.

Look after your tools, keep them clean and dry, and enjoy them: if using the object is giving you positive pleasure, the chances are that you are using it to good effect.

I love good tools. They are sensuous to handle, well-crafted and make the most back-breaking job easier and more enjoyable.

JANUARY

WEATHER REPORT: there is no avoiding it, this is winter. January is either cold and wet or just freezing. This does the garden no harm and potentially quite a lot of good, because a bout of really cold weather will kill off a lot of bugs and diseases and stop the land getting too waterlogged. A spell of unseasonably mild weather is more worrying, as plants will think it is spring, start to grow and then be cruelly cut back by the inevitable cold spell that will come along before spring proper.

Essential
- Prune fruit trees.
- Plant trees and shrubs if the weather is dry and mild enough.
- Dig ground for cultivation.
- Melt frozen surface of ponds so that fish can breathe.
- Protect clay pots from cracking by wrapping against cold winds and ensuring that drainage is good.

Desirable
- Take yew cuttings.
- Check climbers and tie any loose stems in case of high winds.
- Walk round the garden, taking stock of layout and design.
- Get grass-cutting machinery serviced and sharpened.
- Read inspiring and entertaining gardening books, preferably whilst sitting by a warm fire.

- Plant rhubarb and force existing plants by covering with a pot.
- Take chrysanthemum cuttings.
- Take root cuttings of *Anchusa*, oriental poppies and *Anemone japonica*.

You must clear any snow from evergreens as the weight will snap the branches. This is particularly annoying if you are training topiary and it ruins a design that has taken years to develop.

Make the following New Year Resolutions for your garden:

1. Have fun. Enjoy your garden.

2. Keep a garden notebook. A page-a-day Desk Diary is best for this. Each day keep a record of the weather, new blooms, what you have planted and where, any jobs begun or completed, and any memorable moments. It is fun, makes you think about the garden and will be an incredibly useful reference in future years.

3. Be creative. You shouldn't give a fig what anyone else thinks or says about your garden. Do your own thing; make it your own idiosyncratic creation.

PLANTS IN THEIR PRIME

Bulbs: *Crocus;* winter aconites (*Eranthis hyemalis*); *Iris histrioides;* snowdrops.

Perennials: hellebores *(H. niger, H. foetidus):* *Iris unguicularis;* winter pansies.

Shrubs: wintersweet (*Chimonanthus praecox*); dogwood (*Cornus alba* 'Sibirica'); *Daphne mezereum, Garrya elliptica*; winter jasmine (*Jasminum nudiflorum*); *Lonicera fragrantissima;* willow (*Salix alba vitellina*); *Viburnum bodnantense* 'Dawn'; laurustinus (*Viburnum tinus*).

Climbers: *Clematis cirrhosa* 'Freckles'.

Vegetables: broccoli; Brussels sprouts; cabbages; leeks.

Houseplants: water only when surface of compost feels dry. Use soft (rain) water for flowering azaleas. Wash the leaves of foliage plants with large glossy leaves, such as *Monstera*.

WEED CONTROL

Weeds will only grow if there is a mild spell, and then not very much. Keep digging out perennial weeds when you can get on the ground without damaging it. Otherwise enjoy the respite!

Above: Hoar frost makes even the barest winter garden beautiful.

Opposite: Frost sparkles on the stepping stones beside this ornamental pond.

HOUSEPLANTS

The British are keèn on houseplants – by which I mean plants growing permanently indoors – whereas on the Continent people buy many more cut flowers than we do to decorate their houses and give as presents. I have a theory that a lot of people like houseplants because – against all the odds – they manage to survive the rigours of centrally heated houses in the gloom of a British winter, being overwatered, overheated and over here. Most have rich dark leaves and I suppose play the same function as holly and yew have traditionally done, bringing greenery into the house as an act of defiance against the dying of the year.

I am sure that a lot of houseplants are chosen on the basis of the temperature and environment that they evoke – most are bought in the depths of winter in an attempt to bring a tropical or desert climate into our living rooms. We also tend to choose the site for a houseplant on the basis of where *we* would like it to be. Nine times out of ten the plant then quietly curls up and dies within the year. If we positioned it where *it* would like to be, most of these fatalities could be avoided.

Here is a table of suitable positions for houseplants in a centrally heated house.

LIVING ROOM

Full sun: cacti, *Capsicum*, *Hippeastrum*, poinsettia (*Euphorbia pulcherrima*), *Yucca*.

Moderate light: *Begonia rex*, *Ficus elastica* 'Decorata', *Philodendron*, *Saintpaulia*.

Bright, indirect light: *Araucaria*, citrus species, *Cordyline*, *Hibiscus*.

KITCHEN (warm, moistish)

Coleus, *Euonymus*, *Fuchsia*, *Impatiens*, *Primula*, *Tradescantia*, *Zebrina*.

BATHROOM (warm and wet)

Caladium, *Calathea*, ferns, *Fittonia*, *Peperomia*, *Saintpaulia*, *Saxifraga stolonifera*.

BEDROOM (darkish, dry)

Aspidistra, *Chlorophytum*, *Fatsia*, *Ficus pumila*, *Howea*, *Maranta*,.

HALL (dark, draughty)

Aspidistra, *Asplenium nidus*, *Fatsia*, *Ficus pumila*, *Hedera helix*, *Tolmiea*.

GENERAL CARE

A house with central heating is going to make much greater respiration demands on its plants and therefore they will need more water. But as a general rule only plants in full flower need regular watering. Otherwise use your common sense. Only water if the soil is dry (a good way to check that, other than by touch, is if the pot feels abnormally light when you pick it up) and the plant looks as though it is wilting. If the plant is genuinely dry, give it a

Water bromeliads into the 'vase' in the centre of the plant.

good soak rather than continually topping it up, although as often as not when you try to water plants by immersion they squat for an uncomfortable minute, then kick sideways, fart out a drizzle of bubbles and overturn, losing half their compost without seeming to absorb any water. Put a kitchen weight on the surface of the soil until it has absorbed enough water to be weighted down on its own.

Some plants, like bromeliads, will quickly rot and die if the roots are wet. They must be watered into the 'vase' in the centre of the plant.

If plants start to grow lop-sided, turn them regularly so that they receive equal light levels on all sides. Plants with variegated leaves need more sunlight than those with plain green leaves.

CARING FOR CACTI

The most common mistake people make is with cacti. They tend to think of them as desert plants (correctly) and therefore put them in winter in the hottest place in the house (incorrectly). Cacti must be allowed a dormant period over winter.

You are unlikely to kill a cactus with cold. The desert can be absolutely freezing at night. What the plant needs is as much sunlight as possible and no extra heat. A south-facing window-sill in an unheated room would be ideal, or an enclosed porch with plenty of light. **Do not water it at all during the winter.** Then in April give it a good soak and it should do its stuff and produce flowers in the summer.

Glass is a surprisingly poor conductor of light and light levels fall dramatically as you get further from a window. Every foot away from the glass makes an appreciable difference to the plant.

THE SECRET OF POINSETTIAS

When you buy a plant it is usually in a particularly vulnerable state. Christmas houseplants are invariably forced by the growers so that they are in prime condition at this time of year. The problems usually begin a few weeks later when the plant – exhausted from this unnatural pressure to perform – begins to look decidedly ill. Take poinsettias. These originate in Mexico, so are only really comfortable in warmth – which makes them ideal for the centrally heated home. But do not put them next to a radiator – the ambient heat of a living room will suit them fine. The plants you buy will have

Give your houseplants the right amount of sun and shade by positioning them near or far from the window.

been treated with growth retardant to make them stocky. By early February they will gradually extend, becoming leggy. To avoid this you must cut them down to about 10cm (4in) at the beginning of April, pot them on with fresh compost and keep them in a warm, light place. A greenhouse is ideal.

To make poinsettia leaves turn red in time for Christmas – which, after all, is the whole point of the beastly things – you must convince the plant that the days are getting shorter by putting it to bed in a dark room every night at 6p.m. and bringing it out again at 8a.m. the next day. With luck the deception will work and it will react by turning its new leaves bright red over the months before Christmas.

FERNS

I think that the least objectionable houseplants are ferns, which, if luxuriant enough, can look good in a dark, moist, not too warm corner. I cannot be friendly towards the asparagus fern – it is generally too wispy and looks like a prop in a '60s B-movie, but I like cut-leaved ferns like *Microlepia strigosa*, the Boston fern (*Nephrolepis*) and the maidenhair fern (*Adiantum*). All these need to be kept in a moist atmosphere, so must be sprayed if that cannot be supplied naturally, as it might be in the bathroom or kitchen. If they do dry out, cut them right back, give them a soak and start again.

PESTS AND DISEASES

Although attacks by pests are inevitable, one can greatly reduce them by good husbandry. Make sure that your plants get plenty of ventilation, clean the leaves where appropriate, do not overwater and do not reach for insecticides at first sight of an aphid. Derris dust and Pyrethrum are organic

pesticides and will cure most problems. **Overwatering** and **poor air circulation** are the most likely causes of disease. The three main problems are: **black or sooty mould; botrytis or grey mould;** and **blackleg.** The moulds are treatable: wash them with insecticidal soap and discard affected parts of the plant. Blackleg is found where stem and compost meet and spreads upward; it is incurable and the plant should be burned.

Some of the most common pests and how to deal with them are given in the table above.

CONSERVATORIES

It is a sad fact that conservatories are rarely put to any horticultural use. The Conservatory Association surveyed 2,000 owners and found that less than one in ten (8.47%) used their conservatories for plants.

This is a terrible waste. You need know nothing of gardening to enjoy the sensual pleasures of scent and colour that plants such as *Jasminum polyanthum* or Angel's trumpets (*Datura*) inevitably give. And if you do garden a little,

Citrus (oranges, lemons and limes) Semi-evergreen (normally evergreen but will lose some or all of their leaves if very cold). Wonderful, sweet-smelling plants. Not frost-hardy, so need to be brought in in winter. Need a minimum temperature of 5°C (40°F), although limes like a slightly warmer temperature and are best kept above 10°C (50°F). Citrus need generous watering and not too much winter heat. Watch out for scale (see page 21). They can be taken outside in summer.

many of the flowers that grow well in pots during the summer months – such as geraniums of all kinds – will continue flowering well into winter within the warm embrace of a conservatory.

If you are one of the sane 10% intending to grow plants in your conservatory I would advise building in some sort of drainage system. This will enable you to water plants freely without worry and is very simple to install.

If you are one of the 90% ignoring the potential of your conservatory, then it is time to change things. It takes little skill or knowledge, and will create an exotic space that is the ideal link between house and garden.

Double glazing is likely to be an extra cost if you are fitting a conservatory, but makes sense if you are intending to heat it. The secret of double glazing is to have a **minimum of 6mm (1/4in) air gap** between the sheets of glass. The wider the gap, the better the insulation.

Safety is important. Roofs should be of polycarbonate, which is light

and virtually unbreakable. Safety glass is five times as strong as horticultural glass and laminated glass is stronger still.

Don't underestimate how hot a south-facing conservatory can become in summer: easily 35°C (95°F). This is too hot for many plants. It is worth providing some kind of permanent and easily applied system of shading.

Winter-flowering Jasmine (*Jasminum polyanthum*) Very sweet-scented, with masses of small white flowers in midwinter. Prune after flowering. Likes sun and cool roots. Plant in the ground if possible, or in a largish pot, and train against a sunny wall.

VENTILATION

The biggest problem for plants and humans alike in a conservatory is ventilation. The basic rule is the more the better. Even in the British climate a conservatory will get very hot in summer. Automatic hydraulic vents are worth considering and are not overly expensive.

Weeping Fig (*Ficus benjamina*) Requires a minimum temperature of 10°C (50°). It may lose its leaves after you buy it, but don't panic – it is readjusting to the light levels of an English winter and will grow new, smaller ones. The greater the amount of sunlight it has, the larger the leaves. Like all figs, it is relatively unfussy about soil or being dry, so water only when the leaves are looking limp.

Camellia
Evergreen. The *williamsii* group of camellias has the huge advantage of shedding its flowers after they fade (rather than hanging on to the tree in a limp faded way like the japonica camellias). Camellias must have slightly acid soil – definitely not limey – and although they will grow in a frost-free site outside, a conservatory is ideal. Camellias do not need or like too much heat – as long as the temperature is kept above freezing they will flourish. They must be kept well watered – if the buds start dropping off it is because they are dry.

Paradise Palm

(*Howea forsteriana* or *Kentia*)
This can grow to 9m (30ft), so with judicious trimming will easily fill any allotted space you give it and produce the required amount of opulent frondescence. Produces several spikes of small greenish-brown flowers in winter. Needs a minimum of 16–18°C (60–65°F) and humus-rich, well-drained soil. Water freely in summer, but minimally in winter.

Good ventilation lessens the threat of disease and predators; it also reduces condensation, which is a problem if you have soft furnishings in your conservatory.

A number of conservatories open out from the kitchen, which will always be a particularly humid room, what with washing machines, washing-up machines, kettles and cooking. That

Peace Lily (*Spathiphyllum wallisii*)

Evergreen, tufted, rhizomous perennial with clusters of long, lance-shaped leaves. This has fleshy white spadices – which is not some malevolent skin disease but spike-like flower clusters – of fragrant flowers in white spathes (a large bract that surrounds a spadix or an individual flower bud). The temperature must not drop below 15 °C (60°F).

moisture will find itself into the conservatory. You can now get digital thermometers which display temperature and humidity. You should aim to keep the humidity level in a conservatory below 50%. Having stressed this point,

ferns will relish any amount of humidity, but they are the exception that prove the rule.

FURNISHING THE CONSERVATORY

So many conservatories that do have plants treat these as a huddle of houseplants getting a touch more sun than normal. What a waste! What a sad failure to live properly if you go to the trouble and expense of making a conservatory

Polystichum

Members of this genus of ferns may be evergreen, semi-evergreen or deciduous. Fully to frost hardy. Like semi shade and moist but well-drained soil enriched with fibrous organic matter. Remove fronds when they start to fade. Propagate by division in spring.

(or paying extra for a house that has one attached) without using it.

LET THE PLANTS ROMP!

The conservatory should be linked to both house and garden, incorporating colours, textures and themes from both as well as influencing both. Do not make the mistake of treating it as a sunny living room, because invariably you will lose the outdoor qualities. Err on the side of the garden rather than the house – after all, what you are after is the pleasure of sitting in a perfectly warm, sunny garden regardless of the state of the weather.

Garden furniture looks good in a conservatory and so

do hanging baskets, troughs, stone floors, slate and brick staging.

Consider the planting around the immediate vicinity. You should try and have plenty of planting up against the glass, preferably a border and a path through it leading

Baby Tears or Mind-Your-Own-Business (*Helxine* or *Soleirolia*)

Usually evergreen prostrate perennial that forms a dense carpet of foliage. Frost hardy but leaves are killed by winter frost – so a conservatory will keep it in leaf all year round. Prefers moist soil. Good for underplanting around larger plants.

to the door. This links the garden better and gives a greater sense of space when you are inside looking out.

Conservatories need not be for exotic or expensive plants. They need not be heated. Cacti and fuchsias are particularly suitable for a cool conservatory. As someone who is normally unmoved by houseplants, I am very taken with the idea of cacti en masse rather than the odd sad, spiky, phallic totem.

The boxes give a few suggestions for conservatory plants.

Aeonium arboreum

Bushy perennial succulent. Height to 60cm (2ft). Bright green, glossy leaves appear in rosettes. *A. arboreum* 'Schwarzkopf' (not he of Gulf War fame) has narrow, purple leaves. In spring it produces cones of small star-shaped golden flowers. Requires a minimum temperature of 5°C (40°F). Keep dry in winter.

TERRARIA

Terraria (the plural of terrarium) are gardens in bottles. The point about them is not just that you can grow plants indoors – houseplants do that trick well enough – but that you can create an entire miniature garden with its own microclimate; design, tend and enjoy it even if you live at the top of a tower block without a window-sill to put a pot on.

Terraria began by accident. A Victorian gentleman by the name of Dr Nathaniel Bagshaw Ward had tried to grow rare ferns in his docklands garden, but the London air was so polluted that they refused to prosper. Whilst he was observing moths in a closed bottle, he noticed that one of the ferns that would not survive outside had accidentally taken root in the bottle and was thriving. He also noticed that the moisture in the bottle was constantly recycled, the vapour given off by the damp soil during the day condensing at night against the cool glass and trickling back down into the soil, effectively watering it.

Dr Ward developed his bottle into a container for transporting live plants on long voyages. The 'Wardian Case' revolutionised plant collecting, because it meant that rare and delicate living plants could be carried for months protected from the salt spray of the sea and in a self-regulated environment. Plants would arrive home in peak condition to be instantly admired rather than a handful of seeds which might or might not germinate.

The terrarium that you buy today is very similar to the original Wardian case, consisting of a glass bottom, sides and a sloping roof (so the water can run down it) with a door in one side. The door is hinged and opened only for planting and necessary maintenance.

PLANTING A TERRARIUM

If your terrarium's lid lifts off this makes life very easy. Otherwise planting has to be done through the open door or panel. You can easily make tools to help with small containers or big hands (see box opposite).

Cover the base of the terrarium with 2.5–5cm (1–2in) of washed gravel. **This is essential**, as any excess moisture within the terrarium has nowhere to drain away.

Sprinkle a thin layer of charcoal over this. You can either use horticultural charcoal, which is sold anywhere that you can buy a terrarium, or the type used for aquarium filters. The charcoal is to absorb gases that would evaporate in an open container.

Cover this with a layer of potting compost. In principle, any compost will do as long as it is sterile and absolutely weed-free, but in practice a loam-based compost, such as John Innes, is much easier to maintain at a correct moisture level. Bromeliads and succulents certainly do better in loam, but ferns tend to be happier in a peat-based compost, as long as you do not allow it to dry out.

Whatever you use, the soil needs to be slightly moist before you put it in. It should be about 7.5cm (3in) deep for a large container and not less than 2.5cm (1in) for the smallest.

Do not overcrowd the terrarium

and do leave space between plants for them to grow.

Take the plants from their containers and shake off any excess compost, gently loosening the roots from the rootball. This will help them establish quicker.

Scoop out a hollow in the soil (without disturbing the charcoal or gravel layers) and scrape back the compost to cover the roots, pushing the plant in firmly. **Remember to start planting from the outside and work towards the centre.**

When you have finished planting, sprinkle a little more compost between the plants if any roots are exposed.

Place any pebbles or pieces of driftwood in position. Covering exposed soil with stones, wood or moss will both look good and stop the soil drying out.

WATERING

Unless the water balance is correct the plants will die. Because the moisture level is dictated by the plants themselves through respiration, it is impossible to judge how wet the soil should be initially. So start by adding a little water. If in doubt, always put in less than you think will be enough. **Far**

Cross-section through a bottle garden, showing how to build up the soil layers.

POTTING COMPOST
CHARCOAL
WASHED GRAVEL

TOOLS

CUT A THIN CANE ABOUT 30CM (1FT) LONG AND LASH IT TO A SPOON WITH STRING. THIS MAKES A GOOD SCOOP FOR SMALL PLANTS. THE SIZE OF SPOON WILL VARY WITH SIZE OF TERRARIUM, BUT A STRAIGHT HANDLE IS EASIER TO MANAGE.

PUSH AN OLD COTTON REEL ONTO THE END OF A CANE (CUTTING OFF ANY CANE THAT POKES THROUGH). THIS IS GOOD FOR FIRMING THE PLANTS IN.

A SCALPEL BLADE FIXED TO THE END OF A CANE IS USEFUL FOR PRUNING OFF OVER-LARGE OR DEAD LEAVES.

A SMALL BRUSH WITH AN EXTENDED HANDLE IS GOOD FOR CLEANING LEAVES AND THE INSIDE OF THE GLASS.

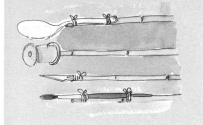

more indoor plants are killed by overwatering than by drought.

When the self-regulating system is working properly, the terrarium should have condensation on the inside of the glass in the morning, when the temperature of the glass is lowest. By about ten or eleven in the morning it should have cleared.

If there is no condensation first thing in the morning, add a little more water. Do this by spraying the plants using a fine mist spray. If the condensation does not clear by midday you have to remove some of the water. Do this by wiping the inside of the glass with a clean cloth to remove the condensation and leaving the lid or the door open for the rest of the day. Repeat this process until the correct balance has been maintained for a couple of days.

Remember: it is easy to add

water, but much harder to remove it and too much water kills. Any sign of grey mould on the plants should be treated as a dire warning that they are too wet.

Keep an eye on the moisture level, but once the terrarium is established, it should maintain a balance. As the plants grow bigger they will both give off and consume more water, but this increase will happen very slowly and the terrarium will only need a very occasional top up to maintain the level.

SITING AND LIGHTING

The first factor to bear in mind is how much light levels vary in different parts of the same room. Our eyes accommodate graduations in light so that we scarcely notice them. However, if you were to check with a light meter you would find that every metre (yard) away from the window showed a marked decrease in light.

The second is that different plants like different light levels. Cacti and ferns will not flourish side by side. Cacti like dry, bright sites and ferns are on the whole happier in moist, shaded spots. Sun-loving plants need the brightest light available in a room.

No terrarium should be placed in strong, direct sunlight because this would heat it up too much and scorch the plants.

Keep the outside of the glass clean, as dust will effectively filter out light, and be prepared to move it closer to a light source in winter if the plants are looking etiolated.

If the container is made of coloured glass, this will filter out as much as half of the available light.

If there is enough light to read a newspaper by, then it should be fine for shade-loving plants.

One of the best places for a terrarium is a bathroom: the humidity helps and most terrarium plants do not mind the generally low light levels.

PLANTS FOR TERRARIA

Do not be tempted to buy your plants too big. If you buy small ones or 'tots' you will find it easier to plant them, easier to establish a balance of humidity and you will have the pleasure of watching them grow.

SOME SUITABLE PLANTS FOR TERRARIA

PLANT	TYPE	MATURE SIZE
Acorus gramineus 'Pusillus'	Grass	38cm (15in)
Adiantum hispidulum	Fern	38cm (15in)
Adiantum raddianum	Fern	30cm (12in)
Asparagus densiflorus	Fern	30cm (12in)
Asplenium nidus	Bird's nest fern	30cm (12in)
Asplenium bulbiferum	Fern	30cm (12in)
Asplenium trichomanes	Maidenhair fern	15cm (6in)
Chamaedora elegans	Palm	38cm (15in)
Ceterach officinarum	Rusty-backed fern	15cm (6in)
Cryptanthus	Bromeliad	10cm (4in)
Cryptogramma crispa	Parsley fern	15cm (6in)
Cyrtomium falcatum	Fern	45cm (18in)
Ficus pumila 'Variegata'	Creeping fig	10cm (4in)
Fittonia verschaffeltii	Creeper	10cm (4in)
Howea forsteriana	Palm	9m (30ft)!
Hedera helix 'Heise'	Ivy	30cm (12in)
Maranta leuconeura	Prayer plant	20cm (8in)
Peperomia marmorata	Silver heart	20cm (8in)
Selaginella martensii	Moss-like perennial	23cm (9in)
Soleirolia (Helxine)	Baby's tears	5cm (2in)
Tradescantia fluminensis	Spiderwort	30cm (12in)

WINTER PRUNING

Most pruning is a human expression of tidiness rather than sophisticated horticulture. Properly done, pruning is a demonstration of control: making the plant do what it does not want to do.

When you do prune, there are three basic rules that help enormously:

First: always use something sharp. It doesn't matter what you use to cut with as long as it cuts cleanly. But it is worth investing in the best secateurs that you can find. These need not be the most expensive. The important thing is that they cut cleanly and strongly, are comfortable and easy to use, and are not too bulky or heavy. This last consideration is important: secateurs should live in your pocket, not in a drawer or on a shelf, so that you can use them when you see something to be pruned without having to scurry off and find the damned things.

The second rule: always cut back to something. In other words, cut back to a leaf or bud, even if it is a lot lower than the chosen aesthetic point of incision. If you leave a length of branch or stem above a bud it will die back to the next bud down anyway and there is a much greater risk of disease getting into the plant. Make the cut on a slight slope, so any water runs away from this top bud.

If you are removing bigger branches with a saw, always do it in three stages. Make the first cut underneath and half through the branch, about 30cm (1ft) from the trunk. This stops it tearing. Make the second cut on top of the branch, slightly further away from the trunk, and saw through until the thing falls. Then saw off the stub, from the top, not flush with the trunk but at a slight outwards angle. It sounds a fiddle, but it is straightforward enough.

Third: hard pruning promotes vigorous growth. If you have a lop-sided rose bush and you want to get it to a more balanced shape, the untutored in-

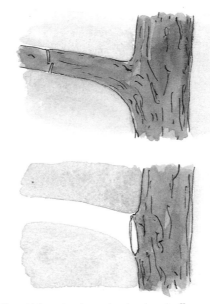

To avoid damaging the trunk, take a branch off 30cm (1ft) or so from the trunk initially and then saw it off close.

stinct is to cut back the seemingly excessive growth of one side, transforming it to smaller, but more uniform, proportions as you cut. The correct approach is the exact opposite. Cut back the weakest growth hardest. Be radical. The harder you cut back, the stronger will be the new growth (remembering always the rule of cutting back to something). This stimulates the weaker side to grow with a vengeance; in a year's time it will have caught up with its better half with balance – and size – restored.

Vines bleed sap from cuts unless they are pruned between November and

PRUNING TOOLS

Secateurs
There are two types: 'Anvil' and 'By-pass.' I prefer By-pass, but it is a matter of personal choice.

Loppers
These are in effect secateurs on long handles. The longer the handle, the greater the cutting power. Unlike secateurs, go for the heaviest model available: it will be easier to use.

Saws
Pruning saws come in two main guises: the bow saw and the curved pruning saw. You can buy double-sided saws, but they are more difficult to use. Bow saws are very good for large branches, but do not be tempted to get one too big. A small one will cut most things and is very much easier to use – particularly when you are perched precariously in the branches of a tree!

Knives
If you want to use a knife for pruning (and a knife can be made to be much sharper than any other cutting tool) it should have a heavy, curved blade with a thick handle for a good grip.

Chainsaws
Invaluable inventions for those of us with log fires and utterly unnecessary for the average gardener. Chainsaws are very good for reducing a hedge or seriously pruning a very tangled tree, but they are frighteningly dangerous. Always wear protective gear and only use a chainsaw if you know what you are doing.

Long-arms
These have a handle up to 3m (10ft) long, with a hook that fits over a branch and a blade operated by a lever at the bottom of the handle which, when pulled, slices the branch off. Very handy for getting at tall branches. Not much use for anything else.

February. They should be pruned back hard to three shoots 90cm (3ft) long each year. Train two shoots horizontally on either side of the leader, then cut them back to three good buds.

Wisteria must be pruned in winter to get a good spring diplay.

make for a bigger tree with lots of leaves but very little fruit. It is done for the health and shape of the tree itself. It should therefore be done only every five years or so, unlike summer pruning, which is geared towards fruit production (regardless of the shape or size of the tree).

Winter pruning of apples should be geared at keeping the tree open so that light and air can get to the fruit and it remains well ventilated.

Prune **wisteria** twice in the year. First in summer after flowering – cut new growth back to 15cm (6in). Then in winter, before it starts to grow again, reduce these pruned stems to a couple of healthy buds.

The main trees that need winter pruning are **apples** and **pears**. All fruit trees flower on 'spurs' of old wood. Vigorous new growth never produces fruit. So winter pruning will

An apple tree should have enough space between its branches for a pigeon to fly through comfortably!

REASONS FOR PRUNING TREES

1. Crossing branches. Where branches cross they rub together, causing wounds that let in infection. Cut back the most inward-growing branch to the point of origin.

2. Tangled branches. Tangled branches stop ventilation, encourage damp and disease. A good rough guide for apple trees is to clear enough space between the branches – particularly in the centre of the tree – for a pigeon to fly through without touching.

3. Weak growth. A puny branch amongst more vigorous growth needs cutting right back. This will either stimulate it to put on more muscle or divert energy into productive wood.

4. Dead wood. Cut this right back into healthy wood.

5. Disease. If the wood looks dodgy, cut back to healthy wood. If in doubt, cut.

ALPINES

The term 'alpine' covers any plant grown at altitude. They were introduced into Britain last century by botanists from mountain expeditions. Because they were found in rocky places it became the vogue to build rockeries in which to plant them, although the truth is that few alpines need rockeries in order to prosper. Most nineteenth-century rockeries were built from vast mounds of soil dotted with lumps of rock, often in shady positions, when **the two things that alpine plants crucially need are sunshine and really good drainage**. The rock has no bearing on either of these factors and is purely decorative.

Rock gardens are often plonked down in unlikely settings and I think to work they need to be either of local stone in as naturalistic a setting as possible – say on an existing rocky bank – or a Spielberg-like production, on a huge scale, like the marvellous rock gardens at Biddulph Grange, or the rockery at Friar Park (now George Harrison's garden), which consists of 23,000 tons of imported rock.

Rock gardens need to be either of local stone in as naturalistic a setting as possible — say on an existing rocky bank — or a Spielberg-like production, on a huge scale.

In a normal town garden the equivalent of this would be to make the entire garden into a rockery. If you had skipfuls of building rubble you could use that as the base and over that create pockets of soil between huge chunks of rock. It would be eccentric, but could look very good.

Plants from the highest altitudes tend to be slow-growing, forming little hummocks on the scree. They hardly need any soil, but must have very good drainage. They are usually under a cover of snow for half the year, which acts as a protective blanket from the cold, keeping the temperature at around freezing.

When the snow melts it provides the water the plants need and the flowers are produced fast, often peeking magically out of the snow. As they only have a few summer months in which to flower and seed, together with year-round cold temperatures at night, alpines remain very small, putting all their available energy into reproduction. When they are moved into the bosom of a warm, lowland garden they continue to behave in this atavistic way, although their need for plenty of cold, wet weather the year round, allied to an aversion to damp soil, makes them need atypical

conditions. In consequence it is often easier to grow this group in a trough or pot.

MAKING A SCREE GARDEN

This is easiest to do on a slope, to make the essential drainage easier to provide. You need to make a basis of loose stone or rubble, which is covered with a layer of sharp sand (this will fall in between the rubble, but put enough on to provide a complete blanket of sand) before being topped by a 'soil' made up of three parts gravel or stone 'dust' from

A rock garden well mulched with grit.

Alpines prefer a soil of 3 parts grit to 1 part loam.

a quarry, to one part loam or potting compost. If you are using garden topsoil it must be completely free of weeds and should really be sterilised. The easiest way to do this is to bake it in batches in a hot oven for half an hour at a time, which is a bit of a caper.

Many scree plants are lime tolerant, so you do not need to add any peat.

The scree can vary in thickness, but aim at 30cm (1ft) for it to be deep enough to plant in. For larger plants you can scoop out hollows and fill these with more soil. Do not worry that the plants seem to be going into an unnaturally poor material – a more luxurious set-up would confuse them.

When it is planted it can then be mulched about 5cm (2in) deep with gravel. Once again, do not be too precious about this: ordinary large-stoned aggregate will do fine.

A scree garden is obviously a good idea if you have very stony soil or if it is full of builders' rubble and impossible to dig. Although all the plants that thrive here will take any amount of exposure to wind and cold, it must be in full sun for at least half the day.

There is a group of alpines that are bushy and shrubby. Most of these can be found naturally in mountains around the Mediterranean or in the Middle East where the winters are cold but the summers hot and arid. The roots work themselves deep into the crevices between rocks and find scraps of sustenance, whilst the leaves have evolved a dry, almost sap-free habit. All their growth and flowering takes place in the brief rainy season before the summer burn. Plants in this group include juniper, thymes, *Hypericum olympicum*, *Genista lydia* or *G. delphinensis*, and *Gypsophila*. Most of these do well planted on or in a wall, where the roots will push deep; this will probably pull the wall down in time, but that seems an acceptable price to pay for beauty.

ALPINES IN A CONTAINER

Perhaps the easiest introduction to alpines is to make a container specifically for them. Stone troughs have become the thing to use for this because of the stone/rock/mountain link, but it could be anything that has good drainage, including a window box. It has to be deep enough for a layer (at least 10cm/4in) of crocks, broken bricks or stones at the bottom. Cover this with enough grit or gravel to form a layer to stop any soil washing down to the bottom. The soil should be normal potting compost mixed 50:50 with gravel or grit.

If the soil is too rich it will make alpines grow too much and too weak, and then they become juicy enough to attract to aphids, slugs and snails. Make sure the soil has enough grit in it and mulch the surface thickly with grit to keep the slugs off.

Most outdoor alpines will not need any more water than that provided by normal rainfall, but in times of drought they should have a good soak rather than a regular sprinkle.

PLANTS FOR AN ALPINE CONTAINER

LATIN NAME	COMMENT
Arenaria	White flowers.
Dianthus alpinus	Rose pink flowers.
Dryas octopetala	'Minor' White flowers.
Edraianthus pumilio	Violet-blue flowers.
Erinus alpinus	Lilac/pink flowers.
Gentiana verna	Intense blue flowers.
Helianthemum lunulatum	Bright yellow flowers.
Linum alpina	Blue flowers.
Myosotis rupicola	Bright blue forget-me-not.
Phlox subulata	Bright, fast spreading.
Saxifraga species	Various colours. Will take shade.
Sedum cauticolum	Pale pink flowers.
Sempervivum	Houseleeks. Grown mainly for their rosettes of leaves.

PLANTS FOR SCREE

Scree plants originate in the highest areas of possible plant life; they tend to be small, cushion-forming and need excellent drainage. The following is a small selection:

LATIN NAME	COMMENT
Androsace villosa, A. microphylla	Pink flowers.
Aquilegia discolor, A. bertlonii and A. scopulorum	Blue columbines.
Armeria caespitosa	Thrift. Pink flowers.
Dianthus alpinus	Alpine pink. Rose-pink flowers.
Draba rigida	Yellow hummock.
Gentiana verna	Intense blue flowers.
Geranium farreri	Soft pink flowers.
Hypericum reptans	Deep yellow, tiny.
Phlox douglasii	Bright carpeting.
Potentilla aurea, P. eriocarpa	Mat-forming, yellow flowers.
Saxifraga (Kabschia and Aizoon sections)	Various colours. Will take shade.
Sempervivum	Houseleeks. Grown mainly for their rosettes of leaves.
Teucrium subspinosum	Late, tiny pink flowers.

COMPOST

Compost makes sense. Everybody has kitchen waste and every garden has plant material that must be disposed of. It is madness not to use this to make the garden look better. It is a magical process really: you bung some dead flowers, tea-bags and outer cabbage leaves in at one end and a few months later out comes sweet-smelling, rich crumbly soil.

That is the theory. In practice a lot of people find that their best efforts at making compost result in a foul-smelling sludge. This need never happen to you if you follow a few basic rules.

In order to make good compost you must remember **AHA. This stands for AIR, HEAT and ACTIVATOR.**

Most problems with compost come from the lack of air and heat, as an activator is only really necessary to speed the process up rather than to initiate it. In time any organic matter will rot down without any outside instigation.

AIR

If you empty a bucket of kitchen waste on to the compost and then top that up with the lawn-mower clippings after a spell of wet weather, you will have problems. The closely packed grass clippings, with their high moisture content, will compact down tightly on top of the rest of the heap, excluding all air. Result: sludge. There are two golden rules that ensure that oxygen gets into the compost.

1. Mix all compostable material up with plenty of dry, fibrous material, such as straw, leaves, dead plant material, dry grass.

2. Turn the compost heap at least

once. The more often it is turned, the faster it will turn itself into compost.

If you can get hold of it, it is enormously useful to buy a bale of straw. Keep this by the compost heap and mix some in whenever you mow the lawn or have some very wet material. It aerates the heap and will decompose itself into good compost.

HEAT

To work properly and kill off all weed seeds, the compost heap must get really hot. The heat is generated by the process of decomposition. There are two ways to ensure you get the temperature required:

1. Make the heap big enough.
2. Use an insulated container.

There must be sufficient bulk to insulate it and retain the heat as it is produced. Most books speak of a cubic metre (just over a cubic yard) as being the minimum size, and I would stress that that is the *minimum*, not the ideal size. In theory the bigger the heap the better. In practice, a heap 1.2m x 1.2m x 1.2m (4ft x 4ft x 4ft) is the most manageable. If it gets too big the thought of turning it is overwhelming, so the job doesn't get done.

There is the problem that if you have only a small garden you never produce enough bulk to create a heap of that size – especially in winter. In that case you must either store your compostable waste

in bags until you have enough to build a heap – which is daft; or you must add something else, such as straw, to bulk your supplies out – which is an excellent idea. Otherwise, take the second option described above and use an insulated container.

There are a number of these on the market, some which you can rotate – usually described as 'tumblers' – which is obviously a good wheeze for aerating the compost; some which fold flat and when opened out have polystyrene insulation – clearly effective in retaining heat; and some which are cone-shaped, with a smallish hole at the top you put your waste into and a trap door at the bottom. Most are made of plastic. While the plastic will insulate to a certain extent, there is no question that a container with an extra layer of insulation will work much faster and better. An old dustbin lagged on the outside and under the lid with fibreglass with a

COMPOST ACTIVATOR	COMMENT	APPLICATION.
Manure	Best fresh.	Spread in a layer 2.5–5cm ((1–2in) thick every 30cm (1ft).
Garden compost	Bonus points for recycling.	Use the end of the last heap just like manure.
Dried blood	Very good.	Sprinkle thinly every 30cm (1ft).
Sulphate of ammonia	High-nitrogen fertiliser.	As above.
Stinging nettles	Use freshly cut.	Mix in with other stuff.
Comfrey leaves	Use fresh.	As stinging nettles.
Urine	!	Pour on.
Seaweed	Excellent material.	Use liberally.

sleeve of waterproofing would work perfectly well. When it is full, tip it all out and refill it, putting the stuff on top in first, thereby turning it.

ACTIVATOR

This is the least important of the three magic makers of rich, crumbly compost, but it does help. You use an activator to instigate and speed up the decomposition. Nitrogen is the magic ingredient and it

All garden waste — except perennial weeds — can go on the compost heap. The more the merrier.

can come in many forms (see box above).

If you fork through a mature compost heap you will see that it is alive with small red worms. These are a sign that the compost is making well, since they are essential to the decomposition process. They are not the same as earthworms, but are called brandlings. You can buy them, but they will come of their own accord if the heap is composting properly.

If you are making a compost heap rather than buying a proprietary container), **keep it simple**. Chicken wire stretched around fencing posts works

well for me, but anything that will provide two or three three-sided bays will work. It is important to be able to get a wheelbarrow directly to the heap and tip on to it. Attention to this kind of small details can save a lot of bother later on.

WHAT IS COMPOSTABLE?

All garden waste. If you can afford it, a shredder will grind up small branches and all tough stalks to make these more readily compostable too. But everything vegetative will go on the compost heap.

All uncooked, unprocessed kitchen waste, including fruit, vegetables, eggshells, tea-bags and coffee grounds.

No meat, bones or fat. All of these will rot down in time, but they will take much longer than vegetable matter and will almost certainly attract vermin to the compost heap.

No paper unless it is shredded finely. If you have a shredder, all well and good. But paper will only rot if it is thoroughly wet; when it is wet it compresses, excluding oxygen, and without oxygen, you don't get compost.

COMPOSTING WEEDS

(For a description of all kinds of weeds see pages 58–59).

All annual weeds – such as nettles, groundsel, chickweed or shepherd's purse – can be freely put on the com-

post heap as long as they are not full of seeds.

Perennial weeds – couchgrass, ground elder, bindweed, horseradish, thistle, dock – can be dealt with in three ways:

1. **Burn them**.

2. **Compost them** in the middle of a really hot compost heap so that any seeds or roots are destroyed.

3. **Keep a 'slow heap'** and put weeds of all kinds on it. A slow heap is one that is left for at least twelve months. It is not turned, no activator is added, but it is left to rot down slowly at its own pace. Inevitably the top will be covered in weeds, which can be pulled and added to the heap. The resulting compost should be weed free, but should equally not be used on borders or with any perennial planting that is difficult to weed. It is ideal for mulching trees.

If you have the space a 'slow heap' is a good idea. It means that you can indiscriminately chuck on to it all weeds, leaves, long grass – anything that takes time to rot.

TIP

KEEP A SMALL DUSTBIN OUTSIDE THE BACK DOOR EXCLUSIVELY FOR COMPOSTABLE KITCHEN WASTE. TAKE IT TO THE COMPOST HEAP WHEN IT IS FULL. THIS WILL CREATE SUFFICIENT BULK AND SAVE THE TROUBLE OF CONSTANTLY TAKING RUBBISH TO THE END OF THE GARDEN.

FEBRUARY

WEATHER REPORT: February usually has the worst weather of the year, but things do not seem so bad because the days are visibly lengthening and the possibility of spring is there. Bird song is noticeably perkier and if you are lucky you will catch a song thrush singing against the elements from the top of a tree. This light at the end of the tunnel must not delude you into over-hasty action, however. Spring is not yet here and any mild, sunny days should be treated as the exception, not the rule.

PLANTS IN THEIR PRIME

Bulbs: *Crocus*; winter aconites (*Eranthis hyemalis*); *Iris histrioides, I. reticulata; Narcissus* 'February Gold'(although it often appears late, making it more March Gold); *Scilla bifolia;* snowdrops; *Tulipa celsiana.*

Perennials: hellebores (*H. niger, H. corsicus, H. orientalis, H. foetidus*); *Iris unguicularis;* winter pansies; pulmonarias; primroses.

Trees: yew; box; holly. All look vibrant and strong when there is little else. Evergreens are vital at this time of year. Alder (*Alnus*) has catkins and thrives in the cold and wet, although hazel (*Corylus avellana*) steals the show with its lemon lambs' tails.

Shrubs: camellias; wintersweet (*Chimonanthus praecox*), dogwood (*Cornus alba* 'Sibirica'); *Daphne odorata, D. mezereum; Garrya elliptica;* witch hazel (*Hamamelis mollis*); winter jasmine (*Jasminum nudiflorum*); *Mahonia japonica; Stachyurus praecox; Viburnum bodnantense* 'Dawn', *V. farreri, V. grandiflorum.*

Climbers: *Clematis cirrhosa* 'Freckles'.

Vegetables: Brussels sprouts; broccoli; cabbages; leeks; early forced rhubarb.

Houseplants: cut poinsettias down to 10cm (4in) to encourage compact new growth for next season. At the end of the month, start to feed established plants with half-strength liquid feed. They must start to grow gradually, so be careful not to overfeed at this stage.

WEED CONTROL

This should be a month when weeds or their absence do not figure in your schedule. You have better things to be doing with your life.

JOBS

Essential
• Finish pruning fruit trees and any diseased wood of other trees (see pages 26 and 27). Cut autumn-fruiting raspberry canes to the ground and summer-fruiting ones to a bud above the top wire.
• Plant trees and shrubs if the weather is dry and mild enough.
• Dig any ground for cultivation in spring so that frost and rain can break it down. **This is now urgent**.
• Melt frozen surface of ponds so that fish can breathe.

Desirable
• Sow annuals under glass, on window-sills or in propagators.
• Finish any repairs to fences or supports for climbing plants.

Optional
• If you live in the milder part of the country, start to prune roses. Prune late-summer flowering clematis down to two healthy buds at the end of the month.
• Check if plants have been lifted by frost and refirm with your foot.
• Finish potting and planting lilies.

Crocuses (opposite) and primroses (right) are among the first signs that spring is on the way again.

MAKING PATIOS AND PATHS

Let's cut the cultural crap and agree that patio, terrace or yard all amount to a level area of hard material close by or attached to the house. Every household is improved with one and I regard it as an essential piece of garden design. Our climate is too wet to have grass right up to the house.

Most houses have too small an area of hard surfacing. A generous space becomes a direct link between house and garden and can be used for eating throughout the summer, every spare inch filled with pots, and the whole thing treated as an extra living space. (At this point cast your two-hour notion to the wind. Consider the hours of hand-blistering, back-breaking labour an investment. And good for you.)

PREPARATION

Whatever the final surface, the preparation is the same:

1. Mark out the area required with string.

2. Dig out the area down to a depth at least 23cm (9in) below the final surface, which must be at least a

course of bricks (10cm/4in) below the damp-proof course of the house.

If the ground slopes steeply from the house, then the spoil nearest the building can be used to build up the level of the slope.

3. Put pegs in a grid over the area every 2m (6ft 6in) and use a straight edge and spirit level to ensure the tops of the pegs are level. Then take out extra soil if any peg has less than 23cm (9in) clearance.

4. If you are still on fairly soft soil it will need to be compacted down firmly to prevent any future subsidence. Compacters can be hired from any tool hire firm.

5. Put a layer of hardcore over the ground. Hardcore can be anything from broken bricks and tiles to ballast. If you are intending to use concrete as your final surface, do not compact the hardcore but leave a rough surface for the concrete to key to. You will also have to build in clear drainage slopes. Ignore the next step too.

6. Cover the hardcore with about 5cm (2in) of soft builder's sand.

Now you are ready to lay the final surface.

STRETCHER BOND

HERRING BONE

WHOLE AND HALF BRICK

STRETCHER FACES

LAYING THE SURFACE

My thoughts on the various surfaces available are given in the table opposite.

A perfectly good option – especially for paths – is to mix whatever materials you can get hold of. I have paths made

TRY STEPPING STONES

IF YOU HAVE A REGULAR ROUTE ACROSS THE LAWN THAT IS MAKING IT WORN AND MUDDY BUT YOU DO NOT WANT TO BREAK UP THE GRASS, SET STEPPING STONES INTO THE TURF SUNK SLIGHTLY BELOW THE SURFACE, SO THAT THE BLADES OF THE MOWER PASS OVER THE TOP OF THEM. BEFORE DIGGING THE GROUND UP AND LAYING THEM, SET THEM ON TOP OF THE LAWN TO GET THE SPACING RIGHT – IT IS MADDENING TO HAVE TO ADJUST YOUR NATURAL STRIDE TO FIT IN WITH A PATH.

of gravel, stone, brick and cobbles. Use your artistic skill and common sense to blend them harmoniously.

In the end, it is likely to be your pocket that will dictate the options. But do not be penny pinching. However you do it it will not be cheap and it costs the same to prepare the site for a cheap, ugly final surface as for York stone.

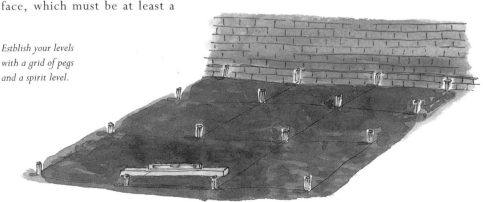
Establish your levels with a grid of pegs and a spirit level.

Always lay slabs in courses running across the longest side of a patio. With paths the opposite rule applies: you should always set slabs in courses across the shortest side (i.e. *across* the path not down its length).

Bricks can be laid in a variety of patterns, including diagonal and square herringbone, basket-weave and all the patterns used for walls. But as a general rule, keep it simple. If you have a curved path, brick can look very good running in lines along the path, following its curves.

Sets and cobbles must be laid like icebergs, so that most of the material is buried in sand or in a thin (6:1) mix of sand and cement. Keep cobbles as close together as they will go.

Gravel should always be laid thinly: ideally only thick enough to cover the surface. The thicker it is the harder it becomes to walk on and the more it scuffs about. Gravel paths must always have a containing edge or border. This can be of timber, held in place with pegs, or brick laid lengthways along the edge of the path can look very good. If you don't have the border the gravel gets everywhere.

When laying slabs, start against the house and work away from it, **making sure each slab is absolutely level before you lay its neighbour**. Use the sand to get the level, packing it in tightly under the slab. If the slab is level it will not wobble at all. Use a spirit level across both faces and diagonally to make sure that each slab is level with the others around it in each direction. If you have kept the underlayer level, this is not too much of a problem with man-made material. **York stone** tends to come in different thicknesses, so adjustments have to be made for each individual stone. Some stone is enormously heavy and has to be ma-

noeuvred with a crowbar and shovel. With the right leverage it is surprising how accurately it can be positioned.

Bricks are laid on the same principle, but because they are so much smaller, each one is easier to adjust. It is better to lay bricks on edge, although this uses far more bricks, so is more expensive.

Always butt bricks and slabs as tightly together as possible. It looks better and is stronger and easier.

When you have finished, brush sand into the cracks between the stones or bricks. I do not normally recommend using mortar. Sand is perfectly firm if laid properly and it lets water drain be-

tween the surface material, meaning that you do not need to set your patio on a slope. There will be a certain amount of plant material seeding itself in the cracks that would be avoided if these had mortar, but they can look good and you can do the job yourself with plants like *Mentha requienii*, which will smell good as you walk over the tiny leaves.

TIP

WHERE PATHS OR A PATIO MEET MOWN GRASS, MAKE SURE THAT THE SURFACE IS LOWER THAN THE GRASS, SO THAT THE MOWN EDGE IS EASY TO CUT.

MATERIALS FOR PATIOS AND PATHS

SURFACE	PROS	CONS
York stone	Always looks wonderful; large pieces look good.	Expensive (up to £30 per sq. m/sq. yd); can be slippery; large pieces very heavy and of irregular thickness.
Bricks	Good colour, texture and rhythm; easy to lay; easy to repair or replace; can be hard wearing; very flexible to arrange.	Expensive (average 50p per brick); slow to lay.
Precast concrete slabs	Cheap; easy to lay; hard-wearing.	Dull, characterless; can be slippery.
Imitation stone slabs	Cheap; easy to lay (regular sizes); can look OK.	Brittle – break easily; coloration wears away; can look really tacky.
Slate	Interesting; easy to lay.	Expensive; can be slippery; dark and dominant.
Cobbles	Good texture; easy(ish) to lay; cheap(ish); very hard-wearing.	Bumpy; a bit fiddly and slow to lay; depend on good supply.
Granite sets	Very hard-wearing; look good.	Expensive; bit fiddly to lay; bumpy.
Concrete	Cheap; easy to lay; can look OK when weathered; hard-wearing	Dull, bland; can be a nightmare to lay; hard to alter – a bit final.
Crazy paving	Um...	Why?
Gravel	Cheap; very easy to lay; looks fine; surprisingly hard-wearing; noisy for burglars	Sticks to muddy shoes; needs weeding; good for paths but not patios.
Quarry tiles	Good colour; easy to lay; uniform.	Not cheap; can look a bit odd.

FENCES

The boundaries of most gardens are defined by fences. In many cases they surround three sides of the visible garden and are not chosen but inherited along with the fabric of the house. For some rather abject reason most of us accept the fence we have as the status quo, whereas replacing it or shopping around for something that looks good is not difficult, time-consuming or expensive, and will radically improve the way that your garden looks.

In summer fences are often clothed with climbers or screened by shrubs and plants. But in winter they are clearly visible, often the single most dominant feature in the garden. The crucial thing to remember is that the fence is part of the way your garden looks, not simply the frame separating it from the neighbour's territory.

So choose your fence with the same care as you choose your clothes. It has to look good and be practical.

March is the windiest month, and wind is the worst thing for the tender new growth just emerging at that time of year. Get your fences bought and in place now before the March winds blow. There is not much you can do about rain, a murky sky or the way the building next door exactly shadows your garden all afternoon, but wind can be filtered and funnelled out of harm's way.

Therefore there must be an interim barrier for these little plants and everything in their lee.

If your fence is primarily to protect the garden from wind, dismiss any idea of using the commercially produced windbreaks in netting form. They are for roadworks and nurseries and whilst

Wind rises up and over a solid wall, creating a damaging back swirl. An open fence filters the wind, breaking it up.

I am sure they work, they are too ugly for gardens. Fences are required.

If a fence is to defend effectively, **it must filter the wind, dissipating its bluster rather than blocking it**. The ideal wind barrier is 60% solid to 40% gap. A solid fence or wall simply lifts the wind up and brings it down in a even more vigorous swirl on the other side at a distance of twice the height of the wall, bashing whatever happens to be there.

CHOOSING THE MATERIAL FOR YOUR FENCE

A lot of fences are pretty hideous, especially the ubiquitous larchlap, so you should take the trouble to exercise the full range of choice available to you. After all, you will have to look at it every day for at least five years, until the hedges can do the job unaided.

When you are choosing a fence your aesthetic senses are more important than a calculator. Choose whatever vernacular materials are appropriate to the area and your house. This does not need to relate to a rural tradition. If you live in the middle of the city it might be that trellis looks ideal, particularly when raised over an existing low wall. You can make your own urban fencing by using painted wood, which is far more in keeping with the bright and often hard colours of normal urban life than the standard orangey stain of most fencing. A white fence will throw the light back at you and distract from an unsightly background, whereas a dark green fence will blend in with plants and a darker background.

If you live in a Victorian or Georgian house, a wooden fence would probably look hopelessly inappropriate, especially for the front garden. Metal

---

A FENCE NEED NOT BE A BOUNDARY

FENCES DO NOT HAVE TO BE RESTRICTED TO THE BOUNDARY AROUND THE EDGE OF THE GARDEN. A FENCE ACROSS OR DOWN THE MIDDLE OF THE GARDEN WILL PROVIDE A SENSE OF MYSTERY AND CONTAINMENT THAT IS ESSENTIAL TO THE SMALLEST BACK YARD. A 1.8M (6FT) HIGH FENCE EITHER SIDE OF A PATH IS INVARIABLY A GOOD THING IN A BACK GARDEN.

HAZEL HURDLES ARE IDEAL FOR THIS. THEY ARE LIGHT, VERY STRONG, EASY TO PUT UP (AND TAKE DOWN) AND WILL LAST ABOUT TWELVE YEARS. THEY ARE TERRIFIC FOR A NEW GARDEN, WITH A HEDGE PLANTED ON THE SIDE AWAY FROM THE PREVAILING WIND. THE HEDGE THEN GROWS TWICE AS FAST IN THE PROTECTION OF THE HURDLE AND IS THICK AND HIGH BY THE TIME THE HAZEL GENTLY ROTS INTO IT.

YOU CAN GET WILLOW HURDLES, WHICH ARE A LITTLE CHEAPER THAN HAZEL ONES, BUT THEY DO NOT LOOK SO GOOD AND LAST ONLY HALF THE TIME. PLUMP FOR HAZEL IF YOU CAN GET IT.

TYPES OF FENCE	DESCRIPTION	COMMENT
Hazel hurdles	Handwoven lengths of split hazel.	Light; excellent against wind; easy to put up and move. The best fencing material.
Larchlap fencing	Machine-woven slats of deal.	Ubiquitous, ugly, weak; cheap.
Closeboard fencing	Parallel feather-edged boards nailed vertically to arris rails.	Very strong.; better in oak than in deal.
Chestnut paling	Thin split chestnut stakes joined by wire.	Rolls up, so very flexible and easy to use; good while hedge is growing.
Picket fencing	Flat pales nailed at 5cm (2in) spacing to arris rails.	A boundary marker; good painted.
Trellis	Thin battens nailed in diamond or square formation.	Flimsy; good windbreak; good for town gardens.
Post and rail	Strong rails fixed to spaced posts.	Cheap, easy to erect boundary marker.
Iron fences	Metal uprights welded to crossbars.	Good for Victorian or Georgian front gardens; surprisingly easy to buy.
Wire fences	Wire mesh attached to posts.	Gives no privacy, but can be good for supporting a vigorous climber like *Vitis coignetiae*.

railings are available in every shape and form from architectural salvage shops or as modern-made reproductions. Try to choose railings that are as strong and chunky as possible. Paint them black or a very dark green.

TWO HOURS OF DIVISION

The range of fencing material may be huge, but the basic system of fence construction and erection is constant. The first thing it must do is be reasonably easy to put up and stay up in all weathers. It should be high enough to provide privacy (though it is worth remembering that you normally to need planning permission for a fence higher than 2m/6ft 6in tall). It must protect the garden from the worst of the wind without creating unwanted shade. Finally, it should fit in with the immediate surroundings.

Putting up a fence does not require any skills and can be done within a couple of hours in most gardens.

Most fences are sold in panels of some kind, supported by posts. **It is important that the posts are put in firmly and absolutely upright.**

Mark the line of the fence with a string, clearing any tree stumps or undergrowth out of the way.

Measure out the site and make sure that the panels will fit accurately.

There are three ways to put the posts in:

1. Hammer the post in. This needs sharpened stakes, which are usually round in section. This is the easiest and quickest method, but also the least secure. However, when using certain fencing materials such as hurdles it is perfectly adequate.

2. For square-section posts, drive a spiked metal sleeve into the ground. Do not bang directly on to the metal sleeve; use a piece of wood placed across it. Check that it is going in upright every few centimetres/inches. When the sleeve has been driven in as far as it will go, insert the post into it. These metal sleeves are available from any garden centre and are the easiest way to fit square posts. They have the added advantage of protecting the base of the post from moisture, meaning that it will not rot so fast.

3. Dig a hole 60cm (2ft) deep and 45cm (18in) square. (The smaller the hole the more difficult it is.) Put a layer of hardcore in the bottom, making sure that you have sufficient to ensure that the post is the same height as the fencing panels. Place the post in the hole and have someone hold it upright as you fill around it with dry concrete.

(Dry concrete will set as hard as wet, is much less messy, easier to mix and easier to tamp.) Tamp the concrete down as you go.

A useful tip is to bang some 15cm (6in) nails into the post bottom so that

A fixed woven fence made from hazel, my favourite fencing material.

10cm (4in) stick out. These will key into the concrete, making the post hold firmer. Leave the concrete to set for at least a day before attaching the panels.

The fencing panels can be secured to the posts either with nails or, if it is an open fence – as it should be – with strong wire.

Strong arris rails – the horizontal bars that fencing boards are nailed to – will hold the fence rigid, and you can fix any type of fencing to them.

GARDENING WITHOUT PLANTS

Far too much of modern garden advice is boring, stuffy, horticulturally difficult and thereby offputting to the beginner. This is very sad, as making a garden is about the most interesting and satisfying thing on this earth. But it is a liberation to see the garden simply as a space that you can do any-

A garden of the mind: Zen simplicity at Ryoan-Ji, Kyoto, Japan.

thing with – and if that excludes plants it can still be gardening.

In England in the early years of the eighteenth century, plants were used merely as a backdrop for the buildings, bridges and lakes of formal gardens, and they were seen as inferior components in creating a landscape.

But with the growth of the Empire came the collection of hitherto unknown plants from all over the world, along with the development of the greenhouse. As a result, gardening

went 'from being a branch of aesthetics to a subdivision of botany'. In other words gardens ceased to be created solely for their beauty and inspiration – they became primarily places of horticulture where as wide a range of plants as possible could be nurtured. Sadly, this is still the predominant view of gardens.

The beauty of using a wide range of non-plant material in your garden is that it gives you freedom to play without the constraints of horticultural convention. You can create patterns out of cobbles, construct weird and wonderful structures in wood and use the Japanese Zen inspiration to have swirling waters made from stones. You can be inventive and creative without limitation other than the boundaries of your imagination.

None of this need be revolutionary. In fact there are very few gardens that do not use 'hard' materials for aesthetic effect as well as practical purposes. These include buildings, seats, pots, bridges, paths, fences, pergolas, walls, gates, as well as the obviously more decorative examples such as sculpture of all kinds, urns, sundials and fountains. The lesson is that one should pay as much attention to how they look as to the function that they perform, because if they are ugly they will make the whole garden ugly.

Use objects to create focal points: put them at the end of a path or a lawn and work your planting around them.

It is much better to position inanimate objects in the garden in winter, when you can evaluate their full aesthetic force. In summer the effect will inevitably be softened, although excessive growth can always be cut back.

You can take the process an imaginative step forward by using less conventional objects in the garden. Mirrors work well, particularly in a small garden, as they reflect not only plants but

THE JAPANESE ZEN GARDEN

THE JAPANESE HAVE BEEN MAKING ZEN GARDENS FOR THOUSANDS OF YEARS. THESE STARTED IN BUDDHIST MONASTERIES AND ARE BASED AROUND AN EXTREMELY SOPHISTICATED AND INTRICATE USE OF STONES OF ALL SIZES, FROM LARGE BOULDERS DOWN TO FINE GRAVEL. EVERY STONE, HOWEVER SMALL, WAS PLACED EXACTLY SO AND WAS PREGNANT WITH MEANING. GRAVEL WAS RAKED TO REPRODUCE THE RIPPLES OF WATER AND RUSHING STREAMS INDICATED BY GRADATIONS OF STONE IN NARROW CHANNELS. THE MOST FAMOUS OF THESE GARDENS IS AT THE MONASTERY OF RYOAN-JI IN KYOTO AND WAS BUILT IN 1490. IT CONSISTS SOLELY OF FIFTEEN STONES ON A BED OF GRAVEL. IT IS THE ALMOST INEXPRESSIBLE SPIRIT OF ZEN MADE CONCRETE. THE JAPANESE COLLECTED ROCKS FOR USE IN GARDENS WITH EXTREME CARE AND THEY BECAME PRIZED POSSESSIONS OF GREAT MONETARY VALUE. DURING TIME OF WAR, GARDENS WERE REGARDED AS BOOTY AND UPROOTED IN THEIR ENTIRETY TO BE USED IN THE PLUNDERER'S OWN GARDEN.

THERE IS A CONVINCING ARGUMENT THAT THE WESTERN MIND CANNOT FULLY APPRECIATE ZEN GARDENS BECAUSE WE DO NOT UNDERSTAND ALL THE LEVELS OF MEANING IN THEM. HOWEVER, YOU CAN TAKE THE JAPANESE INSPIRATION AND EXAMPLE, AND INTERPRET IT IN YOUR OWN MODERN, WESTERN IDIOM.

DON'T BE TOO TASTEFUL WITH COLOUR

THERE IS NO REASON WHY THE COLOUR
OF AN OBJECT HAS TO BLEND IN WITH ITS
SURROUNDINGS. PAINT CHAIRS OR FENCES
BRIGHT PRIMARY COLOURS – WE GROW
FLOWERS FOR THESE QUALITIES, AFTER
ALL. AND IF YOU WAKE UP ONE MORNING
AND FIND THAT THIS BRIGHTNESS OFFENDS
YOU, YOU CAN CHANGE IT THE SAME DAY.
IT IS ONLY PAINT.

the attic of a house that a family has lived in for hundreds of years, full of fascinating but discarded objects. I once decided to get rid of half a dozen pairs of old shoes and rather than throw them in the dustbin I put them neatly against a wall in the garden. As the leather decayed they improved in appearance. A robin nested in one pair and weeds grew out of the lace holes.

A 'Japanese style' stone path recreated at the Hampton Court Flower Show.

also the sky. I have seen an old chest of drawers used to great effect in a border, the drawers half-open and sprouting plants. A friend of mine has a penchant for all things military and has bomb cases flanking a path and ropes of cartridge cases hanging from trees like Christmas decorations. At Stowe, Buckinghamshire, in the 1730s, the landscape architect William Kent had fully grown dead trees dug up and repositioned to create a suitably 'Gothick' effect.

This is the key word – effect. You are striving to create a space that makes you feel good. Even if plants are not your thing, that is no excuse for not gardening.

The use of moveable, non-plant decoration is often most effective in a small garden, where it has more chance to be seen. As with small rooms, it is a mistake to keep ornament small in a limited space.

Use pots and urns that are outsize and the garden will grow to accommodate them, particularly if they are tall rather than broad. The sky, after all, is the same height for everyone, however tiny your back yard.

While Zen gardens use objects sparingly and with minute precision, Western gardens often benefit from a positive clutter of objects. A large pot looks good when set among ten smaller ones. Think of the garden as being like

WINTER COLOUR

Winter light is white and low, casting shadows and displaying everything in high relief. In this light green comes into its own, free from the swamping comparisons of summer colours and unbleached by hot sun. Thanks to the low light levels, even winter grass can shine with an emerald brilliance not seen for the rest of the year.

To get the best out of whatever winter colour is going, you should create as sheltered a spot for the plants as possible. This means a trade-off between shelter from too much rain as at this time of year many flowers are very delicate and can at worst be damaged by the rain and at best get splashed by mud from the ground.

WINTER WHITE

The white light of a winter's day shows white flowers at their best, making them seem cleaner and purer than the white flowers of the kaleidoscopic summer. White flowers in winter – indeed all flowers in winter – are best planted as individuals or in select groups so that you can enjoy them as specimens rather than wedges of colour.

The best known, and first, winter flower is the **snowdrop** (*Galanthus nivalis*), which looks best in small clumps, whether in grass or in a bor-

less exotic.

Camellia sasanqua 'Narumigata' is a white, scented, very early-flowering camellia. It wants to be in as sheltered a position as possible, with good rich soil.

Viburnum tinus 'Laurustinus' will flower all winter, the pinkish buds opening into pure white blooms. A tough, strong-growing shrub, it is a good core for the winter garden. The white versions of *Anemone blanda*, *Cyclamen coum* and *Daphne mezereum* are all less common than their pink cousins, but are excellent plants.

RICH WINTER COLOURS

All the shades of yellow from pale lemon to gold look predictably good in winter, shining with an inner light on the gloomiest day. A splash of yellow flowers can be as cheering as a pool of sunlight, and spring seems possible when the first flush of yellow begins after Christmas. This icteritious rash gathers pace throughout February and March, with aconites, early daffodils, yellow crocuses, primroses, witch hazel, mahonias, winter-flowering jas-

*The Lenten rose (*Helleborus orientalis*) can bring a splash of white, pink or purple to the late winter garden. A wonderful flower for this sometimes depressing time of year.*

sunlight, which in winter means a south-facing or, if that is not possible, east-facing spot (whereas from April to October a west-facing position will get more light than the east), and shelter, as wind will often do more damage than air temperature. You also want

der. It will grow in shade and likes damp soil. It also grows very well in a pot. The most special of all white winter flowers is the **Christmas rose** (*Helleborus niger*). There is another white hellebore, *H. nigercorse*; it is more robust than *H. niger*, but perhaps

> ### DID YOU KNOW?
>
> 'PANSY' IS A CORRUPTION OF THE FRENCH WORD *PENSÉE*, MEANING THOUGHT, AND IS SOMETIMES CALLED LOVE-IN IDLENESS OR HEARTSEASE. THE HORN ON THE BACK OF THE VIOLA FLOWER IS AN INDICATION OF PERENNIALITY AND HARDINESS: THE LONGER THE HORN, THE MORE ROBUST THE PLANT.

mine, hellebores and forsythia. Yellow at this time of year is the colour of hope and promise, and one should revel in it.

Blue always goes well with yellow in any planting scheme and there are im-

Winter-Flowering Plants

White	Yellow	Red/Pink	Blue
Magnolia stellata	Jasminum nudiflorum Winter-flowering Jasmine	Bergenia purpurascens	Iris histrioides 'Major'
Galanthus nivalis Snowdrop	Primula vulgaris Primrose	Viburnum x bodnantense 'Dawn'	Crocus tommasinianus
Camellia sasanqua 'Narumigata'	Helleborus foetidus	Cornus alba 'Westonbirt' Dogwood	Muscari Grape Hyacinth
Helleborus niger Christmas Rose	Helleborus corsicus	Helleborus orientalis Lenten Rose	Scilla tubergeniana
Freesia alba	Freesia 'Yellow River'	Freesia 'Everett'	Freesia 'Romany'
Erica carnea Winter Heath		Erica carnea 'Myreton Ruby'	Erica carnea 'King George'
Rubus cockburnianus	Eranthis hyemalis Winter Aconite	Camellia x williamsii 'November Pink'	Iris unguicularis
Leucojum vernum Spring Snowflake	Cornus mas Cornelian Cherry	Daphne odorata 'Aureo-marginata'	Violas
Daphne mezereum 'Alba'	Hamamelis 'Pallida' Witch Hazel	Daphne mezereum	Iris reticulata
Cyclamen coum album	Mahonia x media 'Charity'	Daphne bholua	Primula 'Wanda'
Lonicera fragrantissima	Stachyurus praecox	Prunus subhirtella 'Autumnalis'	Viola 'Universal Series' Winter Pansy
Anemone blanda 'White Splendour'	Narcissus 'February Gold'	Anemone blanda 'Charmer'	Anemone blanda 'Violet Star'
Rhododendron 'Christmas Cheer'	Chimonanthus praecox Wintersweet	Rhododendron 'Praecox'	
Viburnum tinus 'Laurustinus'	Crocus chrysanthus	Cyclamen coum	
	Forsythia ovata	Magnolia campbellii Pink Tulip Tree	
	Clematis cirrhosa 'Freckles'	Chaenomeles speciosa 'Rubra Grandiflora' Flowering Quince	

portant winter blues, not least from the **iris family**. *Iris histrioides* 'Major' has royal blue flowers on short stems. It likes a sunny, well-drained site (but not stony). *I. bakeriana* is twice as tall and an ultramarine colour. *I. reticulata* has deep violet flowers with golden marks and can be planted in grass like crocus. *I. unguicularis* is amongst the loveliest of flowers at any time of year, and will perform much better if it can have a lot of sun throughout the summer. Apart from planting them in your sunniest spot, you can also achieve this by planting the rhizome half out of the soil. Cut off the leaves in autumn, so that the new flowers stand alone in February.

The **'winter-flowering' pansy** (*Viola tricolor*) is a vital addition to the winter garden, useful either in containers and treated like a bedding plant, or in a border. The 'Floral Dance' and 'Universal' series have been specially selected to tolerate low temperatures and poor light and are thus happiest in winter. Nothing is plusher than a pansy's petal, and few colours richer than their carmines, purples and yellows. Sow the seed in early summer and the plants will flower all the subsequent winter – or buy a tray of plants and bung them in wherever you want them. A rule of thumb for violas is to pinch off the flowers and buds after

Dogwood (Cornus) is a must for winter colour.

planting. This encourages them to put their energy into developing a good root system before flowering with renewed energy.

There are few **pure red** flowers in February, although the **flowering quince** (*Chaenomeles speciosa* 'Rubra Grandiflora') is a vivid exception. Red tends to come suffused with white to make shades of pink. Most of the winter pink is on **shrubs** like *Viburnum bodnantense* 'Dawn', the vivid pinks of both *Camellia japonica* and *C. williamsii*, daphnes, the autumn-flowering cherry (*Prunus subhirtella* 'Autumnalis') and the pink *Chaenomeles*. The **Lenten rose** (*Helleborus orientalis*) comes in every shade from white to deep purple, but it is most typically a wonderfully rich pinky violet. Hellebores are one of gardening's great secrets: they add a richness and fecundity to the winter garden that nothing else provides. See page 184 for tips on how to grow them.

SHRUBS

We tend to assume that we all know what a shrub is, but, for the record, a shrub is a woody perennial, either evergreen or deciduous, that grows a number of stems from the base, unlike trees which tend to grow a single trunk. There are areas of confusion inherent in this definition, as a number of trees will behave like shrubs when pruned to the ground, like hazel, ash, willow and even oak, but the general drift is clear. Shrubs are bushes. With a few exceptions, they have a billowy presence, softening the garden whilst adding shape and structure.

Shrubs are ideal for the gardener who does little gardening, because on the whole they are remarkably undemanding plants. Stick them in the ground with a bit of bonemeal, water them occasionally and watch them

Shrubs provide bulk and form in a garden. Here, spiraea, berberis, honeysuckle and camellias glow in the evening sun.

grow. A bit of pruning does not go amiss with certain species, but even that is not essential.

There are many ways of incorporating shrubs into the garden, but one way

---

> ### SHRUBS AS BARRIERS
>
> SHRUBS CAN MAKE AN INFORMAL HEDGE, PROVIDING THE BARRIER FROM NEIGHBOURS OR THE ELEMENTS THAT YOU REQUIRE WITHOUT THE RIGID FORMALITY OF A CONVENTIONAL HEDGE. *PHILADELPHUS* MAKES AN EXCELLENT FLOWERING HEDGE, FAST-GROWING AND DELICIOUSLY SCENTED.

that I urge you to avoid: do *not* grow specimen shrubs surrounded by mown grass. This is common but usually looks unstructured and ugly unless the grass is there only as an interim ground cover until the shrubs take over the whole area.

If you are lucky enough to have an area of trees in your garden, grow shrubs as an 'understorey'. Many shrubs grow under the canopy of large trees in the wild, and this habit can be usefully adapted to the garden. Even if you do not have any mature trees, walls and fences will provide similarly shaded conditions. Rhododendrons, camellias, magnolias, hydrangeas and bamboos all fit that bill.

Shrubs such as honeysuckle (*Lonicera*) are more usually known as climbers, although in their natural state they form a large bush – and if you have the space that is an excellent way to grow honeysuckle, rambling roses, clematis, wisteria and ceanothus, all more usually trained up a wall.

True herbaceous borders require an awful lot of care for a short flowering season and the 'mixed border' – where shrubs, herbaceous plants, bulbs, annuals and even small trees are all grown together – is now the norm, although a relatively modern concept. It has become a convention that shrubs supply the 'bones' of the border and the rest of the planting fleshes it out. To a certain extent this is common sense, but

---

the shrubs need to be carefully chosen for their flowering as much as their skeletal qualities (see page 66).

It would be perfectly feasible to give the entire garden over to shrubs, blending types of foliage and texture along with a succession of colour, grading size from the smallest at the front to large shrubs such as lilac at the back. Done well, this can be a very satisfactory way indeed of growing shrubs, and is very low on labour of any kind. It need not have the gloominess of the Victorian shrubbery – whose main virtue was as a hidden location for clandestine love-affairs – but with an annual prune and mulch it would provide colour, scent and form. The shrubs should be planted close enough together so that when they mature their branches touch, but not so closely that they crowd each other out. Of course it is not that simple, as different species and different individual plants within species will grow at different rates, so inevitably it would mean some thinning and moving of plants. But overall, the work would be minimal compared to a herbaceous border or vegetable plot.

SHRUBS IN CONTAINERS

If you have a very small garden there is no reason why you should not grow a selection of shrubs in pots. Use as big a container as possible and John Innes No. 3 or a similar compost that is specifically for trees and shrubs. A shrub in a pot will need feeding from time to time and using a slow-release fertiliser like bonemeal twice a year is better than sloshing on a high-nitrogen fertiliser that will provide a lot of leaves but not much else. Liquid seaweed concentrate mixed into its drink every few weeks will keep the shrub completely happy and fit.

As the shrub grows it will need re-

SHRUBS FOR ALL SEASONS

	SPRING	SUMMER	AUTUMN	WINTER
Big	Choisya ternata	Cotinus coggygria	Viburnums	Viburnum
	Ceanothus impressus	Philadelphus	Skimmia	bodnantense 'Dawn'
	Rhododendrons	Viburnum	Sambucus	Camellia
	Camellias	Abutilon		
	Magnolia soulangeana	Oleraia		
	Clerodendrum	Eucryphia		
	Lilac			
	Kerria japonica			
	Spiraea			
	Viburnum			
	Amelanchier			
Medium	Stachyurus praecox	Hydrangea	Pyracantha	Cornus
	Mahonia	Hebe rakaensis	Hamamelis	Eleagnus
	Magnolia stellata	Buddleia davidii	Berberis	Euonymus fortunei
	Forsythia	Deutzia		Fatsia japonica
	Osmanthus	Genista (broom)		Hamamelis
	Pieris	Rubus		Garrya elliptica
	Ribes	Escallonia		
	Eleagnus	Hibiscus		
	Berberis			
	Corylopsis			
Small	Ceanothus 'Blue Mound'	Cistus	Hebe 'Autumn Glory'	Lonicera fragrantissima
	Cytisus 'Lena' (Broom)	Skimmia reevesiana	Cotoneaster	Daphne mezereum
	Dwarf deciduous Azaleas	Lavender	Callicarpa	
	Erica	Potentilla		
	Chaenomeles	Hebes		
	Ribes speciosum	Senecio		
		Salvia		
		Hypericum		
		Fuchsia		

PLANTING SHRUBS

If — as is very likely — your shrub is in a container when you buy it and you want to transfer it to a bed, the first thing to do is to soak it in a sink or bucket of water for at least an hour. At first it will bob about: leave it until it has sunk to the bottom and is fully saturated. Then take it out and let it drain for another hour.

Dig a generous hole (at least twice the size of the pot), fork over the bottom, mixing in some organic material, and sprinkle on a handful of bonemeal. If the soil is heavy, add some potting compost to the topsoil that you fill back in. Take the shrub out of the pot and gently ease the roots away from the shape imposed on it by its confinement. If it has been in the pot for a long time it will be root-bound, which means that the roots will be growing round and round themselves. You must encourage them to grow out into the soil. Plant it carefully, making sure that soil gets around all the surface area of the roots and that the plant is firmly in position. Give it another handful of bonemeal and at least 4.5 litres (1 gallon) of water. When this has soaked in, mulch over an area at least as big as the spread of its branches.

potting, preferably to a larger container. If this is not possible, gently take off the top 2.5cm (1in) or so of the potting compost and replace it with a mulch of organic compost, which will act as a feed and a new root-run.

Shrubs for containers: weigelas, daphnes, hydrangeas, roses, lavender, rosemary, ceanothus, honeysuckle (*Lonicera fragrantissima*).

A number of shrubs have the added bonus of berries in autumn. Shrubs in this category include:

Berberis,
Cornus,
Cotoneaster,
Euonymus europeaus (Spindle),
Hippophae rhamnoides,
Osmanthus,
Pernettya,
Pyracantha,
Spindle,
Viburnum.

A number of shrubs make excellent ground cover (see page 96). A selection of ground-cover shrubs might include:

Berberis wilsoniae,
Ceanothus gloriosus,
Cotoneaster horizontalis,
Erica,
Euonymus fortunei,
Gaultheria,
Hebe albicans,
Hypericum calycinum,
Mahonia repens,
Pernettya prostrata,
Santolina,
Vinca

FOLIAGE PLANTS

Leaves for their leafiness' sake are often a better bet in a small garden than flowers which can only be enjoyed at the cost of months of bareness. A plant that provides texture, colour and shape for great chunks of the year is a powerful aid to making the garden look good with the minimum amount of work. Nevertheless, foliage plants are seen as the poor relations of the garden, backroom boys used to set the scene for the flowering stars. This is a mistake. A garden without a single flower can – often does – look beautiful: a garden with just flowers and no interesting foliage would be horrid.

Foliage inevitably adds depth. That is primarily literal – the branches or stems of a plant will provide layers of leaves – but it also manifests itself via pure colour, layers of green or different purples piling up on top of each other. You can play with the textures and outlines of leaves, so that the soft grey furriness of **lambs' ears** (*Stachys lanata*) is clearly very different from the brittle shiny green of **camellias,** or the delicate cut of the leaf of **Acer palmatum** 'Dissectum Atropurpureum' is, to go to an extreme, utterly different from the aggressive thrust of a **phormium**.

Most shade ground cover has interesting foliage. Don't overlook the virtues of humble **ivy**. It will provide a surprising range of colour in places other plants could not survive, and there is a huge range of leaf shapes and

CROW'S FOOT IVY

colours, from the yellow of *Hedera helix* 'Buttercup' to the crinkled prettiness of *H. h.* 'Cristata' and the zany arrows of **crow's foot ivy** (*H. h. sagittifolia*). I like the **bugle** *Ajuga reptans* 'Burgundy Glow' for its bronzy leaves more than its blue flowers, and the white **deadnettle** (*Lamium maculatum* 'Beacon Silver') shines out in otherwise horticulturally impenetrable darkness.

Feelings are mixed about *Fatsia japonica*. I didn't like it very much until someone I liked even less said that he didn't like it either. Ever since then I have developed a soft spot for the ubiquitous fatsia. The real reason you see it everywhere is that it is so obliging, filling awkward corners of shade. If it has the room to spread I think it earns its aesthetic keep. Almost as common is **mahonia**, with its hard, fishbone leaves. Given its aptitude for shade, I think every garden should have one.

ACER PALMATUM

FOLIAGE FOR COLOUR

I suppose the best known and most widely grown of all 'foliage' plants are **hostas**. Whilst it is worth remembering that their English name of plantain lily comes from their wonderful tall flower

MAHONIA

trumpets, it is the leaves that earn them their spurs. Although hostas are damp soil, shade-loving plants par excellence, they will grow pretty much anywhere. *Hosta sieboldiana* 'Elegans' is a stunner with gloriously blue-grey ribbed leaves. *H. s.* 'Frances Williams' is another favourite, similar to 'Elegans' but greener. I do not like variegated hostas as much, but *H.* 'Gold Standard' is the best of them, a true yellow with gold rims to the leaves. In bright sun it may fade almost to white and in deep shade the colour does not develop properly. Hostas will spread gradually, but this can be accelerated by chopping the clump into divisions with a spade and replanting the resultant bits (each with at least one good bud). Slugs and snails love all hostas, regardless of colour.

HOSTA

Cardoons (*Cynara cardunculus*) with their jagged leaves, spikes and thistleheads (not to mention 1.8m/6ft of height), are quite different to hostas but they are similarly essential foliage plants. A cardoon likes sun and more sun and good drainage. To keep with the silvery greys, **Senecio maritima** 'Silver Dust' is effectively an annual, and although it does produce yellow flowers, these are best cut off to encourage the leaves.

One of my favourite **shrub roses** is *Rosa glauca*. It has diminutive, single, shocking pink flowers not worth the garden space, but its delicate, glaucous, pink-tinted foliage and red stems (rather like dogwood) are fabulous. **Eucalyptus glaucescens** is another of the bluey grey ilk, best kept pruned hard every other year, to keep the leaves round. They become long and less lustrous when mature. If the blue/silver/grey theme is one you wish to persevere with (and I do) try *Artemisia*, rue, *Santolina*, *Hebe pinguifolia* 'Pagei', *Melianthus major* and the **weeping pear** (*Pyrus salicifolia*).

Amid the refinement of greys and silvers, **purple leaves** are essential to intensify the space between other colours in a border. **Cotinus coggygria** 'Royal Purple'

ROSA GLAUCA

does this perfectly. It is best on fairly poor conditions: over-manured soils will stop it colouring as well as it can. **Purple hazel** (*Corylus maxima* 'Purpurea') is another cracker, and is very happy to be cut to the ground every few years, sending up ever-more vigorous shoots in response. It likes well-drained soil. **Heuchera micrantha** 'Palace Purple' is a much smaller plant with dark bronze puckered leaves. It

You have to juggle colour, shape and texture to create the depth of sustained interest. You could, I suppose, see this as an added burden, but if so it is a chore on the same scale as choosing what to eat from a delicious menu.

also has sprays of delicate white flowers, but consider those a bonus.

If you have wet soil you have the

COTINUS

chance to indulge in a range of large, floppy, fat leaves that demand a constant supply of moisture to maintain their dignified turgidity. The biggest of the lot is **Gunnera manicata**, which has leaves the size of umbrellas, but *Rheum palmatum*, *Peltiphyllum peltatum*, *Rodgersia aesculifolia* and the **American skunk cabbage** (*Lysichiton americanus*) all respond to the wet with vast leaves that make their various florescences inconsequential.

The spiky thrust of **phormiums** and **yuccas** leaves me cold, I'm afraid, as does the similar angularity of the **Chusan palm** (*Trachycarpus fortunei*) or the **dwarf fan palm** (*Chamaerops humilis*). You, dear reader, may love them. But for me they have all the tactile allure of an angry hedgehog, and none of the charm.

An exquisite permutation of all the greens at Tatton Park, Cheshire, shows that foliage can be as beautiful as flowers.

MARCH

WEATHER REPORT: 'In like a lamb and out like a lion; in like a lion and out like a lamb' is the old saying about March, and it tends to be true. As I write this at the beginning of March, there is snow on the ground and we have had blizzards and hard frosts for a week. Certainly the weather is roaring! But March is such a dramatic month, such a time of change, that one knows that within days it could all be gone and within weeks spring will be here.

March is always a windy month. A west wind invariably brings rain and an eastern and northern wind cold – sometimes very cold still. But a southerly wind will dry the ground and warm the soil quicker than anything.

The days are lengthening and the sun getting hotter as it rises higher in the sky, so the ground heats up and gradually the garden springs into life. The clocks go forward, too, so there is always the sensation of better weather through lighter evenings. In the warm south, March is the busiest time of the year, preparing the ground, sowing seeds, planting herbaceous plants, cutting grass and weeding. But go by the weather, not the calendar. If the ground is wet enough to stick to your boots, keep off it.

PLANTS IN THEIR PRIME

Bulbs: *Crocus; Erythronium;* snowflake (*Leucojum*); *Muscari;* narcissi; *Scilla;* early tulips.

Perennials: *Anemone blanda;* bergenias; pansies; primroses; pulmonarias; saxifrages.

Shrubs: camellias, flowering quince (*Chaenomeles*); *Daphne odorata, D. mezereum; Forsythia; Magnolia soulangeana, M. stellata; Mahonia japonica;* flowering currant (*Ribes*); *Stachyurus praecox.*

Climbers: *Clematis armandii* at the end of the month.

Vegetables: leeks are still good and spring greens come into their own, but in general vegetables are thin on the ground as winter crops are nearly over and spring ones yet to begin.

Houseplants: increase the watering and feeding regime. Move shade-loving plants away from windows as daylight becomes more intense. Repot mature plants, carefully taking them out of the old pot and knocking off excess soil. Put into fresh compost with a feed.

WEED CONTROL

The single most important thing to do this month is to get rid of as many weeds as you can. Start as you mean to continue. If nothing else grows in March, the weeds will. But they are still small, so pull up, dig or spray them wherever they are. Mulch as heavily as you can with organic material like compost, but do not put mulch on top of unweeded ground.

LAWNS

Most lawns are ready for their first cut. Keep the blades high! You will do much more harm than good by cutting too low. Set the blades at their highest and just trim the top off. Frost does great damage to short grass, so while there is still a risk of frost keep the grass at least 1cm (1/2in) long.

Rake lawns vigorously with a spring-tined rake before and after the first cut and gather up debris for the compost heap.

Opposite: The pink flowers of Magnolia campbellii *appear on leafless branches to dominate this early spring scene.*

Below: Narcissi and crocus growing naturally.

JOBS

Essential
• Prepare seed-bed and ground for vegetables and sow onions, carrots, spinach, leeks, lettuces and brassicas.
• Prune roses and clematis early in the month. Mulch heavily with manure.
• Wash and tidy greenhouse and start sowing seed in trays.

Desirable
• Plant all climbing plants.
• Spray paths with weed-killer.
• Transplant any plants to be moved, taking extra care to provide them with ideal growing conditions in their new home.
• Divide snowdrops from big clumps to smaller groups.
• Sow lettuce in greenhouse.
• Plant chives and mint. Sow parsley.
• Treat lawn with moss-killer.

Optional
• Plant gladioli bulbs.
• Sow grass seed or lay turves if weather is warm enough.

SPRING PRUNING

There is a golden rule for pruning all flowering plants: **you can do no harm by pruning immediately after flowering**. ('After flowering' means when the *last* flower fades – which might be weeks after the first one does so). This is because there will always be a year ahead in which to make new flowering growths, which is all any plant needs.

Clematis and climbing roses show how gentle but judicious pruning can promote healthy growth.

However, this is crude stuff when set against the vast variety of plants with different habits and needs. To get the best out of them it is necessary to be a little more sophisticated in your pruning. So here are two more rules:
1. Plants that flower on this year's growth should be pruned this year.
2. Plants that flower on last year's growth should either not be pruned at all or be pruned immediately after flowering last year.

This is easy to remember, but it is much harder to recall which plant does what. A rough guide to spring pruning is contained in the doggerel

If it flowers before June, do not prune.

PRUNING CLEMATIS

This rule of thumb works particularly well for clematis. But these have to be divided into three groups.

Group 1 clematis include *C. montana*, *C. armandii*, *C alpina*, and *C. macropetala*, all of which are vigorous growers with masses of small flowers in early and mid-spring; they should be pruned after they have finished flowering – at the end of May, beginning of June. But you need to prune these only to restrict their growth: cutting them back will not increase flower production, and the plants are best left to grow unrestricted. If you have to prune them, use shears, giving them a trim rather than performing surgery.

Group 2 clematis are the large-flowering cultivars that flower on new side shoots growing off last season's ripened wood and sometimes again in late summer with much smaller flowers on the current season's wood. Pruning should be done now, but only to get rid of any weak, straggly or diseased wood. Cut back to the first pair of healthy buds you come to. These buds will produce this spring's flowers, so every bud cut off is a flower lost.

The group includes favourites such as 'Barbara Jackman', 'Vyvyan Pennell', 'Nelly Moser', 'Marie Boisselot' and 'The President'.

If you have an overgrown clematis from this group, the best way to rejuvenate it is to cut one third of it to the bottom pair of buds now, one third after the first flowers are over, in June,

and the final third next March. This replaces the entire plant within twelve months without losing out on too many flowers.

Group 3 clematis has to be pruned hard each March. These all flower in late summer and autumn, entirely on growth produced in the same year. If left to their own devices they will produce a flush of flowers at the top of the plant, leaving an increasingly entangled woody mass below. They include all the 'Jackmanii' group, *C. tangutica*, *C. viticella*, 'Perle D'Azure', 'Ernest Markham', 'Ville de Lyon' and many others.

Remove all last season's growth, down to a juicy pair of buds about 30cm (12in) above ground. On a healthy plant this can seem very drastic – but it works.

A similar approach to Group 3 clematis works for shrubs like *Buddleia davidii*, mallow (*Lavatera*), *Fuchsia*, *Spiraea* and *Prunus triloba*. Cut all last year's growth down to the lowest healthy bud (which might well not be the very lowest bud). For woody shrubs like buddleia, you will find that secateurs are not man enough for the job and that strong loppers make life much easier.

PRUNING ROSES

The pruning of roses gets people into a terrible tizzy, but recent research has

---

TIP

DEAD WOOD IS BROWN: LIVING TISSUE IS WHITE OR GREEN IF THE BARK IS SCRATCHED.

IF YOU HAVE OLD, WOODY ROSES WITH BIG THORNS AND A FEW BIG FLOWERS IN SUMMER, IT IS HARD TO REJUVENATE THEM BY PRUNING. BETTER TO DIG THEM UP AND CHUCK THEM AWAY AND START AGAIN, PREFERABLY WITH SHRUB ROSES.

*Rosa 'Francis E. Lester' trained round a window. It
should be pruned after flowering. This job is best
done in October, but can be left as late as March.*

shown this anxiety to be entirely unnecessary. A series of tests was done on
every conceivable type of pruning
method for roses and by far the most
successful – in terms of the health of
the plant and production of flowers –
was an annual trim with an electric
hedgecutter! If you must prune them at
all, and there is no need, this approach
is best for **shrub roses** (see page 98).

Hybrid teas, China and tea roses
are best pruned more radically: remove
all dead and weak wood each year and
shorten healthy stems to about one
third of their length.

Make all cuts just above an out-
ward-facing bud, slanting in and
down at an angle from it so any
water falls off.

Climbing roses are best pruned in
October, but will be improved by
pruning as late as March. The intention
is to remove all old growth (of more

than three years) to the lowest healthy
junction with new growth. Try and
leave half a dozen strong new shoots
fanning upwards, and tie them in. Cut
off all lateral growth from these half-
dozen shoots to the last pair of buds or
leaves.

If you have a very neglected climbing rose it is a good idea to cut a third
of it down to the ground so that it replaces itself over three years, treating
the new growth as described above.

Rambling roses do not need pruning, but may be restrained with a light
trim immediately after flowering (late
July).

COPPICING

This is a method of getting vigorous
new growth from a mature plant.
Traditionally this is done to **osiers (willow)** for basket-making, **hazel** for fencing panels and **oak** and **ash** for

firewood and charcoal. Cutting the tree
or shrub makes it throw up many stems
rather than a single trunk. Although the
above-ground part of the plant starts
anew each time it is cut, the roots go
on growing steadily, so that the growth
becomes more vigorous as the plant
ages.

In the garden this is very effective
with **dogwood** (*Cornus*) and **willow**.
Cut the entire shrub down to the old
growth every other year and the bark
of the new growth will be brilliantly
coloured the following winter. **Purple
hazel** (*Corylus maxima* 'Purpurea'), **eucalyptus** and the **smoke tree** (*Cotinus
coggygria*) also look good when coppiced every three or four years in a
mixed border.

ACID AND LIME

The single greatest influence on the way that your garden looks is likely to be the pH value of the soil. The acidity or alkalinity of the soil is measured on a pH level of 1.0 to 14.0. Pure water measures 7.0: higher than 7.0 is alkaline, lower than 7.0 is acid.

TESTING THE SOIL

PH TESTERS CAN BE BOUGHT FROM ANY GARDEN CENTRE, EITHER AS A LIQUID WHICH YOU ADD TO A SOIL SAMPLE WHICH CAN THEN BE COMPARED TO A COLOUR CHART – DARK GREEN AT THE ALKALINE END OF THE SCALE, ORANGE AT THE ACID AND A BRIGHT GREEN IN THE MIDDLE – OR

ALKALINE   *ACID*

AS A PROBE ATTACHED TO A SCALE WITH A MOVING NEEDLE. YOU NEED TO TEST IN VARIOUS AREAS OF THE GARDEN, ESPECIALLY IF THE SITE IS NEW AND HAS HAD TOPSOIL BOUGHT IN FOR ANY REASON – IT IS SURPRISING HOW MUCH VARIATION THERE CAN BE WITHIN QUITE A SMALL AREA.

THIS IS NOT SOMETHING TO GET DEEPLY HUNG UP ABOUT – THE MAIN REASON FOR TESTING THE PH IS TO AVOID SPENDING MONEY AND TIME ON PLANTS THAT WILL NEVER GROW WELL IN YOUR SOIL. IDEALLY, YOU ARE AFTER 6.5, A SLIGHTLY ACID SOIL, AND MOST THINGS WILL FLOURISH AT THAT LEVEL, INCLUDING SOME AZALEAS AND RHODODENDRONS AS WELL AS MOST LIME-LOVING PLANTS. THE IMPORTANT THING IS NOT TO FIGHT THE PREVAILING CONDITIONS AND TO PUT YOUR LIMITED TIME AND ENERGY INTO GROWING THINGS THAT WANT TO BE THERE.

Most garden plants do best on a slightly acid soil, although on peat soil that is likely to be more acidic (an optimum of about 5.8) than on loam, where it is best to be about 6.5.

TREES AND SHRUBS FOR BOTH ACID AND LIME SOIL	
TREES	SHRUBS
Austrian Pine	Berberis
Beech	Lonicera
Birch	Ceanothus
Oak	Viburnum opulus
Hawthorn	Elder
Holly	Cistus
Yew	
Alder	Buckthorn

A peat soil is always acidic and a chalky or lime soil always alkaline. Sandy soil tends to be acidic, as does clay, but a rich loam in a limestone area will, not surprisingly, be alkaline.

On acidic soils, with a pH reading of 6.0 down to 4.0, rhododendrons, azaleas, camellias, heathers, grass, potatoes, lupins and lilies are going to flourish. Worms dislike acidic soils. On alkaline soils with a pH value of between 7.0 and 8.5, most flowering shrubs, *Dianthus*, *Clematis*, brassicas and spinach do very well.

Certain plants that like an acidic soil – such as rhododendrons and heathers – simply cannot grow in the presence of lime, such as chalk, and are known as calcifuges. So a very good guide to the type of soil in your neighbourhood is to see if there are any rhododendrons growing in the area; if there are it is to a greater or lesser degree acidic — certainly lower than 6.5. If there are none it is certainly alkaline – 7.0 or above.

Going on from there, the easiest way to deduce the general type of soil in your area is to see which trees and shrubs (for no magic reason other than that they are easy to see) that are growing commonly and healthily.

Flowering shrubs tend to enjoy a limey soil more than an acidic one, so the list opposite omits many of the possible candidates within this category if

you live on chalk soil.

Certain trees and shrubs will tolerate extremes of both acidity and alkalinity, and are consequently both useful and generally poor indicators of the soil – thoroughly confusing.

Very few perennials need an acid soil – most will grow best in a pH. of 6.5. However, there are a few that thrive in acidity.

There are more perennials that like lime, which explains why that side of the list is longer. Having said that, very few of these plants will not survive reasonably happily in most garden conditions.

TREES	
ACID SOIL	LIME SOIL
Aspen	Ash
Birch	Box
Grey and White Poplar	Field maple
Juniper	Hornbeam
Rhododendron	Horse Chestnut
Robinia	Laurel
Gleditsia	Whitebeam
Eucalyptus	Apple

CHANGING THE SOIL BALANCE

You can make an acidic soil more alkaline by adding lime (calcium carbonate) or calcified seaweed, but it will not change the nature of the soil — merely neutralise some of the acidity. For certain plants, such as all brassicas, it is part of the growing routine in all but the chalkiest soils, but as a rule you should only lime once every four or five years. Lime should be added in autumn and the maximum effect is achieved as much as eighteen months

pH Ranges within which Minerals can be Absorbed

	4.0	5.0	6.0	7.0	8.0	Effects of deficiency
Nitrogen		••	•••••	•••••	•••••	Stunted growth, leaves yellow.
Phosphorus			•••	•••••		Small, purple leaves, low fruit and seed yield.
Potash		••	•••••	•••••	•••••	Scorched leaves, poor-tasting fruit.
Calcium			•••••	•••••	•••••	Lack of vigour, growth dwindles.
Magnesium			•••	•••••	•••••	Photosynthesis affected, premature leaf drop.
Iron	•••••	•••••	•••••			Yellow or pale upper leaves, thin weak stem.
Manganese	•••	•••••	•••••			Yellowing of leaves; pears and raspberries suffer most.
Boron		•••••	•••••	••••		Misshapen root crops, plants become stunted.

Heather will only grow as abundantly as this on acidic soil.

later. It should not be used at the same time as manure, as they react chemically to produce ammonia and the nitrogen is lost from the manure. Do not plant or sow ground that has been limed for about a month. Mushroom compost is normally very limey, especially when it is fresh, so although it is usual to store it for a few weeks in the open to let the lime leach out of it, on acidic soils it should be spread immediately on the garden to balance the pH.

It is more difficult to make an alkaline soil more acidic, although sulphur (available from garden centres) helps alter the balance a little. It is converted to dilute sulphuric acid in the soil which neutralises the alkalinity, but never to the same degree as lime can neutralise acidity in a soil. Leaf mould or pine bark will help, but only in pretty large quantities. Manure has a tendency to make a soil more acid, although not dramatically so. Aluminium sulphate can be spread to lower the pH, but like lime it has to be renewed regularly. Never add peat in pursuit of acidity, as this is depleting a non-renewable resource. Peat should only be used in containers for calcifuges.

Trace elements are only available within certain pH ranges (see box above), so if for any reason your soil slides off the range, the plants will suffer the resulting shortage of nutrients. Iron, for example, cannot be drawn up by plants in alkaline soils, and some plants, like rhododendrons, must have an good supply of iron if they are to survive.

Shrubs

Acidic Soil	Lime Soil
Burnet rose	Hypericum
Calluna	Senecio
Camellia	Philadelphus
Ephedra	Hebe
Erica	Deutzia
Genista	Elaeagnus
Hibiscus	Euonymus
Kalmia	Rosemary
Kerria japonica	Forsythia
Pernettya	Lilac
Pieris	Weigela

Perennials

Acid	Alkaline
Corydalis cashmiriana	Aquilegia vulgaris
Gentian	Astilbe
Meconopsis betonicifolia	Aubrieta
Trillium	Delphinium
Tropaeolum speciosum	Dicentra
	Avens
	Helichrysum
	Hemerocallis
	Kniphofia
	Nepeta
	Peony
	Penstemon
	Primula
	Rudbeckia
	Saxifrage
	Scabious
	Stachys byzantina

BUYING PLANTS

The garden industry does up to half its annual trade in the few weeks around Easter. There must be millions of people crawling out from under the stone of winter and entering a frenzy of horticultural consumerism. However, you must retain some discrimination despite the green flush of enthusiasm.

DECODING BOTANICAL NAMES

It is helpful to understand how plants are named. At first the vast array of botanical names is as intimidating as learning Mandarin Chinese. But like learning any language, it is much easier to become familiar with names through usage than to try and learn it served up as cold grammar.

If you understand the structure of botanical nomenclature it will not only help you choose the right plant for the right place, it will also help you become familiar with the plants rather than just their names.

Each plant has at least two names. The first is the group name or genus (plural genera) – equivalent to our surnames. This is unique to that group.

The second name, the species – like our Christian names – may crop up in many different groups.

If a plant varies from its true type, it will have a third name describing that variation. This third name is the variety. So you might have:

Jones (the genus), John (the species), the younger (variety.)

Or in plant terms:

Rosa (the genus, which tells you that it is a rose);

rugosa (the species, which tells you which kind of rose);

alba (the variety or which kind of species).

JONES (THE GENUS)	ROSA (THE GENUS)
john (THE SPECIES)	rugosa (THE SPECIES)
the younger (VARIETY)	alba (VARIETY)

If you are listing different species within one genus, it is normal to abbreviate the genus to a capital letter: *Rosa rugosa alba*, *R. gallica officinalis*, *R. macrantha* etc. The genus is always given a capital but the species is always in lower case.

If the variety occurred naturally then the plant's full name is printed in italics – *Rosa rugosa alba*. But if it has been cultivated as a garden variety it becomes a cultivar – a culti(vated) var(iety) – and the cultivar name is printed in normal type with capitals and in single quotation marks. So: *Rosa rugosa* 'Hunter'.

A hybrid is made by two species of the same genus interbreeding. The result is given a name preceded by a multiplication sign, 'x'. So a cross between *R. rugosa* and *R. arvensis* breeds *R. x paulii*.

Hybrids can occur between plants of different genera, in which case the name of the new hybrid genus is preceded by a multiplication sign. The offspring from the cross between *Cupressus* and *Chamaecyparis* is called x *Cuprocessocyparis*; the most vile example being x. *C. leylandii*.

Rosa '*Mischief*' *can be crossed with the climber* R. '*Compassion*' *to produce* R. '*Paul Shirville*' *(left), which is more fragrant than either parent.*

The point of all this is put you in the driving seat: do not be bewildered or intimidated by plant names. There are many botanical names that have effortlessly entered the vernacular, like dahlia, clematis, geranium, fuchsia or magnolia, but there are many more that you will never wrap your tongue, let alone your memory, around. No matter. When you decorate your house no one expects you to understand the chemical make-up of paints or to know how to plaster, yet you would expect to be careful and specific about the colour and texture of your walls. It does not matter if you cannot pronounce the names, but it does matter that you exercise your choice in selecting plants for your garden. Knowledge is power. If you are very busy or only have so much time or energy that you want to give the garden, it is doubly important to choose your plants carefully.

It is far too vague just to decide upon 'a rose'. Think where it has to go, how big you want it, what colour, what the soil is like, how much light it will get, when you want it to flower, will you be able to smell it, do you want it thorny or thornless, what else will be planted around it, do you want hips, does it matter what the leaves are like – treat it like buying clothes or good food: take trouble to inform yourself. I hope that this book will provide a lot of that information, but if you really get into gardening you will soon want much more, which is fine. It is enough merely to whet your appetite.

CHOOSING A PLANT

Having judiciously exercised your choice of species, you go to the garden centre and look at the rows of plants. There are a dozen identical ones to choose from. What do you look for?

1. Go for a strong, even shape with no straggly or withered bits. With annuals, look for strong roots and a bushy top. If a plant has these two qualities it will produce more flowers for longer.

2. Do not be seduced by flowers. Flowers make huge demands on a plant. It will have been artificially forced to produce more flowers than it can do comfortably, just to tempt the likes of you. If it is a healthy plant, it will produce flowers enough where you want it to, in your garden, after planting. This applies equally to bedding plants which are to flower in a few weeks as to shrubs or flowering trees.

3. Buy small. There is usually no advantage in buying a larger plant. The younger the plant the better it will adapt to your garden and the faster it will grow – as well as being much

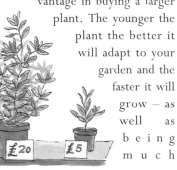

cheaper. The only exceptions to this rule are some herbaceous plants that may be divided later to give you more than one plant.

4. Feel the compost in the pot. Is it dry? if so, avoid the plant. It may be badly damaged through lack of water and the damage is yet to manifest itself. The compost should be pleasantly moist.

5. Are the leaves shiny and turgid? Or are they a bit limp? If the latter, forget it.

6. If practicable, try lifting the plant by the stem. If the roots are poking through the holes in the bottom of the pot it is probably root-bound and has been in the container too long. If the soil comes away from the pot and immediately falls off the roots, the plant has only just been potted up and has not settled down from being transplanted. Avoid it.

7. Look around, including the plants you are not interested in. Is the place shipshape? Do they have the setup to care for the plants? A plant will react to its upkeep instantly and the retailer is the biggest influence on its health.

Finally, I repeat, exercise your discrimination and make yourself sufficiently well informed to choose what you want, rather than accepting blindly what is on offer.

WILD FLOWERS

A wild-flower meadow has become terribly trendy for all horticultural wannabes, even though the nearest most people get to a meadow is a patch of lawn out the back. If the site is right and the gardener skilful enough it can look beautiful. But it usually looks dreadful. More often than not the soil is too good, the grass is cut at slightly the wrong time and the meadow that was to be filled with swathes of flowers reverts to rather scruffy grass with the odd mournful flower.

The truth is that growing wild flowers so that they look natural in the artificial environment of a garden is difficult, both aesthetically and horticulturally.

There is a tendency to assume that, just because a plant grows year after year in a corner of the wild without the benefit of bonemeal, it is naturally tough and will flourish within the tender embrace of the gardener. Not so. The plant has flourished on its natural site for exact and complicated reasons, and has probably taken hundreds of years to get established. It is a tall order to reproduce the precise mix of soil, weather and nutrients on any sort of natural scale within most gardens.

The main problem with the aesthetics of wild-flower gardening is the scale of the operation. The meadow at a grand garden like Powis Castle is tremendous and has certainly led many visitors to rush off and emulate it at home. But much of its success is dependent on its size – getting on for half a hectare (a good acre) I would guess from memory. You need a huge canvas to get the picture in. It looks messy and insignificant on a back-garden scale.

However, I think that you can cheat…

You can still have wild-flower gardens with a range of habitats if you grow your plants in containers. I know that this seems to be against the whole point of creating a 'natural' meadow, but who is fooling whom? Unless your garden is vast or entirely at one with the surrounding countryside you will be creating a completely unnatural, controlled 'meadow' anyway. If you make containers into jewel-like essences of those rolling acres you are likely to be closer to the real thing and have more success in the cultivation.

Never pick or dig up wild flowers. There is no need to possess them. If you want them in your garden, grow your own.

I think that it would be fun to try:
- one container for grassland plants (without the grass);
- another for woodland flowers;
- one for damp-loving plants;
- one for flowers of cultivated ground.

Sow the seeds in seed trays initially and then prick them out either into their final position or into pots before planting them out when they are big enough. The seeds for the broken ground are better sown direct into the soil, but this is only practical in a restricted way. After all, you are not attempting to make a wild-flower meadow itself – just the idea of one.

CONTAINER SIMULATING DRY GRASSLAND

Plants found in open, sunny grassland want soil with low fertility but good drainage. So this pot should have a layer of gravel or pebbles at least 5cm (2in) deep, covered by a layer of soil low in fertility – subsoil from the garden (not clay) or used seed compost would be ideal. This might be topped with 2.5cm (1in) of topsoil. **This is the opposite of almost any other way of preparing a pot, but do not be tempted to give them a bit of extra goodness.** At best it will produce over-beefy plants and at worst it will stop them flowering.

After flowering, let the seed heads form and wait until the seeds have fallen before cutting it all back, removing the cut foliage and stems. This is

likely to be around midsummer. Weeds will inevitably find their way in and it will look a bit scrappy. Hide it (but not in the shade). Then give it another trim around Christmas time so that when the new flowers arrive in early spring they will not be hidden.

Wild Flower Plants for Grassland
Bacon and Eggs or Bird's Foot Trefoil *Lotus corniculatus*
Common Centaury *Centaurium erythraea*
Common Stork's Bill *Erodium cicutarium*
Cowslips *Primula veris*
Dog Violet *Viola riviniana*
Field Mouse-ear *Cerastum arvense*
Field Scabious *Knautia arvensis*
Harebell *Campanula rotundifolia*
Heartsease *Viola tricolor*

Lady's Bedstraw *Galium verum*
Meadow Cranesbill *Geranium pratense*
Oxslip *Primula elatior*
Pasque Flower *Anemone pulsatilla*
Wild Tulip *Tulipa sylvestris*
Viper's Bugloss *Echium vulgare*

CONTAINER PRETENDING TO BE A WOOD

Shade would suit a collection of woodland wild flowers. In a wood the topsoil is made up of layer upon layer of leaves, forming leaf-mould. If you have your own (and if you have access to leaves, you should have your own) this will be ideal. Ordinary potting compost will do, although the drainage needs to be sharp, so mix it with vermiculite or sharp sand.

Some of the plants in the following list need a large container and others will take over the more delicate plants if given the chance; but there is sufficient choice to enable you to have a little 23cm (9in) pot or a large tub.

A covering of moss around the plants would be pretty. It would be best situated getting a little sunlight, so in the lee of an east-facing wall would be ideal.

Woodland Wild Flowers
Bluebell *Hyacinthoides non-scriptus*
Early Purple Orchid *Orchis mascula*
Foxglove *Digitalis purpurea*
Hedge Woundwort *Stachys sylvatica*
Herb Robert *Geranium robertianum*
Lily of the Valley *Convallaria majalis*
Mallow *Malva moschata*

Primroses *Primula vulgaris*
Snowdrop *Galanthus nivalis*
Solomon's Seal *Polygonatum multiflorum*
Spurge *Euphorbia amygdaloides*
Stinking Hellebore *Helleborus foetidus*
White Deadnettle *Lamium album*
Wood Sorrel *Oxalis acetosella*
Yellow Archangel (Deadnettle) *Lamiastrum galeobdolon*

MOISTURE-LOVING WILD FLOWERS

To make a wet meadow in a pot means removing most of the drainage and using a potting compost that will retain moisture (quite a few boggy plants like an acidic soil, so this is one of the rare cases where a peat-based compost would be best). You must also remember to water it. It does not want to be sodden, but should not be allowed to dry out. With the exception of plants like snake's head fritillary, moisture-loving plants tend to be fairly vigorous, so you need a decent-sized container or great discipline in excluding the more boisterous plants.

Wild Flowers that like Moisture
Bistort *Polygonum bistorta*
Comfrey *Symphytum tuberosum*
Common Valerian *Valeriana officinalis*
Devil's-bit Scabious *Succisa pratensis*
Grass of Parnassus *Parnassia palustris*
Hemp Agrimony *Eupatorium cannabinum*
Lousewort *Pedicularis sylvatica*
Marsh Cinquefoil *Potentilla palustris*

Marsh Gentian *Gentiana pneumonanthe*
Ragged Robin *Lychnis flos-cuculi*
Small-flowered Hairy Willowherb *Epilobium parviflorum*
Snake's Head Fritillary *Fritillaria meleagris*
Sundew *Drosera rotundifolia*
Thistle *Cirsium dissectum*
Yellow Loosestrife *Lysimachia vulgaris*

CONTAINER WITH WILD FLOWERS FOR DISTURBED GROUND

The last container should be for the group of wild flowers that move in to colonise broken soil. You often see these on the roadside, rubbish heaps, in agricultural fields that have not been sprayed to death, and in your garden borders.

But the big difference to the normal border is that to make this group of wild flowers grow you need to keep the soil really poor. It will not need nourishment at all — just a riddle with a trowel each winter. It will love this.

Wild Flowers Pretending to be in a Cornfield
Field Poppy *Papaver rhoeas*
Foxglove *Digitalis purpurea*
Ox-eye Daisy *Leucanthemum vulgare*
Aaron's Rod *Verbascum thapsus*
Corn Cockle *Agrostemma githago*
Field Cow Wheat *Melampyrum arvense*
Spurge *Euphorbia helioscopa*

SEEDS

Seeing seeds grow into young plants is tremendously satisfying. Note the clear labelling.

Growing plants from seed is the most satisfying gardening of all, and often the only financially feasible way of producing the quantity of plants that a well-stocked garden needs.

For the Weekend Gardener seeds have the great advantage of doing quite a lot without needing much done to them. If you buy a shrub it changes very slowly for the first few years and then you suddenly realise that it has doubled in size. But with seeds you have the pleasure of ambling over to where you sowed them, noticing that they have grown since the day before yesterday and then ambling away. **An hour spent sowing seeds in an organised fashion will create hundreds of plants.**

Seeds can be sown either in a container, in a seedbed or directly into the place you wish the mature plant to be.

SOWING SEEDS IN CONTAINERS

Seeds can be sown in any container with drainage but the most useful containers are **seed trays**. Do not buy very cheap, flimsy ones. Get the rigid type that cost between 50p and £1 each. There are few things in life more annoying than picking up a seed tray in each hand, both full of carefully grown seedlings, and seeing the trays kink in the middle and the contents fall ruinously to the floor. Rigid seed trays last for years and can easily be carried in one hand.

Square pots are also useful as they can be fitted into seed trays for convenient handling; they are necessary for larger seeds like runner beans. A seed tray will take twelve 7.5cm (3in) pots, each sown with three or four seeds.

You can use seed compost (John Innes No. 1), though I find this too gritty, or a general purpose compost. **Do not use potting compost,** as it will have the wrong blend of nutrients.

Spread compost into the seed tray until it is about 1cm (1/2in) below the rim. Press it down and water it lightly. Sow the seeds as directed on the packet, trying to spread them evenly and thinly. Cover the seeds with a thin layer of compost and water again.

Seed trays can be placed on the window-sill, in the greenhouse or in the dark if the seeds need dark to germinate. You can aid germination by putting the entire tray inside a loose polythene freezer bag, folded under the bottom. This creates a moist, warm microclimate, ideal for germination.

Propagators are enclosed containers for seed trays with clear tops and underfloor thermostatic heating. They range from one to four-tray size and will fit on most window-sills. They dramatically speed up germination for easy plants and improve the success rate for tricky germinators. Their real advantage is that you can start sowing seeds much earlier in the year – unless you have a heated greenhouse.

SOWING SEEDS OUTDOORS

A **seedbed** is incredibly useful. It can be quite small – 90cm (3ft) square is perfectly workable – but the soil must be dug over, well-rotted manure or compost added and broken down into a fine tilth. Remove all stones and, unless your soil is very fast-draining, add a generous amount of grit or sharp sand.

Choose a sheltered, sunny spot for your seedbed and use it as an intensive factory for raising seedlings before they are transplanted to their final position. It is surprising how many different types of seed can be grown in a very small area.

If the soil is very fine, a 'cap' can develop over seeds just sown. This is a hard crust of soil that has been wetted and then baked in the sun. When you subsequently water it the moisture does not penetrate properly but runs off. If the seeds do germinate they have trouble pushing through the hard layer. You can avoid this by covering the seedbed with a layer of sharp sand about 1cm (1/2in) thick. The emerging seedling pushes through it easily and water goes through the sand to the roots in the soil. The sand also acts as a mulch to stop evaporation.

SOWING DIRECT

Many hardy annual flower seeds such as poppies, forget-me-nots, cornflowers, *Nigella*, *Limnanthes*, marigolds and Californian poppies are best sown in the area you wish them to develop. Prepare the ground as thoroughly as possible without disturbing the roots of surrounding perennials (which may not have emerged from their winter dormancy yet) and scratch zig-zag lines with a stick. Sow the seeds thinly in these lines. This will enable you to differentiate between the seedlings of annuals and those of weeds as both appear simultaneously a few weeks later. Thin as soon as the seedlings are large enough to handle, leaving 2.5cm (1in) between plants. They might need thinning again when they are larger.

Seeds germinate in response to

water, warmth and oxygen, so it is vital not let them dry out and pointless to sow outdoors until the soil (not just the air) has warmed up. Farmers used to drop their corduroys and test the warmth of the soil on their buttocks before deciding whether it was the right time to sow their crops, but the neighbours might get the wrong end of the stick if you try that in your back garden. A more genteel, but equally effective, test is to run the soil through your fingers: if it feels at all cold you must wait, regardless of the date. **It is better to sow too late than too soon.** The need for oxygen means that seeds must not be sown too deeply, otherwise the air cannot get through the soil. **Too deep sowing is the most common reason for the failure of seeds to germinate.**

THINNING OUT

When seedlings emerge they must be thinned as soon as they can be handled and the surplus plants thrown away. The secret is to thin out as soon as leaves appear and to hold the seedling by a leaf, not the stem. This is a very easy, quick job, but it is delicate work and women tend to be better at it than men. If you are working indoors this process is called 'pricking out' and involves moving the seedlings to better soil (John Innes No. 2 or a general purpose compost), since seed compost has very little nutrition. Chuck used compost away, as all the goodness will have been used up.

Always be more brutal with your thinning than feels right — the most common mistake is to leave seedlings too close so that the growing plants are competing for nutrients and water and never develop properly.

AND FINALLY

Once the seedlings are growing, they will need to be moved to their final position or 'potted on'. This entails carefully levering the little plants out (holding them by a leaf, *not* the stem) without damaging the roots and replanting them in potting compost at wider spacing. This will enable them to develop a strong root system. Do not be in too much of a hurry to move seedlings grown indoors to the harsh outside world. At the very least they must be 'hardened off' for at least a week: put them outside in a sheltered spot during the day and bring them indoors or cover them over night.

Thin seedlngs as soon as you can lift them by a leaf (not the stem).

Leave plenty of room for each plant to develop.

WEEDS

To begin at the beginning: annual weeds grow from seed and survive only one growing season. Common annual weeds are groundsel, chickweed and annual meadow grass.

Perennial weeds survive for more than two growing seasons – sometimes for many years. Common perennial weeds are nettle, dock, bindweed, ground elder, couchgrass and thistle.

On the whole annual weeds are no problem and can even be seen as a good thing, as they both show that the soil is fertile (something is growing) and are easy to pull up and add to the compost heap so that they return to improve the soil for the things that you want there.

It is perennial weeds that are the buggers. The table opposite divides perennial weeds into two groups – the nuisances and the absolute bastards which must be eradicated at all costs.

ANNUAL WEEDS

That said, annual weeds need to be kept in check for two reasons.

COMMON ANNUAL WEEDS
Annual Meadow Grass *Poa annua*
Black Bindweed *Bilderdykia convclvulus*
Chickweed *Stellaria media*
Common Speedwell *Veronica officinalis*
Fat Hen *Chenopodium album*
Groundsel *Senecio vulgaris*
Hairy Bittercress *Cardamine hirsuta*
Marsh Cudweed *Filaginella uliginosa*
Petty Spurge *Euphorbia peplus*
Prickly Sow Thistle *Sonchus asper*
Red Dead Nettle *Lamium purpureum*
Shepherd's Purse *Capsella bursa-pastoris*
Smooth Sow Thistle *Sonchus oleraceus*

1. There is an old saying 'One year's seeding is seven years' weeding.' A single big plant of fat hen (*Chenopodium album*) can produce 70,000 seeds. A weedy area of ground may produce as many as 50,000 weed seeds per sq. m. (5,000 per sq. ft). Not all of these will germinate, but some will remain dormant in the soil for up to seven years until it is disturbed. So it is vital to destroy annual weeds before they set seed.

2. Weeds are just plants we do not want. They have all the same nutritional and cultivation requirements as the plants that we do want, and compete hungrily with them for available food and moisture. By removing annual weeds we are effectively feeding and watering the plants that remain.

The best way to cope with annual weeds is by a two-pronged attack:
1. Mulch. (see page 150). This keeps the ground dark so most seeds cannot germinate.
2. Hoe. I once asked an old boy what the secret of his wonderful garden was. 'I never lets that hoe rest,' he said.

The time to hoe is when the weeds are very small. Another old gardener once told me fiercely that if you ever needed to hoe, it was a sure sign that you were not hoeing enough. A little extreme, I think, but the point is clear: always keep on top of the weeds.

The best hoe for annual weeds is the Dutch hoe (see page 15), which you push through the soil just below the surface, cutting the weeds from their roots. The sharper you keep it, the easier it is to work and the more effective it is. Hoe when the ground is dry, preferably in the morning. The weeds will die in the sun. Collect big weeds and put them on the compost heap.

There is only one sure-proof method of dealing with perennial weeds: remove the plant before it seeds, dig every last scrap of root from the ground and burn the lot.

It works. There is just one hitch: it involves hours and hours of boring, back-breaking work. You would not be reading this book if you had that sort of time (or that sort of inclination, for that matter).

There are also weeds like horsetail, horseradish and Japanese knotweed with roots of enormous depth and re-

PERENNIAL WEEDS
Nuisances
Bryony *Bryonia dioica*
Buck's-horn Plantain *Plantago coronopus*
Coltsfoot *Tussilago farfara*
Common Stinging Nettle *Urtica dioica*
Cotton Thistle *Onopordum acanthium*
Creeping Thistle *Cirsium arvense*
Curled Dock *Rumex crispus*
Daisy *Bellis perennis*
Dandelion *Taraxacum officinale*
Dog's Mercury *Mercurialis perennis*
Germander Speedwell *Veronica chamaedrys*
Hoary Plantain *Plantago media*
Lesser Celandine *Ranunculus ficaria*
Meadow Buttercup *Ranunculus acris*
Oxalis *Oxalis corymbosa*
Red Clover *Trifolium pratense*
Ribwort *Plantago lanceolata*
Rosebay Willowherb *Epilobium angustifolium*
Sorrel *Rumex acetosa*
White Clover *Trifolium repens*
White Deadnettle *Lamium album*
Yarrow *Achillea millefolium*

silence. Horsetail can go down 2.5m (8ft) and knotweed can be as tough as steel hawsers.

Certain weeds, such as ground elder, bindweed and couchgrass, have a habit of winding in amongst the roots of plants you wish to keep, so have a safe haven from the most diligent of weeding.

Thoroughly depressed? Don't despair – there are answers, if not complete solutions.

THE UNWANTED

Bindweed *Convolvulus arvensis*

Bramble *Rubus fruticosa*

Broad-leaved Dock *Rumex obtusifolius*

Couchgrass *Elymus repens*

Creeping Buttercup *Ranunculus repens*

Ground Elder *Aegopodium podagraria*

Hedge Bindweed *Calystegia sepium*

Horseradish *Amoracia rusticana*

Horsetail *Equisetum arvense*

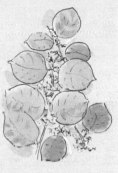

Japanese Knotweed *Polygonum japonicum*

1. Dig where you can. This can be with a hand fork, but however you do it, be meticulous. It is better to clear a square metre (square yard) properly than roughly do ten skimpily. Couch, bindweed and ground elder will grow into rampant plants from a piece of root the size of a half-used match.

2. Use weedkillers. Only a simpleton is politically correct about weeds. But use only Glysophate (Roundup, Tumbleweed) weedkillers anywhere you want anything at all to grow, and nowhere near where anything growing might be eaten. These products should be treated with great care and used strictly according to the instructions on the packaging, but if used responsibly they are safe. They become harmless on contact with soil and kill only green tissue. They are particularly effective on couchgrass, docks, thistles, bindweed and ground elder, but not so good on woody weeds like bramble or nettles, horseradish or horsetail.

3. Cut and cut again. If you have a border that is infested with any of the weeds that resist Glysophate sprays and which you do not have time or inclination to dig clean, regular hoeing with a sharp hoe that slices the plant off just below the surface will dramatically weaken the weeds' growth. Or you can take a long view. Lift the plants you wish to keep (washing the roots under a tap to clean out any trace of weed roots tangled amongst them) and sow the border with rye grass. This should then be mown weekly for at least a year. The mowing will weaken the weeds considerably whilst strengthening the grass, which in turn will suppress the weeds. After a couple of years it can then be sprayed off to kill the grass and converted back to a border.

4. Mulch with black plastic. This should be a last resort: it looks horrible and takes at least two years to be effective, but it does work. Cover the plastic with a mulch of gravel or bark to make it look less hideous.

Finally, weeding is something that **must be done little and often. Never let that hoe rest.**

APRIL

WEATHER REPORT: we all know about April showers, and what they reflect is not so much the wetness of the month but its changeability. One minute it can be positively summery and the next snowing. The moral of the story is to make the most of the good weather, but don't rush into planting anything that would be damaged by frost. The showers are exactly what the garden needs — ideally with warm spells in between. In consequence everything will grow this month. If April is dry — and the only predictable thing is that you cannot predict what the weather will do — start watering gently. The soil can lose as much as 10 litres per sq. m (2 gallons per sq. yd) of exposed soil per week in April and the growing roots near the surface of the soil are moisture-hungry, so keep an eye on things.

PLANTS IN THEIR PRIME

Bulbs: anemones; *Cyclamen repandum;* daffodils; fritillaries; hyacinths; *Trillium;* tulips.

Annuals/biennials: wallflowers (*Cheiranthus*); *Lunaria annua;* forget-me-not (*Myosotis*).

Perennials: aubrieta; *Brunnera macrophylla;* leopard's bane (*Doronicum*); Solomon's seal (*Polygonatum*); primulas; *Pulsatilla vulgaris;* violas.

Trees: maples (*Acer*); damsons; crab apples (*Malus*); bird cherry (*Prunus padus*).

Shrubs: azaleas; *Choisya ternata;* forsythias; magnolias; *Osmanthus delavayi; Pieris;* rhododendrons; flowering currant (*Ribes sanguineum*); *Skimmia japonica; Spiraea; Viburnum burkwoodii.*

Climbers: *Abelia lobata; Clematis armandii, C. alpina.*

Vegetables: the lowest point of the vegetable year. Go shopping.

Houseplants: give cacti their first water since autumn. Ivies, saintpaulias, tradescentias and impatiens can all be taken as cuttings in jars of water.

WEED CONTROL

Hoe lightly and often, trying not to let weeds establish and get on top of you. Collect annual weeds for the compost heap. Glysophate is particularly effective if used this month, so make the most of any sunny, windless opportunity you have.

LAWNS

This is a good month to lay or sow a new lawn (see pages 136 and 137). Keep cutting the grass high, gradually lowering the blades without shaving the grass, however mild the weather is.

Above. Everything is growing fast in April. The colours in the flower garden are at their most vibrant at this time of year.

Opposite: Tulips and pansies provide a swathe of spring colour at the RHS gardens at Wisley.

JOBS

Essential
• Put down slug bait under cover of a tile or pot (so nothing else can eat it) and remove any bodies.
• Sow or turf new lawns.
• Plant summer bulbs.
• Plant and transplant yew, box, holly, laurel, conifers and rhododendrons.
• Plant clematis, honeysuckle and wisteria.
• Stake herbaceous plants before they need it.

Desirable
• Sow hardy annuals outside *in situ* and in seedbeds.
• Continue sowing vegetables.
• Sow herbs in trays or seedbeds.
• Plant out sweet peas.
• Prune all spring-flowering shrubs immediately after flowering.
• Prune lavender and *Santolina,* avoiding cutting back to old wood.
• Dead-head bulbs **but do not cut off leaves** (or tie them up).

Optional
• Plant dahlia tubers and gladioli.
• Prepare ground for chrysanthemums.

TULIPS

When I was small I used to have extra maths lessons in the school holidays, which I hated. But I loved the extraordinary tulips in a narrow border flanking the path to the teacher's door, and the way that the sunlight shone through the petals, making the flower heads shimmer above the ground. Over a few years the colours changed, but the magic of those almost hallucinatory flowers remained as powerful. I had been hit by tulip fever.

I was not the first. When the first tulip arrived in Holland from Constantinople over 350 years ago it was treated as a fabulously exotic rarity. 'Tulipomania' made fortunes and bankrupted others between 1643 and 1647. Individual bulbs exchanged hands for thousands of pounds.

One solitary bulb of a type called 'Viceroy' was exchanged for :

2 cartloads of wheat

2 cartloads of rye

12 fat sheep

2 hogsheads (over 450 litres/100 gallons) of wine

1 bed

1 suit of clothes

4 fat oxen

8 fat swine

4 tuns (4,500 litres/1,000 gallons) of beer

2 tuns of butter

I silver drinking horn

1000lb (about 450kg) of cheese.

That hysteria has cooled a bit, but tulips are still universally loved for their great brazen goblets of bright colour in spring. The range spans from pure white to almost black, but skipping over blue on the way.

Tulips are not quite the labour-free article that most bulbs are, but very effective for the Weekend Gardener because they perform so dramatically that they can cover up some of the deficiencies elsewhere in the garden.

The 'classic tulip' – Darwin hybrids in Springfield Gardens, Lincolnshire.

Time invested on tulips reaps a brash, publicly measurable reward. You do not need – or want – to plant tulips in blocks. Leave that to the Municipal Parks Department. Use their intensity of colour to create ribbons within a border, or plant them in small groups where their brightness is intensified by the green of foliage around them. Of course a single tulip looks rather sad – bulbs require the company of their own kind. The secret is to plant just enough to create an effect but not so many that you spoil it. This takes judgement and experience, both of which are either inherent or easy to acquire.

Tulips differ from other bulbs from the word go. Despite their neat, smoothly conical bulbs they are temperamental about when they are planted. The best time to put them in the ground is November, after the risk of fireblight is past. They must be planted deep – at least three times their own depth.

All tulips come from hot, dry countries. They will not tolerate damp conditions and not many like shade. So give them sun and good drainage, artificially improving the soil with grit unless you have naturally very sharp drainage.

Unlike most bulbs, tulips will not naturalise when planted in grass

Tulips look very good grown in a border among herbaceous plants, before the latter have grown right up. After flowering, the tulip leaves, like those of all bulbs, must be left to die

GROWING TULIPS

AS A GENERAL RULE THE TULIP CULTIVARS ARE BEST TREATED AS ANNUALS, ALTHOUGH IF YOU DEAD-HEAD THE FLOWER AS SOON AS THE PETALS FALL AND GIVE THE LEAVES A FOLIAR FEED, THERE IS A FAIR CHANCE OF THE BULB STORING ENOUGH ENERGY TO FLOWER AGAIN NEXT YEAR, ALTHOUGH IT WILL NEVER DO AS WELL AS IN THE FIRST YEAR. WHEN THE LEAVES HAVE DIED RIGHT DOWN THE BULBS SHOULD BE LIFTED AND STORED IN A DRY PLACE UNTIL REPLANTING IN NOVEMBER. ALL IN ALL THIS IS A BIT OF A PALAVER. WORTH THE TROUBLE IF YOU HAVE PAID A NUMBER OF OXEN, HALF THE LOCAL OFF-LICENCE AND A DOZEN ARMANI SUITS FOR EACH BULB, BUT PERHAPS IT IS ENOUGH TO ENJOY THEM ONCE AND BUY FRESH BULBS FOR NEXT YEAR.

THERE ARE ONE OR TWO CULTIVARS THAT ARE EXCEPTIONS TO THIS: 'KEIZERSKROON' IS A SINGLE TULIP, ABOUT 30CM (12IN) HIGH WITH BULLS-EYE SCARLET AND YELLOW FLOWERS, AND 'COULEUR CARDINAL', A DEEP PLUM COLOUR, WILL BOTH FLOWER FOR MORE THAN A SINGLE SEASON IF LEFT.

DIVISION 1	DIVISION 2	DIVISION 3	DIVISION 4	DIVISION 5	DIVISION 6	DIVISION 7	DIVISION 8
Single Early	**Double Early**	**Triumph**	**Darwin Hybrids**	**Single Late**	**Lily-flowered**	**Fringed**	**Viridiflora**
Single flowers opening right out in sunshine. 'Pink Beauty', 'Diana', 'Keizerskroon' 'Ibis'	Long-lasting, double flowers. 'Mr Van der Hoef', 'Monte Carlo', 'Peach Blossom'.	Single, conical flowers in mid-spring. 'Athleet', 'Purple Star' 'Garden Party', 'White Dream'.	Tall, stately, classic tulips. 'La tulipe noire', 'Oranjezon', 'Big Chief'.	Pointed petals, in late spring. 'Queen of Night', 'Palestrina', 'Dillenburg'.	Long stems, long, pointed petals. 'West Point', 'White Triumphator',' China Pink'.	Same as Division 6 but fringed. 'Burgundy Lace', 'Maja', 'Fringed Elegance'.	Greenish petals. 'Artist', 'Groenland', 'Spring Green', 'Hollywood'.

DIVISION 9	DIVISION 10	DIVISION 11	DIVISION 12	DIVISION 13	DIVISION 14	DIVISION 15
Rembrandt	**Parrot**	**Double Late**	**Kaufmanniana Hybrids**	**Fosteriana Hybrids**	**Greigii Hybrids**	**All the rest**
'Broken' tulips, with patterns caused deliberately by injecting with a virus. 'Absalom', 'Jack Laan', 'Gala Beauty'.	Big, blowsy petals, twisted and frilled. 'Fantasy', 'Black Parrot', 'Blue Parrot', 'Firebird'.	Peony-flowered, 'May Wonder', 'Eros', 'Gold Medal', 'Mount Tacoma'.	Compact, bi-coloured, single flowers, opening flat. 'Heart's Delight', 'Gluck', 'Shakespeare'.	Large flowers opening wide. 'Mme Lefebre', 'Orange Emperor', 'Purissima'.	Large single flowers with wavy-edged leaves. 'Dreamboat', 'Cape Cod', 'Plaisir'.	*T. aucheriana*, *T. greigii*, *T. maximowiczii*.

back uncut, despite the fact that they become very scruffy and dejected. They will soon be hidden by the growing herbaceous plants.

WHICH TULIP?

If bitten by the tulip bug you can extend the precious moments when they are in your life by using the range of flowering season within the vast choice available in the small-flowered species as well as the more common large-flowered hybrids. The first tulip to flower is *Tulipa turkestanica* in March, looking prettily atypical with its yellow star-like petals; *T. saxatilis*, which looks more conventionally tulipy, follows soon after with lilac-pink flowers, each with a yellow internal base. The water-lily tulip (*T. kaufinanniana*) with its narrow petals and big leaves, also flowers in March.

The biggest flowering species is *T. fosteriana*, which appears in early April.

Then the doubles start to get into swing, followed by the lily-flowered tulips, which have pointed petals. The happily named 'Parrot' tulips have raggedy petals and flower in May. Finally the Darwins, nearly 90cm (3ft) tall and everybody's idea of the classic tulip, flower in the middle of May, and *T. sprengeri*, with slender, delicate, flowers of jewel like intensity, can be as late as June.

In fact, there are fifteen divisions of tulip, each with recognisable characteristics, following each other in roughly chronological order (see table above).

A WOODLAND BORDER

Fanciful as it might seem, the gardens of many town houses are rather like woods in that they are often very shaded by a combination of buildings and plants scrambling up walls and fences. By making a border specifically for woodland plants you are distilling the essence of the woods into a back garden and giving them the conditions they enjoy.

These conditions are pretty specific. Plants that grow naturally in deciduous woods get plenty of nourishment from the leaves that create the leaf-mould of the woodland floor, and protection from the worst of the weather, but as the leaves of the trees above them develop they get less and less sunlight and most of the rainfall is filtered away from them. So they have to be able to perform fast in spring, before the leaves of the trees grow. They flower, set seed, then often die right back and hide underground until they get their next brief moment of glory the following spring. Although the leaves overhead keep them from the light, they also keep them from the heat, maintaining the coolness in which this group of plants does best. Although the leaves keep off the light rain, a heavy soaking will evaporate much more slowly than in the open.

So if you have a spot in your garden that is cool and partly shaded – probably getting morning sun only – you can turn the seeming limitations to your advantage by carefully selecting the right plants that will make the most of the conditions.

Of course if you genuinely have an area of trees in your garden, then you can plant amongst them without any urban make-believe at all.

SOIL FOR WOODLAND PLANTS

First you must prepare the soil. I have said that the soil of a wood is largely composed of rotted leaves. This gives it a particularly fibrous, open quality which somehow manages both to hold moisture and to drain well. Nutritionally it is fairly thin, although adding fertiliser will not harm plants that you want to perform above their evolutionary requirements.

Dig the border thoroughly, adding organic matter and mixing it well in to open up the soil structure. Try not to tread on it once it is dug, as this will compact it and make the drainage and root-run less easy. If your soil is clay, it will need opening with horticultural grit as well as manure or compost. If it is very sandy, the manure will bulk it out.

WOODLAND PLANTS FOR MID-SPRING		
	Bergenia 'Silberlicht'	Pink
Bleeding Heart	Dicentra spectabilis	Pink/white
Bluebells	Hyacinthoides non-scriptus	Guess
Coral Flower	Heuchera sanguinea	Pink
Cuckoo Pint	Arum italicum 'Pictum'	Creamy white
Foam Flower	Tiarella cordifolia	Cream
Leopard's Bane	Doronicum plantagineum	Yellow
Lily of the Valley	Convallaria majalis	White
Lungwort	Pulmonaria angustifolia	Blue/pink
Pasque Flower	Pulsatilla vulgaris	Purple
Solomon's Seal	Polygonatum x hybridum	White
Wake Robin	Trillium grandiflorum	White

WOODLAND PLANTS FOR EARLY SPRING		
	Anemone blanda	White/violet
	Crocus	Yellow/lilac
Dog's Tooth Violet	Erythronium dens-canis	Pink
Grape Hyacinth	Muscari armeniacum	Blue
Lesser Celandine	Ranunculus ficaria	Yellow
Navelwort	Omphalodes cappadocica	Bright blue
Primrose	Primula vulgaris	Yellow
	Scilla siberica	Violet blue
Siberian Bugloss	Brunnera macrophylla	Blue
Snowdrop	Galanthus nivalis	White
Stinking Hellebore	Helleborus foetidus	Pale yellow
Winter Aconite	Eranthis hyemalis	Yellow
Wood Anemone	Anemone memorosa	White
Wood Spurge	Euphorbia robbiae	Reddy orange

Midsummer Woodland Plants		
Bugle	*Ajuga reptans*	Blue
Cranesbill	*Geranium macrorrhizum* 'Album'	White
Dead Nettle	*Lamium maculatum*	White/pink
Fern	*Dropteris filix-mas*	Green
Foxgloves	*Digitalis purpurea*	Purple/white
Horned Violet	*Viola cornuta*	White
Lady's Mantle	*Alchemilla mollis*	Yellow

When the border is prepared it should feel right to the hand – you should be able to plunge your fingers in and grasp its loose richness.

Shrubs and Flowers for the Woodland Border

If you have enough space, the best shrub for the woodland border is **hazel**. It likes a well-drained, fertile soil, and is particular happy in alkaline, limey ground. In an area of acidic soil the **deciduous azaleas** will give a balanced backdrop of light and shade. If you have a damp border it might be best to plant a **dogwood** (*Cornus*) or **willow** (*Salix*), which can both be coppiced and which will enjoy the wet. Having said that, go for hazel every time if you can.

Primroses are the most typical flower of hazel coppices and should spread willingly. I find all the gaudy cultivars a vulgar travesty. You cannot improve upon the original, its simple, pale yellow flowers reflecting the catkins hanging above them.

As spring really takes hold in May, the increasing vegetation means that the light is now a dappled shade. On the ground more leaves are pushing up, providing another level of shelter and shade. With careful planning, a new group of plants can take over the responsibilities of flowering.

Then, by June, the canopy has formed so completely that the plants are in almost constant shade. The ground becomes very dry. For gardening purposes you are going to have to water at least once a week, but the plants I am indicating can cope with deep shade and drought.

Finally, plant the **stinking iris** (*Iris foetidissima*) for the wonderful orange-red seeds displayed as the seed-pod bursts in autumn, and the **lilyturf** (*Liriope muscari*), whose spikes of violet-blue flowers in autumn are rather like **grape hyacinths** (*Muscari*).

All the maintenance that this border will need is the removal of any weeds (because of the lack of light there will not be that many); a good soak once a week (not little and often); and a mulch 5–7.5cm (2–3in) thick around Easter each year. The mulch should ideally be of leaf-mould, but failing that mushroom compost or home-made compost is best.

HERBACEOUS PLANTS

The herbaceous border in its full midsummer glory is the very essence of the English garden. It is strange, therefore, to discover that herbaceous borders are no more than a hundred years old and that most herbaceous plants are relatively recent introductions. Also true herbaceous borders are now very rare, because they were only intended to be looked at for a few summer months. For six months of the year they were an event waiting to happen. Nowadays few people would tolerate that state of affairs, especially when herbaceous plants require a fair amount of work in order to keep them looking their best. So most of the borders that we casually refer to as 'herbaceous' are better described as 'mixed', a term which accurately covers the combination of shrubs, annuals, biennials, bulbs and herbaceous plants.

The great beauty of a herbaceous plant is the never-failing element of surprise that comes with its renewal each spring. It adds electricity to a mixed border and the lushness that can only come with rapid growth. So however old-fashioned the true herbaceous border is, herbaceous plants will always be part of any garden.

The herbaceous plant is a non-woody perennial that dies down completely in the winter, although the roots remain alive and healthy, throwing up new, non-woody growth in the spring. This is a device that the plant has evolved to protect itself in its natural habitat, which, in the main, has hot summers and cold winters. The dead growth from the summer acts as insulation against the cold as well as rotting down to provide nourishment. Because its season is so short, the plant has to grow with tremendous vigour in order to flower and set seed before autumn. Hence the dramatic transformation in the herbaceous border in the months from April to the end of June.

CARING FOR HERBACEOUS PLANTS

Because herbaceous plants live a long time and grow so fast, they need a lot of nourishment. This starts with the soil, and **the better the soil the better the plants**. The first thing to do is to dig it really well, double-digging it if possible (see pages 152 and 153). At the very least fork in a good amount of organic material as well as a liberal sprinkling of bonemeal. (Bonemeal works slowly and does not get washed out of the soil, so the plant can draw upon its goodness as it grows).

Plant each individual plant with more manure and bonemeal and water it well in. The best time to plant is in the dormant season when the shock of moving is minimised. I always think of moving a plant as being like surgery: however successful the operation, the patient – or plant – must be given time and care to recover properly.

Each spring you must weed carefully around each plant (a job best done grovelling on your hands and knees with a hand fork), sprinkle it with bonemeal and then mulch between the plants as thickly as you can with good compost. It was always the done thing to take all the plants out of a herbaceous border every third winter, split them (see page 162), double-dig the ground, adding vast quantities of manure, and replant it. This was a major performance, and quite beyond the scope of even the keenest Weekend Gardener. Nowadays we have learnt that deep mulching with well-made compost will replenish the goodness that the voracious growth of the plants takes out of the soil and work its way down to keep the soil structure good. But it is necessary to put a mulch of at least 5cm (2in) and ideally 15–18cm (5–6in).

Herbaceous plants have no backbone. Because they grow so fast they are very soft and will bend, buckle and

BY THE TIME THAT YOU READ THIS, MY LIST WILL HAVE CHANGED. THAT IS ONE OF THE JOYS OF GROWING HERBACEOUS PLANTS – EVERY YEAR ONE SEES THEM AFRESH.

break in bad weather. So they must be supported. The secret is to provide support before they need it, and not as a salvage job after a storm. You can use bamboos, which are effective but ugly; proprietary metal supports, which are pricey; string, stretched between inconspicuous uprights and around each clump of plants; or best of all, twigs and branches cut specially for the job the previous winter. Stick these into the ground around each clump – they will become hidden as the plants grow.

DESIGNING YOUR BORDER

It is vital that you do not just plonk the plants down at random. **A border must be composed with all the care of a picture**, paying attention to colour, shape, height and texture. You need height at the back, using plants such as *Macleaya cordata* (4.5m/15ft), *Rudbeckia*, *Filipendula* and *Inula* to give the border a sense of scale. These tall plants need to be planted in groups so that they do not look too spindly. Oriental poppies, lupins, phlox and plants with bare stems should go in the middle of the border, so the plants in front of them will hide their naked nether regions but not obscure their flowers. Low-growing plants such as sedums and *Alchemilla mollis* are ideal for the front of the border, spilling over on to a path or lawn.

Be aware of the effect of colours upon each other. Whites and blues look cool and distant and may look best in semi-shade. Reds, yellows and oranges are 'hotter', leaping out at you.

If you want to see what a herbaceous border on a grand scale can look like, visit the Royal Botanic Gardens in Edinburgh in July and August. The border there is 6.5m (21ft) deep and the longest in the country, planted in great groups of colour and form. The lesson to be learnt is that one should plant boldly and not in dabs of this and that. **Herbaceous plants should always look vigorous, not chaotic.**

Do not forget the role of the green foliage, which will dominate the border in April and May. The intensity of all their greens and the fantastic rate of growth of their foliage in spring is one of the surprising joys of growing herbaceous plants.

A herbaceous border in early summer. Delphiniums, penstemons and poppies in the foreground; geraniums, crambe, lilies and catmint behind. Note the paved edging to protect the lawn.

CLIMBERS

To garden with abandon you need to be private. This is not simply a matter of marking boundaries, but also of light and vision. If neighbours overlook you that can be a hostile invasion.

It is important to take into account the time of day that you want your privacy. Most people use their gardens only on summer evenings and at weekends. So if you have an office block hanging over your back garden, you may effectively have complete isolation. On the other hand, if there is only one window with a view into your garden, and it is unlooked out from all day save for the one hour when you want to sit and unwind, the result is violation.

So analysis of aspect is vital.

To protect your privacy, you are trying to create a bower, not a barricade. This means that it must look and smell good – by whatever yardstick you use. High hedges are fine in the country but do not work so well in the town. It is usually better to use a combination of climbers.

GROWING CLIMBERS

Most climbers can be grown in a pot, although do not expect them to reach the height of a similar plant in the open ground. The secret is to get as large a container as you can manage – big climbers have big roots. Make sure it has decent drainage holes. Put at least 5cm (2in) of crocks or pebbles in the bottom and fill it to within 5cm (2in) of the top with a specific tree or shrub compost (as John Innes No. 3 used to be). Plant the climber with a good handful of bonemeal. Do not overfill, as this will not leave enough room for watering. Water well at least once a

TIP

REMEMBER THAT THE BASE OF A WALL IS ALWAYS DRY, SO MAKE YOUR HOLE AT LEAST 45CM (18IN) FROM THE WALL AND WATER FREQUENTLY. IT IS BETTER TO WATER THOROUGHLY ONCE A WEEK THAN A LITTLE EVERY DAY. THE LATTER PROGRAMME ENCOURAGES SHALLOW ROOTS, WHICH WILL IN TURN BE MORE VULNERABLE TO DRYING OUT.

week and even daily in the summer.

Tie in climbers as they grow. Use a soft string or raffia that will not bruise the tender new growth.

CHOOSING PLANTS

If you have a small garden with high walls, the chances are that these walls shade the garden for much of the day. However, there are climbers that are very happy in shade.

If you have a sunny wall or fence, don't waste it – use it to grow climbers that will make the most of the situation.

Lots of gardens have a wall – often east-facing – that is very exposed to winds. There are climbers for this situation, too.

A selection of suitable climbers for these different conditions is given in the table (left).

CLIMBING ROSES

These are divided into two types, climbers and ramblers.

Climbers are less vigorous

Shade Climbers

LATIN NAME	COMMON NAME	COMMENT
Chaenomeles	Quince	Early blossom. Spiny, attractive fruits.
Clematis		Many varieties, especially 'Jackmanii' cultivars.
Hedera helix	Ivy	Evergreen and self-supporting.
Hydrangea petiolaris	Climbing hydrangea	Self-supporting. A slow starter.
Jasminum officinale	Common jasmine	Sweetly scented white flowers. Also grows in sun.
Lonicera tragophylla	Chinese woodbine	Very vigorous. Yellow flowers.
Rosa 'Souvenir de Dr Jamain' and 'Zéphirine Drouhin'		

Climbers for Full Sun

Ceanothus	California Lilac	Lovely blue flowers, evergreen leaves.
Clematis armandii		Evergreen leaves, white flowers .
Ficus	Fig	Likes dry, poor soil.
Humulus lupulus	Golden hop	Perennial. Likes moist, rich soil.
Jasminum officinale	Common jasmine	Very sweet-scented.
Rosa		Most climbing roses like full sun.
Wisteria		Vigorous with drooping racemes of flower.

Climbers for an Exposed Position

Clematis montana, C. vitalba		White flowers.
Cotoneaster horizontalis	Fishbone cotoneaster	Low-growing.
C. 'Hybridus pendulus'	Weeping cotoneaster	Fast-growing, fan-shaped
Euonymus fortunei var. radicans		Grows well in shade too.
Forsythia suspensa	Weeping forsythia	Needs plenty of space
Jasminum nudiflorum	Winter jasmine	Butter-yellow winter flowers.
Lonicera	Honeysuckle	Most varieties will do well in this position.

Training vines or other climbers carefully over a trellis will provide a dense summer screen.

than ramblers, have fewer, much larger flowers and often flower though the season. They must be pruned annually (see pages 48–49). Typical examples are 'New Dawn', 'Climbing Iceberg' and 'Madame Alfred Carrière'.

Ramblers grow powerfully, producing a froth of flowers for a few splendid weeks only and should only be pruned to contain them. They are ideal for scrambling up a tree, over a building or on a large bank. My favourites include 'Albéric Barbier', 'Paul's Himalayan Musk' and 'Rambling Rector'.

Do not be lured into planting rambling roses of violent growth such as *R. filipes* 'Kiftsgate'. Most people wildly underestimate both their rate and ultimate extent of expansion. You want to screen the neighbours, not smother them. My current favourite rose for a shady wall or trellis is 'Souvenir de Dr Jamain' a hybrid perpetual with wonderful, deep crimson flowers from late May to September.

OTHER CLIMBERS

You need a **honeysuckle** and my favourite is *Lonicera americana*. It has yellow flowers with purplish shading and a rich scent of cloves. It is not too happy on very alkaline soils, but grows pretty easily. Honeysuckles are best allowed to bush and scramble rather than being trained too severely. Their scent

is much better in the cool of the evening or early morning than during the day – which fits in neatly with a working timetable.

The **vine** (*Vitis coignetiae*) covers a vast space with its huge leaves and colours well in autumn. It can romp away a little alarmingly, but is easy to prune and clothes trellis faster than almost anything.

Annual climbers can be planted when the last frosts have gone. **Scarlet runner beans** make a good screen, as do **sweet peas** (*Lathyrus odoratus*) and the more exotic annuals such as *Ipomoea*

tricolor 'Heavenly Blue' or *Cobaea scandens* – both subtropical species that will grow until the first frost.

Ivy may be ubiquitous, but it is not to my mind a sexy plant. It has two main virtues to the gardener, though. The first is that it will grow almost anywhere, in any conditions other than bog. The second is that it is self-clinging, which means that it will cover a smooth wall without needing to be tied up. Ivy thrives in the shade and drought, although a young ivy plant should be watered for its first year to help it establish.

It is easy to create mysterious and shady walks if you grow climbers like this wisteria over arched support.

RHODODENDRONS AND AZALEAS

I was brought up on the chalk downs of northern Hampshire, where rhododendrons simply cannot survive. But I went to school – less than 30km (20 miles) away – in the acidic heathlands of Berkshire, where they ranged unfettered. And that is the way with rhododendrons and azaleas. They do like their soil acid. If you live on chalk or limestone, then forget it. Of course you can grow them in a peat-filled container, but if everything around the plant is lime-loving, it looks stupid. If you only have a back yard, treat them like an outside houseplant rather than as part of the garden.

Deciduous azaleas in spring. Unlike rhododendrons, they like full sun.

In the right setting rhododendrons look magnificent. Out of place they look sad. For me they are not shrubs and trees of small gardens unless small varieties are chosen. But if you have plenty of space, an unnaturally high rainfall, cool temperatures, woodland shade and intensely acidic, peaty soil then you can use the big boys such as *R. arboreum*, *R. barbatum* or *R. falconerii* and let rip. A few years back I was visiting the gardens of the west coast of Scotland, and although the weather was filthy, the rhododendrons were sublime. Gardens like Crarae, Arduine, Ardtornish, Inverewe, Benmore and Castle Kennedy are blazing with glory in April and May.

There are 800 species of rhododendrons, ranging from tiny alpine scrub to vast tree forms. They belong to the Ericaceae family, which includes heathers, pieris, blueberries and bilberries, all plants that look well with rhododendrons. They attract each other. They also attract a particular brand of gardening fanatic, charming people who get a mad glint in their eyes when they hear of or see a rhododendron that they have not grown.

Azaleas are botanically a type of rhododendron, although most gardeners treat them as a separate group, and I shall do the same.

RHODODENDRONS

Rhododendrons proper are broken into two groups, lepidote and elepidote. Lepidotes contain over 500 species, including most of the tiny ones, and elepidotes most of the garden species.

Elepidotes are in turn broken down into sixteen 'series', each series named after its best-known member. I shall not burden you with a list, but even the least interested gardener will have heard of *R. ponticum*, whose mauve-pink flowers are to be seen everywhere save on alkaline soil. In Snowdonia it has become the major pest, eating up acres of countryside every year. I can see no possible reason for planting it into yet another garden.

Rhododendrons are actually very easy to plant and undemanding once established. They are surface feeders, so the area around their roots must not be disturbed and should be mulched generously every spring, preferably with manure. This habit of surface feeding has the advantage that even big specimens can easily be dug up and moved. The leaves and flowers do not particularly want shade, although their roots do. This shade is provided in the mature plant by the branches, but the young specimen will need a thick mulch to provide the necessary cover.

What they cannot tolerate is dry air. They do not want to be in sodden ground, but adore sodden air. Cold winds are hateful to them and ice alarming, although they cope perfectly well with snow. In very dry weather, the best way to treat them is to set a fine spray or sprinkler on them for an hour or so a day.

THE HARDY HYBRIDS

These were bred from a cross between the unremarkable North American species and those introduced in the early 1800s from the Himalayas. The flowers from the latter were universally lusted after, but it was found that they were produced in March and could not survive frosts. So nurserymen manically set about crossing the two types to

make plants that would produce the sexy flowers later in the year when most of the danger of frost had passed. Most of the results are horrid. But there are a few that have subtlety and make superb plants rather than backdrops for lipstick-coloured flowers.

AZALEAS

Whereas rhododendrons are almost always evergreen, azaleas lose their leaves in winter. As they do so they give off a wonderful autumnal display. Although there is a group of 'evergreen' azaleas, they do lose their leaves every year, but wait until spring before doing so. Their flowers are more plentiful and smaller than rhododendrons and completely cover the bush. The best azaleas are far nicer than any rhododendron, the worst as bad as so many of the hardy hybrids.

Azaleas differ again from rhododendrons in that they will take open sunshine in any quantity, although they also like damp soil and a moist atmosphere.

The evergreen azaleas are all low, spreading shrubs, with brightly coloured flowers in shades of white, red and mauve. The Japanese shear them regularly to encourage dense bushes, whereas standard Western practice is to pinch out the growing tips.

Deciduous azaleas have a complicated history, but can be divided into the following groups:

Every shade of lipstick under the sun! Azaleas strutting their stuff. You either love them or you hate them.

I cannot finish without putting my cards on the table. While I can enjoy many deciduous azaleas, I cannot feel at ease with rhododendrons. I find the combination of dark green leaves and oversized gaudy flowers disturbing and oppressive. But I am a product of my own geology, and there is an incompatible seam of chalk running through my tastes.

Ghent Hybrids	Open, deciduous shrubs up to 3m (10ft) high. Delicate, sweetly scented flowers.
Rusticas	Double-flowered Ghent hybrids.
Occidentale Hybrids	Late-flowering, pale coloured. Drought tolerant.
Mollis Azaleas	Bred for winter colour in Victorian conservatories. Yellow to orange-red. Fragrant.
Knap Hill Azaleas	Brighter, larger flowers. Bushes to 1.5m (5ft).
Exbury Azaleas	Big, bright flowers. Very hardy.

ANNUALS

Annuals are the sprinters of the horticultural world. All their lives are crammed into one year, in which time they must germinate, grow, flower, set seed and – die. Biennials set leaf and strong roots the first year, then flower and die in the second. Some perennials are also usually treated as annuals. Because it is essential that they pollinate fast and produce viable seeds, annuals and biennials tend to have the most colourful flowers of all plants.

They are particularly useful in the first five years or so as a new garden is establishing. The gaps between plants that are inevitable until they mature can be filled with annuals, bringing colour and volume to otherwise scant borders.

Annuals need some indulging. Give them rich soil, thin them, weed them and water them well. Pamper them – they will repay the trouble tenfold.

There is a strong possibility of many annuals and biennials self-seeding in a border, so be careful how you weed or dig around them until you know what is a weed and what the offspring of last year's flowers.

HARDY ANNUALS

Hardy annuals will withstand frost and can be sown directly outside.

1. Clear the area to be sown of all weeds.

2. Mix in 2.5cm (1in) of organic compost and rake to a fine tilth.

3. Sow in zig-zags or a cross so that when the seedlings emerge you will be able to tell which are weeds and which your flowers-to-be. Water and mark the area with a label or stick with the seed packet attached.

4. Thin the seeds as they grow to a final spacing of about 7.5–15cm (3–6in) per plant, depending on size.

Hardy annuals need cold weather to germinate. They are normally sown outside in March – as soon as the soil is fit to be raked to a fine tilth – although some, including forget-me-nots, love-in-a-mist and poppies, are better sown in autumn, overwintering as small plants.

HALF-HARDY ANNUALS

Half-hardy annuals cannot take low temperatures; they have to be raised under glass and not planted out until after all chance of frost has passed. They need a temperature of at least 10°C (50°F) in order to germinate.

A cold frame is easy to make and invaluable for hardening off and growing half-hardy annuals.

HARDY ANNUALS

Sunflower *Helianthus annuus*
Opium Poppy *Papaver somniferum*
Love-in-a-mist *Nigella damascena*
Tobacco Plant *Nicotiana sylvestris*
Poached Egg Flower *Limnanthes douglasii*
Borage *Borago officinalis*
Cornflower *Centaurea cyanus*
Mallow *Lavatera trimestris* 'Mont Blanc'
Pot Marigold *Calendula officinalis*
Anchusa capensis
Corncockle *Agrostemma*
Larkspur *Delphinium consolida*
Californian Poppy *Eschscholzia californica*
Alyssum *Lobularia maritima*
Candytuft *Iberis*
Clarkia
Rudbeckia hirta
Toadflax *Linaria*
Scabious *Scabiosa*
Sweet Pea *Lathyrus odoratus*

HALF-HARDY ANNUALS

Bells of Ireland *Moluccella laevis*
Cosmos Bright Lights series
Cosmos bipinnatus
Everlasting Flower *Helichrysum bracteatum*
Busy Lizzies *Impatiens*
Tobacco Plant *Nicotiana alata* and *N. affinis*
Petunia: Resisto series
Zinnia elegans
Sage *Salvia splendens*
African Marigold *Tagetes erecta*
Snapdragon *Antirrhinum majus*
Phlox drummondii
Begonia semperflorens
Mexican Sunflower *Tithonia rotundifolia*
Night-scented Stock *Matthiola longipetala bicornis*
Aster *Callistephus chinensis*
Swan River Daisy *Brachycome iberidifolia*
Pink *Dianthus*
Butterfly Flower *Schizanthus*
Verbena

BIENNIALS

Foxglove *Digitalis purpurea*
Pansy *Viola wittrockiana*
Sweet William *Dianthus barbatus*
Daisy *Bellis perennis*
Canterbury bell *Campanula medium*
Wallflower *Cheiranthus cheiri*
Forget-me-not *Myosotis*

If you are not growing them from seed yourself, you are best buying them in trays after 1 June, even though they are often on sale well before that date. Look for sturdy, compact plants with healthy foliage and moist compost. Do not buy plants already in flower or 'leggy'.

If you have grown them from seed in a heated greenhouse or propagator, remember to harden them off before planting out. At least a month before planting, transfer them to a closed cold frame which is gradually exposed to more air as the weather improves.

BIENNIALS

Sow your biennials in May and June so that they develop strong roots this summer, overwinter and flower next spring and summer. If you have the space, a corner of the vegetable garden is ideal for this. Transplanting biennials to their final position in October will produce earlier flowering than moving them in spring. If they produce flower buds in the summer after sowing, pinch them off so as not to reduce the quantity and quality of flowering next spring.

OTHER USES FOR ANNUALS

Some annuals grow very big very fast and are best used to fill a space. My favourites for this job are the **giant thistle** (*Onopordum acanthium*), **sunflower** (*Helianthus annuus*), **mullein** (*Verbascum nigrum*), **delphinium** (*Delphinium ajacis*) and **larkspur** (*Consolida ajacis*).

Not all annuals are grown for their flowers: *Senecio maritima* 'Silver Dust' is usually grown as an annual for its silvery, fern-like leaves. Very effective it is too.

*A border of annuals dominated by African marigolds (*Tagetes*) and tobacco plants (*Nicotiana*).*

WEATHER REPORT: *May is my favourite month. No other month moves into such voluptuous richness. If it is wet all the greenery becomes lush and full and if it is hot and dry the flowers race ahead. Just to keep us on our toes and to stop the flow of poetry becoming a gush, May can also produce quite sharp frosts, especially in a dry spell with warm daytime temperatures, so be wary about putting out tender plants such as tomatoes, half-hardy annuals and pot plants like citrus. 'Ne'er cast a clout until the May is out' does not refer to the month of May but to the hawthorn (may) blossom, which traditionally was at its best around May Day. The calendar was moved forward by eleven days in the mid-eighteenth century, so the old May Day is now 11 May – about the time the may blossom is at its peak and you can start to throw your clothes (clouts) off with abandon.*

PLANTS IN THEIR PRIME

Bulbs: alliums; bluebells; *Cyclamen repandum*; *Fritillaria imperialis*; snowflake (*Leucojum*); tulips.

Annuals/biennials: daisies; wallflowers (*Cheiranthus*).

Perennials: aquilegias; bleeding heart (*Dicentra spectabilis*); *Euphorbia griffithii, E. wulfenii*; bearded iris; lily of the valley; lupins; catmint (*Nepeta*); peonies; Solomon's seal (*Polygonatum*); Pasque flower (*Pulsatilla vulgaris*).

Trees: maples (*Acer*); amelanchiers; apples; cherry; Judas tree (*Cercis siliquastrum*); hawthorn; horse chestnuts; laburnum; crab apples (*Malus*); pears (*Pyrus*); false acacia (*Robinia pseudoacacia*); whitebeam (*Sorbus*).

Shrubs: *Buddleia globosa*; *Ceanothus; Kolkwitzia amabilis*; lilac; mock orange (*Philadelphus*); rhododendrons; *Rosa pimpinellifolia*, *R*. 'Nevada', *R. primula; R. sericea;* weigelas.

Climbers: *Clematis montana, C. macropetala; Rosa xanthina* 'Canary Bird'; *Wisteria sinensis*.

Vegetables: asparagus; broad beans; baby carrots; spring greens; lettuce; radishes; spinach.

Houseplants: remove old flowered bromeliad stems. Move plants off hot window-sills.

Above: The cherry blossom signals that spring is really here.

Opposite: A laburnum tunnel designed by Rosemary Verey at Barnsley House, Gloucestershire, lures one irresistibly towards the 'feature' at the other end.

WEED CONTROL

If you have been away or have not had time to get into the garden, do not panic. The situation is still retrievable. At this time of year weeds pull up easily and many have not yet seeded. An excellent tool for crisis weeding is a mattock, with which you chop all the weeds, however terrifyingly rampant, just below the surface. Rake them up and make a heap of them. In twelve months they will have composted down. This creates a physical and psychological space in which to manoeuvre.

LAWNS

Cut once a week, collecting cuttings if possible. Mix with straw or other dry material in compost heap.

JOBS

Essential
• Stake herbaceous plants.
• If you are buying bedding plants, choose strong, healthy plants with bright green leaves.
• Hedges such as *Lonicera nitida* or privet need their first trim now.
• Sow biennials.
• Plant out half-hardy annuals at end of month.
• Plant window boxes and hanging baskets (see pages 92 and 93).
• Sow herbs.

Desirable
Trim the foliage of *Iris unguicularis* when it has finished. This lets sun and air in to ripen the roots for next year.
• Prune *Kerria japonica, Prunus triloba, Forsythia*.
• Make ponds (see pages 78 and 79)
• Plant waterlilies.
• Plant out alpine strawberries.
• Earth up early potatoes.
• Plant out tomatoes in greenhouse.

Optional
• Prune *Clematis montana* and *C. ar mandii*, cutting back only as far as tidiness and size limitation dictate.

CREATING A POND

Let me start by making one vital point: **if you have children under the age of six, do not put any sort of pond into your garden. If you inherited a pond when you bought the house and have small children, don't think twice about it: fill it in.**

The principles of making a pond are simple. You dig a hole, line it with something waterproof and fill it up with water. In practice you can refine this down somewhat.

The first thing is to **choose the site**. This wants to be an open, sunny position, away from overhanging trees which will provide unwanted shade and fallen leaves in autumn. It also wants to be as level as possible. It is perfectly possible to make a pond on a slope, but it does make life more difficult.

Next **work out the shape**. If you are having an informal pond, a flowing shape is ideal. If you are including the pond in a formal design, a rectangular or circular shape works best. Avoid tight corners or narrow angles.

Mark out the outline of an irregular pond with a hosepipe or heavy rope. Then calculate the size of liner needed. The liner should measure the maximum width of the pool plus twice its depth, by the maximum length plus twice its depth. Add 15cm (6in) on to both width and length to allow for a flap at the edge to prevent leakage. Thus a 60cm (2ft) deep pool measuring 2m x 3m would require a liner of 3.5m x 4.5m, and one of 6ft x 8ft would require a liner of 11ft x 13ft.

Now you have to **choose the type of liner**. Butyl is undoubtedly the best.

It is very strong and pliable and will last for fifty years. But it is expensive. You can use PVC or polythene, but I do not recommend it. It would have to be replaced after a few years and this would be a false economy. Rigid liners made from fibreglass or plastic impose a shape on your pool and are more difficult to install, as the hole has to be dug to exact dimensions.

Next **dig a hole**. A mini-digger can be hired for around £100 per day and makes the job a lot more fun.

The hole needs a shelf around the edge about 23cm (9in) deep, for marginal plants whose roots are under water but whose crowns are dry. It is not necessary to dig down more than 60cm (2ft) for horticultural reasons, although if you are to keep fish in the pond you need part of it to be at least as deep as this so that they can avoid freezing in the winter. Dig the sides at an angle of 20° to stop it caving in.

Use a spirit level to check that the top is level and if you are on a slope build up the lower side with spoil from the higher.

When the hole is the shape and size you want it to be, **take out all stones and roots**. This is to stop the lining being punctured. Then spread a layer of soft sand, glass fibre or proprietary material over the entire surface to protect it further. Do not skimp on this — it is essential.

Wait for a sunny, dry day. Spread the liner out in the sun away from the pool. This gives it a chance to warm up and become more flexible.

Spread the liner fairly tautly over the hole so that it just touches the deepest bit and weigh the edges down with bricks or bits of stone. Fill the pond with water from a hose. Stand back and admire your handiwork as the water slowly seeps in.

The weight of the water will expand and mould the liner to the contours of the pool. Inevitably there will be some wrinkles, but do your best to minimise them by keeping the liner taut. You have to ease the pressure on the butyl gradually by adjusting the weights around the edge as the water fills.

When the pond is full, remove the weights and trim off any excess liner, leaving an edge of about 30cm (12in).

Now **make an edge for the pond** by laying the edging material over the top of the protruding liner and letting it overhang the pool by 2.5cm (1in) or so.

Stone is the best edging material as it keeps a firm edge, but if you want to encourage wildlife, turf is more natural and does perfectly well. Whatever you use, make sure that the surface around the pond is firm and level, so that there will be no future subsidence. Also take particular care to have any bricks or slabs fitted closely and absolutely

CREATING A PEBBLE BEACH

A PEBBLE BEACH CAN LOOK VERY GOOD IN A POND. IT IS EASY ENOUGH TO CREATE.

1. MAKE A LARGE SHALLOW SHELF AT THE EDGE OF THE POND WHERE YOU WANT THE BEACH TO BE.

2. SINK A KERBSTONE INTO THE SOIL AT THE EDGE OF THE SHELF JUST BEFORE IT DIPS MORE STEEPLY DOWN TO THE BOTTOM OF THE POND.

3. PUT THE PROTECTIVE LAYER OVER THE TOP OF THIS KERB AND RIGHT OUT OVER THE SHELF.

4. ALLOW ROOM FOR THE BUTYL LINER TO BE SUNK BACK DOWN INTO THE GROUND 30CM (12IN) BEYOND THE EDGE OF THE SHELF.

5. COVER THE SHELF WITH PEBBLES (THE KERB WILL STOP THEM FALLING INTO THE POND) SLOPING GENTLY UP TO THE DRY GROUND AT THE EDGE OF THE POND.

Goldfish add an important dash of colour to any pond.

smooth to avoid the danger of someone tripping and pitching headlong into the water.

If you are edging with turf you should slope it down to the water's edge rather than set it over the liner, otherwise water cannot drain and the grass roots will sit permanently in water. Which would do them no good at all *unless* you were deliberately creating a bog garden, of which more on page 80. Stones could be set in the grass like stepping stones through a river, enabling you to walk round with dry feet.

SAFE ALTERNATIVES TO PONDS

If you have small children or want the sight and sound of water in the garden without having a pond, there is an extremely good alternative, which is to have water bubbling through stones and soaking back into a reservoir beneath them. The stones are constantly wet-ting and drying and there is the gentle sound of murmuring water. You can buy kits which consist of a plastic basin with a lid, and a pump that goes inside the basin. You can also buy bags of smooth pebbles or collect your own. It needs water and a power supply, but a hose and an outdoor cable will provide these easily enough. It takes about half an hour to dig out a suitable hole and rig it up.

A slightly more imaginative idea is to drill a hole through a large piece of rock and have the water bubbling through this and falling over its sides, before falling into the unseen tank below. The rock can be set on and surrounded by pebbles, hiding the mechanics of the reservoir. Once again, this is completely safe for small children and avoids the whole business of looking after a pond.

Finally, you can combine the virtues of a pond, a reservoir beneath it and a small container by using an old stone trough or even a basin fed by a small pipe above it. The water pours into the trough with a splashy sound, the trough fills and overflows (more watery sound effects) over stones and into the reservoir below where the pump brings it round to the pipe again.

A POND IN A BARREL

YOU MAY NOT BE ABLE TO DIG A HOLE IN YOUR GARDEN. YOU MAY NOT WANT TO DIG A HOLE. BUT YOU COULD STILL HAVE A PERFECTLY INTERESTING POND.

BUY THE BIGGEST HALF BARREL THAT YOU CAN FIND. LINE IT WITH BUTYL. (AS WITH A FULL-SCALE POND, ANY WATERPROOF MATERIAL WILL DO, BUT BUTYL DOES NOT CRACK WHEN COLD AND LASTS MUCH LONGER.) YOU NEED NOT BE OVER-ANXIOUS ABOUT PUNCTURING THE LINER, AS THE BARREL SHOULD BE WATERPROOF TO A DEGREE. I HAVE FOUND A STAPLE GUN TO BE THE BEST TOOL FOR THIS. TRIM THE TOP JUST BELOW THE RIM.

COVER THE BOTTOM WITH A LAYER OF CLEAN TOPSOIL OR PROPRIETARY COMPOST ABOUT 7.5CM (3IN) DEEP.

MIX A LITTLE WATER WITH THE SOIL SO THAT IT TURNS TO MUD.

THE BARREL HAS ALL THE QUALITIES OF A LARGER POND AND ALL THE POSSIBILITIES FOR GROWING SMALL AQUATIC PLANTS AND KEEPING FISH.

Staple a waterproof liner such as butyl inside a half-barrel, and plant as a miniature pond.

PLANTING A POND

Your pond should have a deep and a shallow end and shelves around the sides. You will need different types of plants for the three situations.

DEEP-WATER AQUATICS

These are the plants – such as water-lilies – that have all but their necks submerged under water. Plant them in special plastic planting baskets, which you can buy from any supplier that will provide the plants. Line the baskets with hessian before planting. This will eventually rot away, by which time the roots of the plant will be well established.

Line a plastic planting basket with hessian before filling it with compost.

Half-fill the basket with compost and then put the plant firmly into it. It is important to pack the compost tightly around the roots so that there are no air spaces to decrease the volume of compost as the water drives the air out.

The best compost is good, clean topsoil or special aquatic planting compost from a garden centre. **Do not use a light potting compost.**

Water the plant thoroughly.

Spread a layer of pea shingle about 2.5cm (1in) deep over the surface of the compost around the plant to stop fish nosing into the earth and disturbing the roots.

Place the basket so that the crown of the plant is level with the top of the water. The best way to achieve this is to put as many bricks as necessary under the basket until you have the right level. As the plant grows the bricks can be removed, keeping the foliage just at the surface.

If you are planting straight into a natural (unlined) pond, do not use the baskets: plant straight into the hessian.

Lay a square of the material on the ground and heap some compost on to it. Place the plant into the centre of the soil and wrap the four corners of the hessian into a bundle, tying it just below the crown. Then put it into the water, where it will sink. The hessian will rot, by which time the roots of the plant will have established themselves in the soil floor of the pond.

The leaves of **waterlilies (***Nymphaea***)** grow in spring, spreading out across the water before fading and sinking, which they do in succession until autumn. The flowers need heat to bloom, so usually appear sometime in June. They open in the morning and close in the afternoon, lasting a few days before sinking tragically below the surface. To flower successfully they must be in a sheltered, sunny site.

Although a smallish lily may look puny at first, do not be tempted to put too vigorous a variety in your pond unless you have plenty of space. When it gets established it will romp across the water. As a rule of thumb, the larger the lily, the deeper the water it will grow in.

There are a lot of lilies to choose from and the table above is intended only as an indication.

Other deep-water aquatics include:

Water hawthorn (*Aponogeton distachyos*). White blossoms from spring until autumn with almost oblong leaves.

Nymphoides peltata. Rather like a tiny waterlily with bright yellow flowers that each last only a day

Orontium aquaticum. An odd plant. White pokers with yellow tips poke out from glaucous, lance-shaped leaves. It can be increased by freshly gathered seed in trays of mud.

SUBMERGED AQUATICS

These are the most unglamorous of pond plants but are vital for keeping the pond clean: they feed off the dissolved mineral salts on which algae thrive. Thus the algae cannot grow and cover the pond in green slime. If you are planning to keep fish in the pond, oxygenators are essential in order to provide oxygen for the fish.

Hornwort (*Ceratophyllum demersum*) does not root like other oxygenators and can simply be chucked into the water with a lead weight to hold it down.

Canadian pondweed (*Elodea canadensis***)** is a very good oxygenator, with whorled leaves and tiny lilac flowers. Invasive but easily managed.

Autumnal starwort (*Callitriche hermaphroditica*). Goldfish love to eat the cresslike foliage. If it flourishes it is a sign that the

WATERLILIES		
LARGE	MEDIUM	SMALL
N. alba (white)	'Hermine' (white)	*candida* (white)
'Col. A.J. Welch' (yellow)	'Moorei' (yellow)	*odorata* 'Sulphurea'
'Colossea' (pink)	'Fabiola' (pink)	'Turicensis' (pink)
'Sirius' (crimson)	'William Falconer' (red)	'Gloriosa' (red)
	'Comanche' (orange)	'Graziella' (orange)

chemical balance of the water is right.

Water violet (*Hottonia palustris*) has spikes of pale lilac flowers and bright green foliage. It is better to introduce this plant only after the balance of the water has been achieved, as it needs clear water.

Water crowfoot (*Ranunculus aquatilis*). The submerged foliage gives this plant its common name: it looks like a bird's claw. Just before it flowers in midsummer it produces dark green deeply lobed leaves followed by the gold buttercup flowers.

Lobelia dortmanna makes dense, upright clumps of foliage with lavender flowers on thin stems. Does not want to be in the deepest part of the pond.

FLOATING PLANTS

There are a few plants that need no planting at all. Simply plonk them into the water and the roots paddle freely beneath them. Do not be concerned if they tilt a little at first: the larger floating plants take a few days to get their balance.

Generally speaking, floating plants only flourish in frost-free areas and are usually treated as annual additions to a pond after the last risk of frost has passed.

Water fern (*Azolla*) is a carpeting, floating plant that can rapidly spread with its tiny fronds. Its growth is controlled by cold weather.

Water hyacinths (*Eichhornia*). These weird plants have roots like wispy feathers and fat, waxy leaves. The flowers are lilac-coloured. Very frost-sensitive.

Duckweed (*Lemna*).Can be very invasive and is frost-hardy. Ivy-leafed duckweed (*Lemna truscula*) has leaves that hang just below the surface and does not spread too much.

Water soldier (*Stratiotes aloides*). This floats like a pineapple top with a small white flower just breaking the surface. In winter it sinks to the bottom. Hardy.

Bladderwort (*Utricularia*). Fine foliage containing bladders in which insects are caught floats below the surface. In late summer bladderwort produces small yellow flowers.

MARGINAL PLANTS

Marginal plants (which does not mean that they are a bit iffy, but that they like to be on the shelves on the margin of the pond) are planted in compost in baskets just like all other pond plants, unless it is a natural pond without any lining, when they can go straight into the ground. Most will grow in conditions ranging from mud to 15cm (6in) of water.

Always plant one type of plant to one container, or they will intertwine inseparably, and one will invariably crowd the others out. But plant two or three of a type to each basket so that you quickly get a filled-out effect.

If you buy marginal plants that have been growing in peat compost, remove this from the roots, or they may rot.

Iris laevigata. The blue-flowered aquatic iris. Easy to grow, clump-forming. Flowers in early summer. Increase by division immediately after flowering. There are many cultivars.

Yellow flag iris (*Iris pseudacorus*). Vigorous plant, really too big for a small garden pond. *I.p.* 'Variegata' has cream and green sword-shaped leaves and a less rampant habit.

Iris versicolor has purple-blue flowers which appear a little later than those of *I. laevigata*. There are a number of cultivars, of which 'Kermesina' is the best known, with its rich plum colour.

Lobelia fulgens. Often grown as a border plant, this will grow well in a pond. Bright red flowers and maroon foliage.

Mimulus. Nothing could be easier to grow. Plant it right at the edge or in running water. It produces flowers in late summer. There are a number of cultivars with flowers of yellow, blue and red.

Water mint (*Mentha aquatica*) can take over if left to its own devices, but is easy to control.

Giant spearwort (*Ranunculus lingia grandiflora*) develops from spear-shaped leaves into a giant buttercup. Vigorous.

Lesser spearwort (*Ranunculus flammula*) is less invasive and flowers earlier on red stems. Plant right at the edge of the pond, so it can spill over on to the ground.

Arum lily (*Zantedeschia aethiopica*). Another plant that is more often grown in a border, but is perfectly happy in water. Great goblets of white flowers and arrow-shaped dark green leaves. The cultivar 'Crowborough' is the most hardy.

MARGINAL PLANTS

FLOATING PLANTS

SUBMERGED AQUATICS

The different planting levels of a pond.

BOG GARDENING

Most people have bog gardens by default. They have a piece of ground that never drains and yet can hardly be called a pond. This embraces anything from ground that is 'damp' to a veritable swamp. Bog gardening covers the same wide range. The one real definition of a bog garden is that it is in an area of ground that never dries out. It can be very small and completely containable, because in the main plants that like boggy conditions will not spread to surrounding, drier areas.

I like bog gardens because they make a virtue out of necessity. Rather than dry and drain the ground and impose a man-made cultivation on to it, you go with the flow and only plant what will prosper.

In fact it makes much more sense to make a bog than to try and drain one.

MAKING A BOG

If you are starting a bog garden from scratch, it will look most natural in the lowest part of the garden. It looks good flanking a path or below a bank. Bog gardens tolerate more shade than a pond and need some shade to protect tender plants in early spring.

It might seem easiest to create an area of bog at the edge of a pond. You do this by placing a kerb or boulder along a shelf at the edge of the pond, lining it with the butyl liner as though it was to be filled with water and then backfilling it with soil before filling the pond with water. The soil-filled shelf will become saturated with water and the liner will stop it ever draining.

However, the problem here is that the water will drain back into the pond, taking with it nutrients which will make the water a foul, murky green. The area of bog is very wet indeed and digging will damage the liner. In short, it makes a bog but a bad bog.

Ideally one wants a bog where the top is dry but the roots go down into wetness. This is easy to make.

Dig an area about 45cm (18 in) deep to the side of the pond. Line the hole with butyl, but perforate it. For a bog garden, old polythene sacks are ideal. If possible, take the lining from the pond down into the bog area so that the water can overflow into it.

Fill the hole in again, adding compost or well-rotted manure.

If the pond will not overflow into the bog area, sink a perforated drainage pipe into the ground, blocked at the bottom. This can be filled with water and will keep the roots moist without puddling the surface.

Your bog is now ready for planting. Some suggestions for suitable plants are given below. Bog plants need plenty of nutrition. Mulch the surface between the plants each spring with compost or manure, which will both conserve moisture and rot down to feed the roots.

American skunk cabbage (*Lysichiton americanus*). A must for the bog garden. It appears each spring with bright yellow spathes growing like bananas from the mud; these are followed by huge, spinach-like leaves.

Astilbe has ferny foliage and plumes of feathery flowers in late summer. It grows to 1.2m (4ft).

Comfrey (*Symphytum*). Has fuzzy leaves that are wonderful medicine for the garden, used as an infusion, on the compost heap or as a direct mulch. *But* they are very invasive.

Ferns. The following ferns will love the soggy conditions of a bog garden.

Marsh buckler fern (*Dryopteris palustris*). Will creep towards water.

Royal fern (*Osmunda regalis*). Looks like large, stately bracken.

Sensitive fern (*Onoclea sensibilis*). Arching pale green fonds that spread.

Ostrich fern (*Matteuccia struthiopteris*). Green fronds like a giant shuttlecock.

Gunnera manicata. One of my favourite plants. Fully grown it is an absolute whopper, like rhubarb on steroids, with the largest leaves in the northern hemisphere, growing like elephant's ears. It is not a plant for a small garden, but an essential addition to any garden that can house it. Must be protected from frost.

The ideal place for a bog garden is next to a pond, so that the water can spill over into it.

Lysichiton americanus, hostas and primulas make an ideal waterside composition.

Hostas. Another genus of border plants that are more at home in a bog. Hostas have fleshy, ribbed leaves that die right down each year, growing back bigger, making large clumps. Although hostas are primarily grown for their leaves, they produce wonderful flowers, usually mauve or white, on spikes. There are many species and varieties, of which the following are a selection particularly suited to a bog.

H. crispula. Green leaves with white rim.

H. fortunei. Greyish green leaves

H. f. 'Aurea marginata'. Dark green foliage with pale gold margins.

H. sieboldiana. Has deeply ribbed bluish grey leaves.

H. s. elegans. Larger leaves than the species, much bluer in colour.

H. lancifolia 'Kabitan'. Dwarf cultivar with yellow leaves with a green margin.

Irises. Again, there are lots of species and varieties, but here are a few:

Iris kaempferi (*I. ensata*). Has a branched stem, producing around a dozen purple or plum-coloured flowers. There are hundreds of varieties.

Iris ochroleuca. Big yellow and white flowers with tall, sword-like leaves

Iris sibirica. Blue flowers on long stems with grassy foliage. Divide immediately after flowering. Many different cultivars.

Ligularia. A member of the daisy family that grows to 1.8m (6 ft) and flowers in late summer. There are a number of varieties, of which *L. stenocephala* 'The Rocket' is one of the best, growing as tall as a man with tall wands of bright yellow flowers on black stalks. *L. przewalskii* also has black stems, but has deeply cut leaves and spires of daisy-like flowers.

Monkshood (*Aconitum napellus*). A cottage garden plant that thrives in the wet. Looks a bit like a delphinium with spikes of blue flowers.

North American daisy (*Rudbeckia*). Golden daisy petals with cone-shaped black centres. As long as the soil remains wet, they are improved by being in full sun.

Ornamental rhubarb (*Rheum palmatum*). Will grow where *Gunnera* fails and is the nearest substitute in scale and type. Has deeply cut apple-green leaves 90cm (3ft) across and 1.8m (6ft) stems of creamy white flowers.

Primulas. The best reason for a bog garden. There are too many different types of primula for a book of this scope to deal with, but the candelabra type are particularly good with their wedding-cake tiers of flowers in whorls.

Candelabra primulas for the bog garden:

P. bulleyan. Easy to grow with bright orange flowers.

P. chungensis. Pale orange blossoms in early summer.

P. aurantiaca. Reddish orange flowers. Can be divided as they emerge.

P. japonica. First to flower (in May) with crimson tiers.

P. helodoxa. Large buttercup-yellow flowers.

Of the **non-candelabra type of primulas**, the following grow well in waterlogged soil:

P. denticulata. The flower emerges low to the ground and is then pushed up by the stem until it is like a lollipop.

P. florindae. Late-flowering (July/August), with cowslip-shaped heads of sulphur yellow.

P. pulverulenta. Has 60cm (2ft) stems with deep burgundy-red flowers.

P. secundiflora. Almost purple flower bells in June.

P. sikkimensis. Bright yellow flowers with sweet scent.

Rodgersia. Although this has clusters of white flowers, it is grown for its foliage, which is bronze when young, becoming green in maturity. The plant grows to 1.2m (4ft).

R. tabularis is unlike all other rodgersias in that it has round, slightly scalloped leaves.

Trollius. Buttercup-like flowers on wiry stems.

Umbrella plant (*Peltiphyllum peltatum*** or *** Darmera peltata***).** The round leaves are over 30cm (1ft) across and grow profusely after the flower spikes have appeared in spring. A perennial that grows anew profusely each year.

HERBS

There is absolutely no mystery to growing herbs; there are simply two essential growing conditions – good drainage and sunshine. The sunshine is prescribed by uncontrollable forces, but you can make the most of what you get by siting your herbs in the sunniest (south-facing) spot in the garden. Good drainage depends upon digging the ground, putting in plenty of organic matter and adding grit or sand if the soil is heavy. Most herbs do not want too rich a soil, so adding plenty of horticultural grit is the ideal way of getting the soil right for them.

The herbs that you use regularly need to be as close to the kitchen door as possible. Plant a few essential herbs such as **parsley**, **mint**, **sage**, **chives** and **rosemary** in pots and treat them like a living store-cupboard.

Although there are many types of **mint**, only two are really useful in the kitchen: **spearmint** (*Mentha spicata*) and **applemint** (*Mentha rotundifolia*). **Peppermint** (*Mentha piperata*) is used for making mint tea. Once established, mint will take over an entire border.

HERBS THAT WILL GROW IN MOIST SHADE		
COMMON NAME	LATIN NAME	COMMENTS
Angelica	*Angelica archangelica*	Biennial. Grows to 1.8m (6ft).
Bergamot	*Monarda didyma*	Wonderful flowers.
Chervil	*Anthriscus cerefolium*	Annual. Must be used fresh.
Chives	*Allium schoenopragasum*	Hardy perennial.
Lemon Balm	*Melissa officinalis*	Hardy perennial.
Lovage	*Levisticum officionale*	Perennial, lasting several years.
Mint	*Mentha* species	All mints are rampant, so restrain!
Parsley	*Petroselinum crispum*	Make three sowings: in March, July and September
Sorrel	*Rumex acetosa*	Don't let it flower.

HERBS THAT MUST HAVE DRY SUNSHINE		
Basil	*Ocimum basilicum*	Tender annual killed by first frost. Pinch out the tips of plants before they flower – this will make them produce more leaves.
Bay	*Laurus nobilis*	A tree that needs protection from frost.
Dill	*Anethum graveolens*	Needs moisture to grow.
Fennel	*Foeniculum vulgare*	Perennial; comes in bronze or green.
Feverfew	*Tanacetum parthenium*	Easy to grow, with pretty flowers. Self-seeds.
Rosemary	*Rosmarinus officinalis*	Woody shrub. *Hates cold damp.*
Rue	*Ruta graveolens*	Will tolerate the poorest soil.
Sage	*Salvia officinalis*	Cut back each spring to encourage new growth.
Sweet Marjoram	*Origano marjoranum*	Perennial, but treat as an annual.
Tarragon	*Artemisia dracunculus*	Perennial with yellow flowers.
Thyme	*Thymus vulgaris*	Wonderful scent.

Sink an old bucket or plastic pot in the ground with the bottom knocked out and fill it with soil. Plant your mint in this to stop it spreading.

Horseradish (*Armoracia rusticana*) is another invasive plant. My garden is infested with the stuff and as its roots go down 1.8m (6ft) or more, it is almost impossible to dig out. Sprays seem to have no lasting effect. It has brittle roots and a fresh plant will grow from every tiny scrap left in the ground. Grow it like mint – in

Parsley-tasting in my herb garden. The dog wants some too.

an open-bottomed container. Horseradish likes rich, fertile soil and is best harvested in autumn, when the flavour is at its most intense.

A herb that appreciates a certain level of dampness is **angelica** (*Angelica archangelica*), which grows to be over 1.8m (6ft) tall. The seeds of this used to be used to decorate cakes and it makes the most wonderful structural plant in a flower border.

Two other herbs that are grown primarily for their structural value prefer a sunnier, drier position. **Fennel** (*Foeniculum vulgare*) comes in two shades, green and bronze. The leaves make a wonderful aniseedy addition to a grilled trout and their tall but delicate outline is something that I would not be without in any mixed border.

Lovage (*Levisticum officinale*) grows

Herbs grow well in an informal, loose arrangement mingled with decorative plants.

to over 90cm (3ft) high and has a hollow stalk with fleshy green leaves. It can be eaten like celery and the leaves added to salads and stews.

Wild marjoram (*Origanum vulgare*) makes a low mound rather than a pillar, but is perhaps one of the most useful herbs to grow. As its Latin name suggests, it is closely related to **oregano**. Another mound-maker is **lemon balm** (*Melissa officinalis*), with its strong lemony scent.

Rue (*Ruta graveolens*) has a distinctive bluish-green cast to its leaves and an equally distinctive smell that one either finds irresistible or nauseous. It also has the unfortunate habit of causing bad burns if the sap comes into contact with skin in hot weather. I write from blistered experience.

For a small garden the **rosemary**

HERBS WITH ROSES

HERBS ARE VERY GOOD COMPANIONS TO ROSES, ESPECIALLY THE OLD-FASHIONED SHRUB ROSES (SEE PAGE 98). PLANT BRONZE AND GREEN FENNEL, DILL, SAGE, CATMINT (*NEPETA*) AND LAVENDER AMONGST THE ROSES FOR AN EXQUISITE COMBINATION.

Rosmarinus officinalis 'Miss Jessopp's Upright' is ideal because it makes a tall, upright bush as opposed to the rather lax, sprawling habit of most rosemary (which can, of course, be its charm in a larger garden). Rosemary loves heat and dry soil and is one of the few plants that thrives when planted under the eaves of a south-facing wall. I have seen rosemary trained as an espalier in this position – and very handsome it looked too.

Parsley (*Petroselinum crispum*) loves a good, rich soil with plenty of water and will grow happily in partial shade.

There is much debate as to the relative virtues of flat-leafed parsley against curly-leafed, but I think every garden needs both types. Flat-leafed has the edge on flavour but curly-leafed looks wonderful grown as a low hedge alongside a path and tastes almost as good.

Common sage (*Salvia officinalis*) is another perennial herb that will take a lot of rough treatment and benefits from a good cropping back each spring. **Purple sage** (*S.* 'Purpurascens') looks good in a border with its bronze leaves and **white sage** (*S. farinacea* 'Alba') has white flowers as opposed to the pinky-purple ones of common sage. Sage is one of the easiest garden plants to take from cuttings.

HERBS IN CONTAINERS

Herbs can be grown very easily in any kind of container, be it a window box, pot, gro-bag or old bucket. While drainage is very important, you will need to keep the soil a little more moist than if they were growing in open ground.

Herbs for large containers: I recommend borage, dill, fennel, lemon balm, rosemary (Miss Jessopp's Upright), sage, savory, tarragon.

Any kind of container will do for growing herbs, as long as it has good drainage.

Herbs for a smaller space: try basil, chives, marjoram, mint (retained in its pot), parsley, thyme.

Make sure that the container has plenty of decent drainage holes (window boxes bought ready-made from garden centres are nearly always under supplied with these) and that there is room for the water to drain away from the bottom.

Cover at least the bottom 2.5cm (1in) – more if the container is large – with pebbles, crocks or coarse gravel to ensure good drainage.

Use standard potting compost. You will find that the compost the plants are potted up with will take up most of the space and that all you need to do is fill in the gaps around them. Arrange the plants so that the taller ones are at the back and allow space for them to grow a bit, but plant them more tightly together than if they were in a border. If one plant fails you can hoick it out and replace it.

CHILDREN'S GARDENS

Every child needs a garden, but they want it to be a playground, not a sophisticated mix of colour, scent and foliage. They want sandpits and paddling pools, tyres on a rope, treehouses and obstacle courses, camps and football pitches. Trees are for climbing and hedges for hiding behind. Shrubs provide cover from baddies and paths are for doing wheelies on and then blocking with a thrown-down bike.

SAFETY AND COMMON SENSE

ON THE WHOLE I BELIEVE THAT CHILDREN ARE PRETTY GOOD AT LOOKING AFTER THEMSELVES AND MOLLY-CODDLING THEM WILL RETARD THEIR OWN ACUTE SENSE OF SURVIVAL. BUT THERE ARE EXCEPTIONS TO THIS RULE.

★ THE FIRST IS **NO WATER**. A TODDLER CAN DROWN IN 5CM (2IN) OF WATER. TOO MANY DO. UNTIL CHILDREN ARE STRONG ENOUGH TO GET THEMSELVES OUT OF ANY WATER UNAIDED – ABOUT FIVE – **NEVER LET THEM NEAR WATER UNSUPERVISED**.

★ THE SECOND IS TO DO WITH **POISONS**. DON'T USE ANY POISONOUS SPRAYS, FEEDS, PELLETS OR WHATEVER WITH CHILDREN AROUND. THEY WILL EAT THEM AND IT IS A PAIN CARTING THEM OFF TO HAVE THEIR STOMACH PUMPED.

★ MAKE SURE THAT YOU HAVE AN AREA OF HARD SURFACE NEAR THE BACK DOOR THAT CHILDREN CAN PLAY ON, OTHERWISE YOU WILL HAVE AN AREA OF MUD AROUND THE BACK DOOR FOR HALF THE YEAR.

★ GET THEM THEIR OWN TOOLS.

★ **DON'T BE TOO AMBITIOUS**. A CHILD CAN HAVE A LOT OF FUN WITH JUST A FEW PLANTS IN A TINY PATCH OF SOIL OR A CONTAINER. MAKE SURE THAT IT IS ALWAYS PLAY – NOT REAL GARDENING. **IT DOESN'T MATTER IF THEY DO IT ALL WRONG**.

Most of the best known gardens are solemn, grown-up places. 'Serious' gardening and children don't mix. Children prefer common but colourful plants to rare (but dull) specimens, get bored in three minutes and are unimpressed by Latin names.

You *can* try and tempt children out of the playground into horticulture, although it is humbug to pretend that this is for the sake of the children. You do it to buy a little time to garden yourself. All you want is half an hour to plant out the sweet peas without stopping to break up a fight and mend a puncture.

The mistake that most people make in providing a garden for the kids is to find a dank corner with poor soil where least harm, practical and aesthetic, can be done. This won't do. You have to give up a plot in full sun with perfectly prepared soil so that everything will grow fast and flourish. It can be small – less than 2m x 1m (6ft x 3ft) is enough to start with, or even just a pot or tub – but position it so that it can expand if the enthusiasm is there. Prepare the soil yourself, but let them manure it with you. Until the age of about nine the allure of poo is always irresistible.

PLANTS FOR CHILDREN

Only use plants that will give quick results. It is difficult to get grown-ups to take the long view in gardening, and impossible with children. Top of the list are **sunflowers** (*Helianthus annuus*). The variety called 'Russian Giant' will grow to 3.5m (12ft) or more and is the one for children. Each flower will need strong staking – which can be part of the game. If each member of the family plants one now you can race them, with a weekly measurement and an overall winner on a momentous final reckoning in September. Buy a healthy plant for each child and get a packet of seed at the same time, partly to show how this enormous thing can come from a seed and partly to have a reserve if there is a disaster. Sunflowers grow best in heavy soil and, of course, in full sun. If you are using seed, sow three seeds in each place where you want a flower, removing the two smallest seedlings to leave one strong plant.

Runner beans are the other guaranteed success. Plant or sow them with a wigwam of beansticks for each child, one at each corner and another in the middle. If sowing, it is as well to make doubly sure and put in two or three seeds for each plant, again thinning to leave the strongest. Runner beans need a lot of moisture and nutrients, so it pays to dig a pit beneath each wigwam site and put in plenty of organic muck. If that proves hard to come by, old newspapers will act as a sponge to hold moisture. In their native mountains of Mexico runner beans get heavy rain in July, August and September with not too much heat (tending to grow in the north shadow of the hills), so you have to try to recreate this to get the best from them. Again, you must not be tempted to fob children off with second best; to hold their attention and imagination each plant has to perform at the top of its bent, a sort of horticultural Olympics, so treat each plant as a prize specimen.

Sticking to edible plants, **radishes** grow quicker than any other vegetable and can be intercropped with **little gem lettuce**. Sow them in drills about 60cm (2ft) long. If you allocate a special 4 1/2litre (1 gallon) – anything larger is too heavy – watering can the chances are that everything will be diligently drowned, so it is as well to grow things will relish the damp.

The final food plant that is always fun is **sweetcorn**. The variety 'Polarvee' matures in 52–55 days, a month or more quicker than more traditional varieties. Sweetcorn should always be sown or planted in blocks, each plant about 15cm (6in) apart.

It is good to grow plants that change in a day – which for most children under eight is as long a time as they can be patient for. **Morning glory** (*Ipomoea*

tricolor) grows fast up a sunny wall and the flowers open early in the morning and close by mid afternoon. The **Californian poppy** (*Eschscholzia californica*) gets up to the same thing, opening and closing during the day. **Daisies** and **thistles** will remain shut in wet weather.

An excellent flower for children to grow – and eat – is the **pot marigold** (*Calendula officinalis*). 'Geisha Girl' is a brazen vermilion shout with exactly the right lack of subtlety required. (When you add them to a salad do so after you have dressed it – a coating of oil and vinegar does nothing for them.)

Nasturtiums (*Tropaeolum majus*) have exactly the right combination of fast, magical growth and bright colour. Grow the 'Jewel' or 'Whirlybird' series and they should flower into November. If these are over-nourished they develop more leaf than flower, so this is a case for starved, dry conditions. They have the very important virtue for children of winning friends and influencing people, because you can casually pick a flower in passing and

pop it into your mouth. I suppose over-anxious parents will fret that this is a progression down the slippery slope from nasturtiums and marigolds to indiscriminate petal-popping, but I would rather they ate flowers than junk food. And while you are creating this brash, childish area in order to buy a little time for serious, proper gardening, you might just discover that one ingredient that grown-ups often omit from their gardens—

fun.

MAKING A SANDPIT

A SANDPIT SHOULD BE TREATED LIKE A DRY POND.

1. DIG THE HOLE OUT AND DITCH THE SUBSOIL, USING THE TOPSOIL WHERE NEEDED IN THE GARDEN. (STORE IT IF YOU DON'T NEED IT NOW, SOONER OR LATER YOU WILL.)

2. DIG THE HOLE AT LEAST 30CM (1FT) DEEPER THAN THE INTENDED DEPTH OF SAND.

3. FILL THE BOTTOM 23CM (9IN) WITH HARDCORE OR LARGISH STONES. COVER THIS WITH A LAYER OF 7.5CM (3IN) OF SHINGLE. THIS WILL ENSURE DRAINAGE.

4. PUT IN SAND (AT LEAST 30CM/1FT). SILVER SAND IS BEST FOR DRAINAGE, BUT IN THE END ANYTHING IS MUCH BETTER THAN NOTHING.

5. IT IS A GOOD ADDED EXTRA TO BUILD A WOODEN FRAME AROUND THE TOP OF THE SANDPIT FROM 15CM X 2.5CM (6IN X 1IN) TIMBER. THIS SHOULD BE 2.5CM (1IN) OR SO PROUD OF THE TOP OF THE HOLE AND WILL STOP THE EDGES COLLAPSING, CONTAIN THE SAND AND ACT AS A FRAMEWORK FOR A LID THAT YOU MAY WISH TO PUT ON IT.

WHEN THE CHILDREN ARE OLDER, THE PIT CAN BE EMPTIED AND THE SITE USED FOR A POND.

A sandpit must have plenty of drainage material at the bottom if it is not to become waterlogged.

EASY VEG

I have deliberately omitted most vegetable growing from this book, as it means a bigger commitment in time than the Weekend Gardener is prepared to give it, and it is something that must be done regularly rather than in odd bursts. However, anybody with a garden bigger than a window box can grow certain vegetables with practically no trouble at all.

But it is not cheaper, not easier and not much healthier to grow your own veg. If you live in a city it could even be less healthy, as the vegetables from the

Aubergines and tomatoes growing under a black plastic mulch. Both plants need plenty of sun and moisture.

supermarket will have been grown in East Anglia, Worcestershire or some such clean-aired place, while your own right-on organically grown crops will be loaded with lead from the polluted

air you choose to live in. Personally, I would take the risk and stick with growing my own, but it is not a position to pontificate from.

If you cost your time, home-grown veg are much pricier than bought. But you would not dream of being so dull. You grow vegetables because it improves the quality of your life. They taste good. It makes you happy. There is no better reason.

GROWING LETTUCE

The vegetables that most people want to grow most are what the horticultural world manages to call – in a frenzy of ugliness – 'salads'. Most vegetables that are eaten raw grow very fast and can therefore be fitted in around other, slower-growing crops. In short, you can bung them into any decently prepared bit of ground that gets some sun. Which suits the Weekend Gardener just fine.

Lettuces like a rich soil with good drainage. They need to be kept constantly watered if they are not to bolt. 'Bolting' is the process by which the plant, sensing a crisis as a result of lack of water, forces itself to flower and produce seed as fast as possible before its own demise. This is bad for those of us who eat lettuce, but jolly good for the survival of the species. Regular watering will stop this and keep all intimations of mortality at bay until you eat it.

Most varieties of lettuce are best sown as thinly as possible in drills about 1cm (1/2in) deep. Make sure that your hands are absolutely dry, hold

the seed in the palm of one hand and squeeze a pinch of seed at a time between the thumb and forefinger of the other hand as you move down the row.

It is not a bad idea to **water the drill before you sow the seed**, so that it lies on wet ground. Flick the soil back over the sown drill and mark it. Lettuce needs cool temperatures to germinate, and may become dormant if the soil temperature is above 20°C (68°F).

In about a week a green rash will spread down the drill line. **As soon as the plants are big enough, they will need thinning.** I find that the initial thinning is best done in clumps, reducing the width of the row to one plant if possible. The next thinning, after about four weeks, will be edible, dozens of tiny lettuces making a salad. It varies from variety to variety, but I would say that no lettuce needs to be more than 15cm (6in) from its nearest neighbour. It is far better to have two small plants than one whopper.

The main problem with growing lettuce is that it is too easy. Most households have only a couple of lettuce eaters in them and it is surprising how far a little lettuce goes. A packet of seed produces far too many plants too quickly for two people to eat before they start to bolt, however much you water them.

There are two ways round this problem.

The first is to sow short rows 60cm (2ft) long at ten-day intervals. One packet should do up to half a dozen rows like this. This will provide enough lettuce for a week in each row.

The second is to use the thinnings to transplant. Carefully pull up every other lettuce in a row, trying not to damage the roots (which you are bound to do). They respond to this open-transplant surgery by flopping alarmingly and take a couple of weeks to catch up, thereby giving you an extra fortnight or more of lettuce from the same crop.

OTHER 'SALAD' VARIETIES

Radicchio, **chicory** and **endive** are closely related, although most chicory needs blanching to get rid of its bitterness. Endive can be made sweeter by tying the leaves together at the top, but I like the slight bitterness of moss-curled endive when mixed with a sweet lettuce like 'Lobjoits Green' cos. Radicchio is slow to develop, best sown in mid-May for harvesting from September. I have forced chicory, but it is a bit of a fiddle and the supermarkets will provide it as well and for a lot less effort. You grow the plants from seed all summer and then dig a few up, cutting the top off to about 2.5cm (1in) and reducing the roots to 23cm (9in). These are put in moist peat in a pot with another pot inverted over it. After

about three weeks they will have grown white, flame-shaped 'chicons'.

Purslane is hardly grown here, although it is supposed to reduce heart disease and its name in Malawi translates as 'Buttocks-of-the-wife-of-a-chief', which seems to be reason enough to grow it all over the garden.

Rocket is both terribly easy to grow and utterly distinctive. I grow it broadcast, plucking handfuls of leaves as and when needed, rather than letting them develop into mature plants. A patch a metre (yard) square would keep most households going for a couple of months.

It is a mistake to think of lettuce as a summer vegetable. **Lamb's lettuce** prefers the cold, and if sown in September will last through to spring. **Winter purslane** or miner's lettuce is easy to grow and very good — you just pick off the tops of the plants — and there are a number of 'ordinary' lettuces like 'All the Year Round' and 'Valdor' that have been bred to grow and mature in winter. The chicory family is sown in early summer and grows slowly for harvesting in winter, being tolerant of frost but not of too much wet, so may have to be protected from the rain.

LETTUCES AND OTHER 'SALAD' VARIETIES

NAME	TYPE	SIZE	MATURATION	NOTES
'Tom Thumb'	Early Crisphead	Small	65 days	Slow to bolt. Old variety.
'Little Gem'	Cos	Small	80 days	Delicious. One lettuce per person.
'Valdor'	Butterhead	Medium	Winter	Sow autumn for early spring harvest.
'Salad Bowl'	Loose Leaf	Large	80 days	Leaves picked throughout summer.
'Red Salad Bowl'	Loose Leaf	Large	80 days	Red leaves regrow when picked.
'Lollo Rossa'	Loose Leaf	Medium	80 days	Leaves frilled with red.
'Webb's Wonderful'	Crisphead	Large	80 days	Crispy heart, slow to bolt.
'Lobjoits Green'	Cos	Large	80 days	Upright, crisp, delicious.
Red Cos	Cos	Medium	70 days	Red leaves. grow quickly with lots of water. Tough plant, tender eating.
'Saladin'	Iceberg	Large	80 days	Crisp, predictable lettuce.
Green Curled	Endive	Medium	80 days	Slightly bitter leaves good in salad.
'Sugar Loaf'	Chicory	Medium	90 days	Good sown late summer for autumn/winter eating. Does not need blanching.
'Alouette'	Radicchio	Small	150 days	Essential growing! Sow May to August for autumn/winter
'Witloof'	Chicory	Small	150 days	Chicory for blanching and making 'chicons'.
	Lamb's Lettuce	Small	Winter	Excellent winter crop.
	Celtuce	Medium	75 days	Celery-flavoured lettuce.
'Sigmaleaf'	Spinach	Medium	50 days	Pick young leaves as they appear for salads. Needs water.
Winter Purslane	Miner's Lettuce	Small	Winter	Very good winter crop. Needs shade and water. Pick leaves only.
	Purslane	Small	75 days	Very fleshy stems and leaves. Very good for you. Pick shoots when young.
Flat-leaf Parsley	Parsley	Small	75 days	Grow for salads. Water well.
	Rocket	Small	75 days	Very distinctive taste. Pick when young.

WEATHER REPORT: June is the month with the most sunshine, although July and August are often hotter. We are now in summer proper and should relish it. The days are at their longest and it is possible to enjoy warm evenings outside. Having said this there are very few Junes without a cold and wet week, although there is no danger of frost as there sometimes is in May. The ground is losing around 25 litres of water per sq. m (5 gallons per sq. yd) per week, so unless it is exceptionally wet you will have to water regularly to replace this loss and maintain lush growth.

Plants in their Prime

Bulbs: alliums; irises; *Lilium martagon*, *L. regale*.

Annuals/biennials: alyssum, snapdragons (*Antirrhinum*); calceolarias; Canterbury bells; poached egg plant (*Limnanthes douglasii*); lobelias; nasturtiums; pelargoniums; poppies; sweet peas, sweet Williams.

Perennials: *Acanthus mollis*; *Achillea*; *Anchusa*; *Aruncus*; *Astrantia*; *Campanula*; columbines; delphiniums; *Dianthus*; lupins; geraniums; oriental poppies (*Papaver orientale*); peonies; *Iris sibirica*; *Dicentra spectabilis*; *Tradescantia virginiana*; London pride (*Saxifraga umbrosa*).

Trees: false acacia (*Robinia pseudoacacia*). All deciduous trees in first full flush of leaf.

Shrubs: all shrub roses; *Buddleia alternifolia*; *Ceanothus dentatus*; *Cistus*; *Cotoneaster*; *Deutzia*; hebes; *Kolkwitzia amabilis*; *Philadelphus*; *Potentilla fruticosa*; *Pyracantha*; *Weigela*.

Climbers: all climbing roses by end of month; all early-flowering clematis such as *C.* 'Nelly Moser' and *C.* x *durandii*; honeysuckle (*Lonicera*); *Hydrangea petiolaris*; jasmine (*Jasminum officinale*); *Wisteria sinensis*.

Vegetables: asparagus; broad beans; lettuce; mangetout peas; spinach; early potatoes; carrots.

Fruit: cherries; strawberries; gooseberries.

Herbs: chives; parsley; thyme; fennel; sage.

Houseplants: place tougher houseplants like *Citrus* and scented-leaved geraniums outside.

Weed Control

Keep hoeing on dry days. Five to ten minutes' weeding each morning before breakfast will help you keep on top of the situation.

Lawns

Cut once a week, collecting cuttings if possible. Mix with straw or other dry material in compost heap. Cut long grass with bulbs in it for the first time in the year. Collect all cuttings and make a separate compost heap.

Opposite: The striking pink and white flowers of Lilium regale *against a background of delphiniums.*

Below: Clematis *'Nelly Moser' in full flower. Left unpruned, it will flower again in late summer.*

Jobs

Essential
Dead-head roses as they fade. This involves cutting back to a leaf or bud, not just pulling off faded petals.
• Finish planting out dahlias.
• Take softwood cuttings (see pages 104 and 106).
• Water all containers regularly.
• Plant out tender annuals.

Desirable
• Plant out basil plants.
• Mow long grass with wild flowers after Midsummer's Day (24 June).
• Keep picking sweet peas to encourage new growth.
• Sow lettuce every two weeks to get a steady supply of young plants.
• Plant outdoor tomatoes.
• Plant out leek seedlings and celery.

Optional
• Plant marrows and courgettes.
• Net fruit against birds and watch out for slugs.
• Thin apples and grapes.

DRY GARDENS

A British garden typically needs 2.5cm (1in) of rain every week to keep it looking its best. When we have a dry summer it gets nothing like that unless you water intensively. This is time-consuming and costs money. For some things – like vegetables – this is unavoidable and part of the general game, but you can reduce the problems of drought by choosing plants that will thrive without wet-nursing.

When you consider the conditions from which many of our now very familiar garden plants originated, it is quite extraordinary that so many tolerate our damp, cold climate. Something

Wind dries plants and soil out more than sun. Protect delicate plants by screening them from the wind with larger, tougher ones.

like lavender, which comes from Mediterranean hillsides, feels as English as tea in the garden and yet is only really at home in conditions that we would regard as exceptionally dry.

Wind dries leaves exactly like washing on a line. If there is not sufficient moisture in the soil to replace it, the plant will wilt. **So make sure that drought-susceptible plants have protection from the wind**.

PLANTS FOR A DRY GARDEN

There are certain outward signs which indicate that a plant is likely to cope well with drought.

The first is a **silvery colour**. This comes from a coating of fine hairs on the leaf surface, giving a felted or woolly texture as with **lambs' ears** (*Stachys byzantina*) or **Artemisia schmidtiana**. The coating reflects light and reduces the amount of moisture lost through transpiration.

A bluish tinge to the leaf is often caused by a waxy protective coating, which retains moisture. This is found in **rue** or **eucalyptus**, for example.

Another clue is the **size of the leaves**. As a rule, the bigger the leaf, the more water it needs. So a plant like **rosemary**, with its thin, hard leaves, positively dislikes the wet.

Many **bulbs** are designed to fight drought by growing fast and flowering after the short spring rains, or melting and storing food for next year before the summer gets going. This early dormancy can also be seen in **oriental poppies**, which die back immediately after flowering in June, thus protecting the plant against desiccation.

You might think that plants adapted to drought would develop as shrivelled up affairs, but many grow fast and large, adding real drama to the parched garden.

One of my current favourite dramatic plants is the **giant silver thistle** (*Onopordum*). This is a biennial that will grow to 2.5m (8ft) and not mind a total absence of water once it is established. It flatters to deceive in its first year, making a neat rosette of spiky leaves that then rocket up the following spring to a stag's head of prickles. After flowering, it collapses into a horribly prickly brown heap that is a bugger to clear away, but there you are, there is a

price to pay for everything. It tends to seed itself and can become invasive, but is worth the space in any garden.

Cardoons (*Cynara cardunculus*) are similar and like the same kind of conditions, although they only grow to two-thirds of the onopordum's height and lack its wild bifurcation.

As different from onopordum as it can be is **Crambe cordifolia**, except that it is also a giant of a plant. It has a cloud of tiny white flowers hovering above great fat leaves (which are the

exception proving the rule that the bigger the leaves the more moisture they need). These take up rather a lot of lateral space, so don't plant anything too close to it. However, most of its growth happens in a spurt from mid-spring, so daffodils or even early tulips would have died back before the crambe hid them.

Altogether more modest but still strikingly upright is the deliciously-

Dry-loving plants: fennel, iris, rue, phlomis, euphorbia and rosemary all relish drought.

scented **tobacco plant** (*Nicotiana sylvestris*), which will keep flowering through to the first frosts without a drop of water near it. **Mulleins** are another plant happy in the dry, the sulphur flowers of *Verbascum olympicum* growing to over 1.8m (6ft).

Anchusa azurea 'Loddon Royalist' grows spectacularly tall and will need staking, but it is the bluest of all blues and is worth supporting. While they are temperamental on heavy, wet soils, they should be placidly accommodating in a well-drained, sunny border. The **rosemary** that best complements this mix of upstanding drought-lovers is 'Miss Jessopp's Upright' (which sounds like the caption to a saucy seaside postcard), growing tall and spire-

like, contradicting the natural rosemary tendency to droop languidly. If you find the flowers of Miss Jessopp's too pale a blue, try the more brilliant 'Benenden Blue' or 'Severn Sea'.

If you have dry shade the choice of planting is more limited. But **Corsican hellebore** (*Helleborus corsicus*) will like it, as will *Acanthus*, although this flowers better if it gets a good baking from the sun. *Geranium* x *oxonianum* 'Claridge Druce' will spread thickly under any

tree and thrive in deep shade. **Hypericums** also make a good deep-shade ground cover, with *Hypericum* x *inordum* 'Elstead' doing best in the dry. **Lonicera japonica** 'Halliana' will twine up into the tree causing the lack of moisture, relishing the natural woodland conditions. **Comfrey** is usually associated with boggy conditions, but the species *Symphytum ibericum* (*S. grandiflorum*) is a compact, ground-covering comfrey with tubular creamy flowers in spring that doesn't seem to mind drought or shady conditions.

TIP

A DEEPLY DUG SOIL WITH PLENTY OF ORGANIC MATTER IS THE BEST DEFENCE AGAINST DRY CONDITIONS. NOTE THE DRIEST PARTS OF THE GARDEN NOW AND RESOLVE TO DIG THEM IN THE AUTUMN.

PLANTS FOR DRY GARDENS

SHRUBS	BORDER PLANTS	BEDDING PLANTS
Artemisia	*Acanthus*	*Brachycome* (swan river daisy)
Cotoneaster	*Achillea*	*Cheiranthus* (wallflower)
Euonymus (evergreen varieties)	*Agapanthus*	*Dianthus barbatus* (sweet William)
Genista (broom)	*Alstroemeria*	*Iberis umbellata* (annual candytuft)
Hebe (veronica)	*Artemisia*	*Limnanthes douglasii* (poached egg flower)
Hypericum	*Dianthus*	*Malcolmia maritima* (Virginia stock)
Lavender	*Echinops* (globe thistle)	*Nicotiana alata* (tobacco plant)
Philadelphus (mock orange)	*Eryngium* (sea holly)	*Verbena*
Potentilla fruticosa	*Euphorbia*	
Rue	*Oenothera* (evening primrose)	
Russian Sage	*Geranium* (cranesbill)	
Santolina	*Kniphofia* (red hot poker)	
Senecio 'Sunshine'	*Nepeta* x *faassenii* (catmint)	
	Papaver orientale (oriental poppy)	
	Penstemon	
	Verbascum	

Hanging Baskets and Window Boxes

Hanging baskets come in various guises – be they made of a pre-formed cardboardy-type of material, a wire frame or an ordinary shopping basket, they all share the common factor of being a porous container viewed from below. To my mind a hanging basket – indeed, any container – only looks good when it is treated like a living flower arrangement. You should apply the same rigour and criteria to them as you would to the flowers on the table at a dinner party.

Any hanging basket is prone to drying out and many have to be watered twice a day. Wind, not sun, is the greatest enemy, so siting it in a sunny but sheltered position will radically improve its water retention.

You will have to feed your hanging basket to keep it growing well. Mix some slow-release fertiliser granules into the compost when planting. I find that a seaweed feed (obtainable at garden centres) sprayed on once a week makes a big difference. Any fertiliser high in potash will increase flowering. A feed high in nitrogen will increase green growth, but not flowering.

Planting a Wire Hanging Basket

1. Rest the basket on a bucket or pot so that it hangs down as you fill it.

2. Line the bottom and the first 2.5cm (1in) or so of the sides with sphagnum moss, green side facing outwards. Use as few pieces as possible – the larger the pieces the longer they will live.

3. Cover with potting compost so that the basket is about half full. Hanging baskets are one of the few occasions that there is a valid reason for using a peat-based compost, as it is lighter than a loam-based one. Whatever compost you use, mix in a handful of vermiculite to aid water retention and keep the weight down.

4. Start planting into the compost through the bars of the basket, pushing the roots in from the outside, so that they sit on top of the compost. Work round the basket so that it is visually balanced.

5. Put more moss round the sides and more compost, to within 2.5cm (1in) of the top, covering the roots.

6. Plant the remainder of your plants, starting in the middle and working out towards the edge, where it is best to place those plants that will trail down.

7. Water the basket thoroughly but gently and then cover any bare soil with more moss to slow down evaporation.

8. Put into position.

Plants for Hanging Baskets

When choosing the plants for a hanging basket, do not be tempted to put in too much variety. A basket with a single variety of plant will look very striking if it is done with panache.

It is sensible to choose plants that can survive with restricted water, so the list below gives a few that are drought-tolerant. Do not plant out until all risk of frost has passed, which in most areas is the first week of June.

Busy Lizzies (*Impatiens*). Repeat flowering. Will grow in partial shade.

Fuchsias. Use trailing varieties such as 'Cascade', 'Marinka', 'Summer Snow' and 'Tom West'.

Helichrysum petiolare. Tumbling shoots of silvery grey foliage look great in a large hanging basket.

Ivy (*Hedera helix*). Best to use mature plants, as most ivy grows too slowly to make an effect in the few summer months suitable for a hanging basket. One exception, 'Manders Crested', is rapidly vigorous.

Ivy-leafed pelargoniums (*Geranium*). Try 'Ailsa Garland', 'L'Elegante', 'Lady Plymouth', 'Mini-Cascade'.

Lobelia. Try the cultivars 'Blue Basket', 'Sapphire' and 'Red Cascade'.

Balance the hanging basket on a bucket or pot while you are planting it up.

Marigolds (*Tagetes*). Loads of different varieties, all in yellow and orange.

Nasturtiums (*Tropaeolum majus*). Easy to grow. Can be sown directly into the basket.

Pansies (*Viola* x *wittrockiana*). Use single colours rather than buying trays of mixed. Very easy to grow from seed. Try the 'Crystal Bowl' series, 'Floral Dance' series or 'Azure Blue'.

Senecio maritima. Silver foliage – a good foil and filler.

Snapdragons (*Antirrhinum*). Spikes of flowers in lots of different colours.

Tobacco plant (*Nicotiana*). Only *N. alata* (*N. affinis*) has the typically delicious scent. It is best for larger baskets. The 'Domino' series is bushier, but opens during the day.

Verbena. Use 'Lawrence Johnston', 'Loveliness' or 'Pink Bouquet'.

WINDOW BOXES

Whatever it is made from, a window box must have plenty of large drainage holes in the bottom. Window boxes that you buy from garden centres –

particularly plastic ones – are invariably deficient in this, so you will probably have to make extra holes. Always put in at least 2.5cm (1in) of drainage material over the bottom of the container so

Some of the best window boxes I have ever seen were in Venice. In such an intensely urban place they made all the difference, and yet every single one was composed of ivy-leafed geranium. The moral of the story is that a simple planting scheme with one or two types of plants can often be much more effective than a window box crammed with different plants.

that the holes do not clog with soil and the roots do not sit in water. Gravel is probably the best thing to use, but crocks or even pebbles work well. Anything is better than nothing. Make sure that the box is standing on some chocks of wood or pieces of tile – anything that will leave a space between it and the window ledge so that the water can actually drain away.

Half fill the window box with compost. Use a potting compost and mix in

Window boxes must be carefully composed. Although bright, note the limited range of colours used here.

a few handfuls of bonemeal to provide a slow-release fertiliser. As with hanging baskets, mix in a quarter of the volume of vermiculite to lessen the overall weight and increase water retention.

When choosing plants, consider the direction that the box will be facing: if it faces north your options are going to be restricted. If it faces south, you could grow almost anything, including vegetables and herbs. Water your window box weekly in dry weather, even more in a hot summer. But if you have your drainage worked out it will never become waterlogged.

When you have planted the window box, top up the soil level with more compost if necessary, but leave the surface at least 1cm (1/2in) below the rim so that you have room to water.

In summer I have a great fondness for window boxes stuffed with gaudy single-colour annuals. See page 72 for a list of easy-to-grow annuals.

SHADE

Too much shade is the most common complaint of the town gardener. Country gardeners can cut down trees or choose sunny spots within their generally larger gardens, but there is little that you can do about a dark urban back yard.

No matter. The secret, as ever, is to go with the situation and use the shade for plants that will enjoy it. See it as a chance to grow all the lush, verdant plants that would wilt in direct sunlight. There is an incredible range of plants for shade, and most gardens do not begin to have room for half of them. Good gardens invariably look good because they make the most of the conditions forced upon them rather than applying rules and regulations that are inappropriate to their individual situation. So relish the opportunity the gloom presents you!

Shade-loving plants originate from woodland. Those that will grow in coniferous wood, such as **ivy** or **holly** will tolerate deep shade. Plants of deciduous woodland have learned to flower early, before the canopy of the trees shades out all light, and to put on healthy growth despite the shade overhead. They are ideal for a garden that gets only early morning sun.

The ideal soil for shade plants is woodland soil: if you walk through a beech wood the soil is almost black, distinctly springy and composed of pure leaf-mould. This is rich but light, holding moisture and yet well drained. **If you have very heavy soil in a shady garden, add plenty of organic matter and grit or sharp sand to it** (builder's sand will not do).

The sun rises higher in summer than in winter, casting much less shade. Nevertheless, many gardens have corners in perpetual shade.

If you are planting under a tree, it can be almost impossible to dig because of the roots. So go up rather than

---

PLANTS FOR SHADY GARDENS

TREES
Canadian Hemlock (*Tsuga canadensis*)
Holly
Juniperus x media 'Pfitzeriana'
Yew (*Taxus*)

SHRUBS
Berberis
Box (*Buxus*)
Camellia
Choisya ternata
Cotoneaster
Daphne
Euonymus
Fatsia japonica
Flowering currant (*Ribes sanguineum*)
Fuchsia
Golden privet (*Ligustrum ovalifolium* 'Aureum')
Guelder rose (*Viburnum opulus*)
Hazel (*Corylus avellana*)
Mahonia aquifolium
Mock orange (*Philadelphus coronarius*)
Osmanthus decorus
Rosa alba; R. rugosa
St John's Wort (*Hypericum*)
Skimmia japonica 'Rubella'
Vinca major; V. minor

CLIMBERS
Clematis 'Marie Boisselot'; *C.* 'Vyvyan Pennell'; *C. viticella*; *C.* 'Nelly Moser'; *C. alpina*; *C. tangutica*
Garrya elliptica
Honeysuckle (*Lonicera japonica* 'Halliana'; *L. periclymenum* 'Belgica'; *L. x brownii* 'Dropmore Scarlet')
Hydrangea petiolaris
Ivy (*Hedera helix* 'Hibernica')
Nasturtium (*Tropaeolum speciosum*)
Pyracantha
Rosa 'Madame Alfred Carrière'; *R.* 'Golden Showers'; *R.* 'Paul's Lemon Pillar'; *R.* 'Alberic Barbier'; *R.* 'Gypsy Boy' (Zigeunerknabe); *R.* 'Zéphirine Drouhin'
Virginia creeper (*Parthenocissus*)

PERENNIALS
Anemone x hybrida
Aquilegia vulgaris
Astrantia
Brunnera
Bugle (*Ajuga*)
Comfrey (*Symphytum grandiflorum*)
Dicentra spectabilis
Foxgloves (*Digitalis*)
Geranium phaeum
Helleborus corsicus; H. foetidus; H. orientalis
Hosta
Iris foetidissima
Kohleria digitaliflora
Ladies' mantle (*Alchemilla mollis*)
Lamium
Liriope
Loosestrife (*Lysimachia*)
Pulmonaria
Spurge (*Euphorbia amygdaloides robbiae*)
Streptocarpus saxorum
Tellima grandiflora
Tradescantia zebrina 'Quadricolor'
Waldsteinia ternata

FERNS
Adiantum pedatum; A. venustum
Ceterach officinarum
Davallia canariensis; D. mariesii
Dryopteris filix-mas
Hard fern (*Blechnum spicant*)
Hart's Tongue (*Phyllitis scolopendrium*)
Nephrolepis exaltata
Polypodium vulgare 'Cornubiense'
Pteris cretica

BULBS
Cyclamen (*Cyclamen hederifolium*)
Dog's tooth violet (*Erythronium dens-canis*)
Grape hyacinth (*Muscari armeniacum*)
Snowdrop (*Galanthus nivalis*)
Winter aconite (*Eranthis hyemalis*)
Wood anemone (*Anemone nemorosa*)

ANNUALS
Busy Lizzie (*Impatiens*)
Nemophila insignis

down. I have a large nut tree outside my back door and have woven a low fence around it with hazel. This creates a retaining wall for a raised bed. Put in as much good topsoil, organic matter and grit as you can to create a free root-run for your plants before they reach the massed roots of the tree. You will have to put a good layer of organic

mulch down each spring (and autumn too if you can) to maintain the nutrition and depth of the topsoil. The tree will greedily consume most of any nutrients you put in, so add a top dressing of bonemeal around each plant at the beginning of April.

COLOUR AND LIGHT

Colour is much trickier in shade than in full sun. On the whole plants that grow well in shade tend to have white flowers, as these attract what light is available much better than any other colour. This applies within species, so a white rose will usually do better on a north wall than a pink one. There are notable exceptions to this rule (such as the rose 'Zéphirine Drouhin', which is a strong pink), but they are few and far between.

Use a mirror to reflect light and to make a dark space appear bigger. This is an old trick but very effective. It can be leant against a wall (reflecting more sky than ground, so picking up more light) and surrounded with ivy so that it appears to be an open doorway

Paint any walls or fences white or off white so that they reflect the light.

Hostas and any number of ferns will flourish in shady corners.

Use pale surfaces for the ground.

The smaller the space, the more intensive the planting has to be. Therefore you should cram a small yard with pots and be prepared to keep moving them around so that the sun reaches the plants that need it most on that day or at that time of year.

DEALING WITH SNAILS

A PROBLEM THAT TENDS TO GO WITH SHADED URBAN GARDENS IS SNAILS. THIS CAN BE VERY BAD NEWS INDEED FOR PLANTS LIKE HOSTAS, WHICH SNAILS DEVOUR WITH AMAZING GREED. THEY BREED IN LOOSE MASONRY, SO THE FIRST THING TO DO IS TO MOVE ALL PILES OF BRICKS AND POINT UP ALL LOOSE BRICKWORK. THIS WILL NOT ERADICATE THE SNAILS, BUT IT DOES MAKE

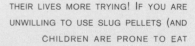

THEIR LIVES MORE TRYING! IF YOU ARE UNWILLING TO USE SLUG PELLETS (AND CHILDREN ARE PRONE TO EAT THEM), TRY PUTTING DOWN A SAUCER OF BEER. SNAILS ARE ATTRACTED TO IT AND FALL INTO THE SAUCER IN A DRUNKEN STUPOR. SLUGS AND SNAILS HATE SHARP SURFACES, SO MULCH BETWEEN SUCCULENT PLANTS LIKE HOSTAS WITH GRAVEL OR GRIT.

GROUND COVER

Ground cover is a modern phrase for a modern approach to gardening. It is based on the assumption that we do not have the time to cope with the garden as we might wish to, or as we might do if we had plenty of cheap labour. So rather than let weeds fill the spaces between plants, we plant things that will spread and keep the ground covered.

The point of keeping the ground covered is that this blocks out the light and thus stops anything growing beneath the low canopy – so no weeds.

NO WEEDS = NO WEEDING

Clearly the eyes of the Weekend Gardener start to light up at this point. Here is a group of plants that will do half the work in the garden for you.

That is the good news. The bad news is that most ground-cover plants are pretty dull and that the idea has been used to death by municipal authorities. So if you don't want your garden looking like a particularly dreary shopping-precinct planting plan or a ring-road roundabout, you need to choose your plants with care.

The first thing to remember is that ground-cover plants do not need to be small. The only prerequisite is that they be sufficiently thickly growing to dominate a position. So **rhododendrons** or **bamboos** make good ground cover, even though they hardly fit in with the preconceptions of spiralling growth.

The great aesthetic virtue of judicious ground-cover planting is that it can unify a garden, filling in disparate

Creeping Jenny creeps unobtrusively sideways to cover the ground.

A SELECTION OF GROUND-COVER PLANTS

SHRUBS	PERENNIALS
Dry, Sunny Places	
Artemisia	Acanthus
Ceanothus 'Cascade'	Achillea
Cistus	Aubrieta
Cytisus (broom)	Feverfew
Juniperus (juniper)	Geranium renardii
Lavandula (lavender)	Nepeta (catmint)
Rosmarinus officinalis 'Prostratus'	Sedum
Salvia (sage)	Stachys (lambs' ears)
Santolina	Teucrium (germander)
Light Shade	
Arundinaria (bamboo)	Ajuga (bugle)
Cotoneaster	Alchemilla mollis
Elaeagnus	Bergenia
Escallonia	Geranium (cranesbill)
Hypericum	Hemerocallis (daylily)
Rhododendron	Saxifraga (London pride)
Vinca (periwinkle)	Symphytum (comfrey)
Deep, Dry Shade	
	Blechnum
	Buxus (box)
Fatsia	Euphorbia amygdaloides robbiae
Hedera helix (ivy)	Lamium (deadnettle)
Hypericum calycinum	Symphytum grandiflorum
Prunus lusitanica	Waldsteinia ternata
Damp Places	
Cornus (Dogwood)	Humulus lupulus 'Aureus' (golden hop)
Salix repens (willow)	Aruncus (goat's beard)
Sambucus niger (elder)	Gunnera manicata
Viburnum opulus (guelder rose)	Hosta
	Luzula maxima 'Marginata' (woodrush)
	Lysimachia nummularia (creeping Jenny)
	Rheum palmatum
	Rodgersia

spaces with the same or similar plants in a way that so rarely happens in small gardens. **The moral to this is that you should be consistent within each area**. Do not dot different types of ground cover around. One type of plant will look much better.

The most obvious ground-cover plant to achieve this unity is **grass**. But one of my pet gardening hates is grass dotted with shrubs. It seems to have the opposite effect to unity. The shrubs look spotty and awful and the grass is broken and meaningless. A good rule of thumb for grass is to mow it only where you have unbroken sweeps or areas. They might only be 30cm (1ft) wide, they might curve and swerve, but they must flow.

Ground is seldom uncovered in nature. Brambles, for example, are a perfect ground-cover plant inasmuch as they spread fast, stop animals treading the area – and thus compacting it

blanket the ground and nourish the soil with an annual fall of leaves. However, it would be fairly eccentric to plant brambles in your garden as ground cover.

PREPARING THE GROUND
Before you start to plant ground cover, **clear the area of any weeds**. The most certain way of doing this is to hand dig it, picking out every scrap of root. But that is often not possible and nearly always too much of a pain to contemplate. I would spray the area to be planted with a glysophate weedkiller ('Roundup' or 'Tumbleweed'), which will kill most things and yet be completely harmless once it hits the soil. It is particularly effective for grasses, thistles, docks, bindweed, ground elder and any annual weeds. Glysophate makes nettles feel unwell, but tends not to kill them. Try digging these out. Horseradish and horsetail are almost impossible to eradicate without either regular cutting or a plastic mulch.

Leave the ground for six weeks before planting to make sure everything is dead.

PLANTING GROUND COVER
Plant your ground cover at decent spacings. Too close and it will not develop properly and grow into lumps. Too far apart and there will always be gaps between the plants.

It is better to plant a number of small plants than a few big ones.

It is a good idea to underplant low-growing ground cover with **bulbs**. The

Ground cover can be bushy and striking.

crucial factor is that the ground cover should not obscure more than half the leaves of the bulbs, as these need sunlight in order to manufacture and store next year's food for the flowers. Crocuses go well under bugle, daffodils are fine poking through a mat of ivy and tulips will prosper under a carpet of prostrate rosemary.

Prostrate woody shrubs and trees make the longest-term ground cover.

Taxus baccata 'Cavendishii' is a prostrate yew, growing sideways rather than up, as does the juniper *Juniperus* x *media* 'Pfitzeriana', which is often used to provide impenetrable cover. Both are 'proper' trees that choose to progress crabwise rather than up. Both are very shade-tolerant.

In the table opposite I have included a short selection of plants for a few different positions. Remember that some will spread inexorably and that although they might start life as weedy-looking specimens they will cover yards and yards of ground very quickly. For all that, until they are established, even the thickest ground-cover plant will need to be kept weed-free.

> *Remember that some ground cover plants will spread inexorably and that although they might start life as weedy-looking specimens they will cover yards and yards of ground very quickly.*

TIP

GROUND-COVER PLANTING IS PARTICULARLY SUITABLE FOR STEEP SLOPES, WHICH ARE AWKWARD TO TEND AND DRAIN VERY FAST. THE FOLIAGE OF THE PLANTS WILL SLOW DOWN EVAPORATION AND AS THEY SPREAD THEY WILL COVER THE BANK. I HAVE USED RAMBLING ROSES VERY EFFECTIVELY FOR THIS. THEY MAKE MOUNDS RATHER THAN FLAT PLAINS, BUT DO THE JOB WELL AND EXTREMELY HANDSOMELY. *R. FILIPES* 'KIFTSGATE' SHOULD ONLY BE USED WHERE THERE IS A LOT OF ROOM: IN A SMALLER GARDEN TRY 'ALBÉRIC BARBIER', 'FÉLICITÉ PERPÉTUE' OR 'PAUL'S HIMALAYAN MUSK' INSTEAD.

SHRUB ROSES

Shrub roses have the advantage of being remarkably tough and undemanding, whilst producing the most wonderful flowers of any plant group in the world. There is a tendency (which I once shared) to think of roses as ugly plants with beautiful flowers, but most shrub roses have attractive foliage and hips and should be planted in mixed borders surrounded by other flowering plants rather than in stark 'rose beds'.

There is not the space here to ex-

For me, shrub roses in full romp exemplify the best in British gardens.

plore the full range of roses, but I shall try and demystify the various groups within the realm of shrub roses:

Gallica roses were brought to this country from the Middle East by Crusaders – probably in the mid-twelfth century. They are tough shrubs, flowering only once in June/July, and include some of the greatest glories of the plant world, such as 'Charles de Mills', 'Cardinal de Richelieu', 'Rosa Mundi' and 'Tuscany' as well as the famous *R. gallica officinalis*, the Red Rose of Lancaster.

Damask roses come from a similar background to gallicas and simple varieties such as *R.x damascena* would have been known to the ancient Greeks and Romans. This group is also tough and single-flowering; it includes 'Kazanlik' (ideal for pot-pourri), 'Madame Hardy', the ancient and repeat-flowering 'Quatre Saisons' and the deliciously scented 'Ispahan'.

Portland roses are compact shrubs – mostly about 90cm (3ft) high – and often keep on flowering all summer. I grow 'Rose de Rescht' very happily in a pot.

Cabbage or **Centifolia roses** are, as the name implies, usually full to the point of blowsiness. Most were bred 300–400 years ago in Holland and are typically seen in still lives of that period. These are voluptuous flowers with petals like silk; most smell heavenly (I use the word advisedly). I have grown and can recommend 'Fantin-Latour', 'Juno', 'Robert le Diable', 'Rose de Meaux' and *R. centifolia*.

Moss roses (*R. centifolia muscosa*) have whiskers. They were very popular 150 years ago, but are now less widely grown. Which is a pity. The green fuzz (hence the 'moss') on their unopened buds adds curiosity to the charm and loveliness of their flowers. I currently grow 'Chapeau de Napoleon' (so-called because the bud looks like a tricorn hat), 'General Kleber', 'Madame de la Roche-Lambert', 'Henri Martin' and 'William Lobb'. This list will certainly be increasing.

Albas are the hardiest, least demanding and often most beautiful of all roses, always with wonderful scent. *R.x alba* is

the White Rose of York, with lovely matt-grey foliage. The following selection is intimately known to me: 'Celestial', 'Queen of Denmark', 'Cuisse de Nymphe' (or Great Maiden's Blush), 'Maxima', 'Madame Legras de St Germain', 'Madame Plantier' and *R. alba semi-plena*.

Rugosa roses have become very well known through being much used in municipal planting. But it is a shame to think of them as a kind of flowering motorway barrier. They will grow in any soil, ignore atmospheric pollution, flower all summer and are a perfect introduction to growing roses for the novice gardener. *R. rugosa alba* is one of my favourites – pure white flowers with vigorous growth. 'Blanc Double de Coubert' is justly renowned and should be in every garden; 'Hunter' is a bright crimson and 'Roseraie de l'Hay' an equally bright pink.

Bourbon roses came from the island of Réunion in the Indian Ocean about 200 years ago. They are mostly continuously flowering, vigorous shrubs.

The hips of Rosa rugosa *are extremely decorative.*

grow and love 'Souvenir de Malmaison', 'Louise Odier', 'Madame Isaac Pereire', 'Zigeunerknabe' and the famous climber 'Zéphirine Drouhin'.

An array of David Austin roses – 'Seagull', 'Claire Martin' and 'Fred Loads'.

Hybrid perpetuals are vigorous and re-peat-flowering, with a tendency to-wards large flowers. 'Souvenir de Dr Jamain' is a classic climber, flowering from May till October and growing best in shade. The three shrubs I grow and can recommend from experience are 'Reine des Violettes', which is practically thornless with rich, velvety, crimson flowers, 'Paul Neyron', a smallish bush with huge flowers of warm pink, and 'Ulrich Brunner' which has a very upright growth.

Species roses are those described only with a Latin name and undoctored by man. They flower only once, often with small or single flowers and nearly always with great charm. Most have very decorative hips. Those making a deservedly popular comeback include *R. pimpinellifolia* (the 'Burnet Roses'), *R. foetida*, *R. eglanteria* and *R. sericea*.

There are some excellent modern shrub roses, including the group that has come to be known as **English roses**, which were bred by David Austin, crossing older roses with mod-ern hybrid teas and floribundas. They have the shape of shrubs and yet bloom all summer. The biggest complaint I have against them is that their foliage rarely matches the delicacy and beauty of older roses. There are too many to list here, but 'Troilus', 'Chaucer', 'Pretty Jessica' and 'Mary Rose' are noteworthy.

Other modern shrub roses such as 'Nevada', 'Fruhlingsmorgen', 'Fruhlingsanfrang' and 'Golden Wings' have been developed from burnet roses and are exceptionally ro-bust and floriferous.

PLANTING SHRUB ROSES

It is always best to buy roses from a specialist nursery which will provide them 'bare-root' in winter (November–March), when they should be planted, although you can plant con tainer roses from a garden centre at any time of year, even when they are in flower. All roses, of whatever type, should be planted in the same way as follows.

1. Dig a hole to a spade's depth and big enough to spread the roots out in every direction. Loosen the bottom of the hole with a fork.

2. Dig some manure into the loosened layer and sprinkle a handful of bone-meal over it.

3. Position the plant in the middle of the hole so that the 'union' (the cal-loused join between the rootstock, which is the same in all roses, and the top, which varies from variety to vari-ety) is about 2.5cm (1in) below the surface. This is important. Roses are invariably potted up so that the union is standing well above the soil level, but you must ignore this precedent. When properly planted the branches of the shrub rose should stick out of the ground like separate twigs.

4. Replace the topsoil carefully, mak-ing sure that it is worked right around the roots. Firm the soil in well with your boot.

Plant all roses so that the union (the point where the species is grafted on to the rootstock) is below the surface of the soil. This protects it from frost and wind damage. When you buy a rose in a container the union is invariably above the surface.

5. Sprinkle another handful of bone-meal and plant a clove of garlic to deter greenfly (see pages 112 and 180).
6. Water well and mulch with manure.
7. Prune all branches back to two or three healthy buds. This will ensure and stimulate healthy, vigorous growth from the bottom of the plant.

SCENT IN THE GARDEN

Nothing makes a garden more exotic or sensually pleasing than the scents of sun-warmed flowers.

It is perfectly possible to organise the smelliness of your garden with a little careful planning, so that not only are the best scents in the right places but there is also a decent spread of perfume across the year.

It is amazing how powerfully evocative the faintest trace of scent can be. When I was a child we would use a tiny swimming pool in a neighbour's garden which was surrounded by a box hedge. Now, thirty years later, the smell of box on a sunny day still instantly recalls those swimming expeditions. The real point of this story – other than sharing details of my riveting past – is that you do not need exotic plants to create wonderful scents. Any local garden centre can supply you with plants enough to fulfil the possibilities of this essential component of a rewarding garden.

Whereas a scent might waft to you on a gentle breeze, wind invariably blows nice smells away and nasty ones to you (I live downwind of a chicken factory-farm, so I know). To make the most of the delicacy of scent you need a sheltered garden. Ensure that there are trees, shrubs and fences around the perimeter to trap the scent in.

The other great boost for developing the full possibilities for scent is sun. Try and use the available sun to best advantage. Make sure that the borders are there and every inch of sunny wall space is used.

CHOOSING PLANTS FOR SCENT

Scented plants do not have to be big. There are a number of small but powerfully scented plants that will enrich the smallest garden. These tend to be **herbs**, and camomile, mint and thyme should be in every garden, planted in the cracks in paths, in the risers between steps and in containers raised up by seats. Most herbs are worth their place in the garden for their scent alone. So lavender, rosemary and bay will reach out their scent to you. Other herbs will release their scent if you brush past them or pluck a leaf.

It makes sense to bring the plants as close to the nose as possible, so use raised beds and pots to surround a seat with nose-height scents.

The most conventionally perfumed of plants are the **roses**. Actually not all smell and some smell a lot better than others. Some smell horrid. As I have made clear on the previous pages, the only sensible roses for the Weekend Gardener to grow are shrub roses and preferably old-fashioned shrub roses at that. The *albas* and *rugosas* have fabulous scents on plants as tough as brambles. *Rosa* 'Alba Semiplena' and *R. rugosa* 'Blanc Double de Coubert' are absolute essentials for anybody with a nose to smell them. The Bourbon roses are less subtle but none the less worthy for that. *R.* 'Mme Isaac Pereire' is one of the most powerfully scented of all roses as well as being a strong pink colour. It can be trained to climb over a support or left to grow into a bush.

The most obvious scented plants, and most useful for the small garden, are **climbers**. While we are on the subject of roses, it goes without saying that every garden should have at least one

Perennials

Cosmos	C. atrosanguineus	Summer
Crambe	C. cordifolia	Summer
Geranium	G. endressii	Summer
Hellebore	Helleborus foetidus	Early spring
Iris	I. germanica	Early summer
Lupin	Lupinus polyphyllus	Early summer
Catmint	Nepeta	Summer
Phlox	P. paniculata	Summer
Violet	Viola odorata	Spring

Shrubs

Butterfly Bush	Buddleia davidii	Late summer
Box	Buxus sempervirens	Perennial
Rock Rose	Cistus	Summer
Broom	Cytisus	Late spring
Daphne	D. mezereum	Early spring
Deutzia	D. compacta	Summer
Eleagnus	E. commutata	Early summer
Eucryphia	E. lucida	Late summer
Witch Hazel	Hamamelis mollis	Early spring
Juniper	J. communis	Perennial
Magnolia	M. sieboldii	Summer
Osmanthus	O. x burkwoodii	Spring
Mock Orange	Philadelphus	Summer
Lilac	Syringa	Spring
Viburnum	V. x bodnantense	Winter
Rose	All old roses	Summer

Trees

Indian Bean Tree	Catalpa bigonioides	Spring
Eucalyptus	E. glaucescens	Perennial
Crab Apple	Malus	Spring
Balsam Poplar	Populus balsamifera	Spring

climbing rose for the scent alone. One of the easiest to grow is R. 'New Dawn', which has a delicate fragrance. A couple of French madames are more powerfully perfumed: R. 'Mme Grégoire Staechelin' and R. 'Mme Alfred Carrière', which, unlike most roses, will perform well in shade.

If you grow a **honeysuckle** and a **jasmine** in conjunction you can spread the smelling season from spring to autumn. Unlike roses, honeysuckle smells best in the evening or early morning, when it is a little cooler. Plant a honeysuckle by the back door so that its scent is the first thing to greet when you poke your nose out on a summer's morning, or against a wall

summer. *L.japonica* 'Halliana' is a vigorous, almost evergreen climber with white flowers and a fruity smell; *L.x americana* smells of cloves and yellow flowers appear in midsummer.

The **common jasmine** (*Jasminum officinale*) is a strong brew and can fill the evening air with cheap perfume – heady stuff, but a little overwhelming. Go steady with it or else it swamps the scent of its more subtle neighbours. *J. beesianum* is a more restrained alternative and *J. x stephanense* the offspring of the two. It has gently scented pink flowers.

One does not normally think of **clematis** as being notable for its scent, but there are a few varieties that are worth growing for this alone. *C. montana* smells of vanilla in spring and *C. flammula* of meadowsweet in September. *C. rehderiana* has a delicate primrose fragrance and *C. serratifolia* the scent of lemons. As far as I know there is not a clematis that smells of clematis.

One of the most evocative off all scents comes from the **sweet pea** (*Lathyrus odoratus*). Plant a line of these against a sunny fence and you will have wonderful cut

flowers and their unique scent. Do not use the modern 'Spencer' varieties as these have had the scent bred out of them. Buy an Old Fashioned or Grandiflora mix.

Another annual that is essential for scent alone is the **tobacco plant** (*Nicotiana sylvestris*). This smells only at night, but nothing else has such a musky, exotic perfume. *N. affinis* is a smaller, less dramatic plant, but still wonderfully scented.

As its name suggests, **evening primrose** (*Oenothera odorata*) is another plant that gives off its scent at night. *O. biennis* is the more common version, but it can be rather invasive for a small garden.

Climbers		
Clematis	*C. montana*	Spring
	C. flammula	Summer
	C. rehderiana	Late summer
Jasmine	*Jasminum officinale*	Summe
Honeysuckle	*Lonicera x americana*	Summer
	L. caprifolium	Summer
	L. japonica 'Halliana'	Summer
	L. periclymenum 'Belgica'	Summer
Wisteria	*W. floribunda*	Late spring
Rose	R. 'New Dawn'	Summer
	R. 'Mme Grégoire Staechelin'	Summer
	R. 'Mme Alfred Carrière'	Summer

Bulbs		
Crinum	*C. x powellii*	Late summer
Cyclamen	*C. purpurascens*	Autumn
Cape Hyacinth	*Galtonia candicans*	Summer
Bluebell	*Hyacinthoides non-scripta*	Spring
Madonna Lily	*Lilium candidum*	Summer
Regal Lily	*L. regale*	Summer
Daffodil	*Narcissus jonquilla*	Early spring

or fence, you sit in the evening contemplating the follies of the working day. *Lonicera fragrantissima* starts flowering at about Christmas time and is grown purely for its ravishing scent. The common honeysuckle (*L. periclymen* 'Belgica') is next in late May/early June, with *L. p.* 'Serotina' having darker flowers that come out later in

Annuals and Biennials		
Snapdragon	*Antirrhinum*	Summer
Wallflower	*Cheiranthus*	Spring
Sweet William	*Dianthus*	Summer
Sweet Rocket	*Hesperis matronalis*	Summer
Sweet Pea	*Lathyrus odoratus*	Spring/Summer
Sweet Alyssum	*Lobularia maritima*	Summer
Tobacco Plant	*Nicotiana sylvestris*	Summer
Evening Primrose	*Oenothera odorata*	Summer
Verbena	*V. x hybrida*	Summer

Deliciously scented honeysuckle trained against a wall.

JULY

WEATHER REPORT: my birthday is in July, so I have always thought of it as a turning point of the year. Although it is the middle of summer, the days are getting shorter and that fresh lusciousness that characterises May and June has gone. By the end of the month the garden can get tired and drab. Thunderstorms are common and can do a lot of damage to fruit and unstaked plants. The general rule is that if it is hot it is very hot, if wet, very wet. St Swithin's Day is on 15 July and the prophecy is that if it rains on this day it will do so for forty days. I don't know if this is true, but I do know that Billy Bragg wrote a very good song called 'St Swithin's Day'.

PLANTS IN THEIR PRIME

Bulbs: *Galtonia candicans*; lilies; gladioli.

Annuals/biennials: *Alyssum*; foxglove (*Digitalis*); *Ageratum*; *Phlox*; pinks (*Dianthus*); marigolds (*Calendula*); Californian poppy (*Eschscholzia*); snapdragons (*Antirrhinum*); *Calceolaria*; Canterbury bells (*Campanula*); poached egg plant (*Limnanthes douglasii*); lobelias; nasturtiums; pelargoniums; poppies; sweet peas; sweet Williams; petunias; *Tropaeolum*.

Perennials: hollyhocks (*Althaea*); *Acanthus mollis*; *Achillea*; *Anchusa*; *Aruncus*; *Astrantia*; *Campanula*; daylily (*Hemerocallis*); delphiniums; *Eryngium*; geraniums; hostas; *Inula*; *Lavatera*; *Macleaya*; evening primrose (*Oenothera*); *Rudbeckia*; *Verbascum*.

Shrubs: all shrub roses; *Ceanothus*; *Cistus*; *Escallonia*; hebes; hydrangeas; *Hypericum*; lavender; *Phlomis fruticosa*; *Potentilla fruticosa*; *Spiraea*; vincas.

Climbers: all climbing roses; all hybrid clematis; honeysuckle; *Hydrangea petiolaris*; jasmine (*Jasminum officinale*).

Vegetables: beans; beetroot; carrots; cauliflowers; cucumbers; lettuce; onions; peas; potatoes; tomatoes.

Fruit: all currants; gooseberries; raspberries; strawberries.

Herbs: all herbs.

Houseplants: gloxinia.

WEED CONTROL

Do not let weeds seed. Weed little and often. Weed hedges and trees and mulch the clear ground.

LAWNS

If it is very dry, raise mower blades and only cut lightly once a week. Water lawns. Trim edges.

Opposite: Herbaceous borders at Bramdean House, Hampshire. Note how the plants cover the ground, giving an impression of continuity without looking in the least bit squashed.

This page: You don't need a garden to garden. Herbs will grow on the smallest window-sill. However, you would need a garden to grow these wonderful redcurrants.

JOBS

Essential
• Eat outside at least once a week.
• Water all containers regularly.
• Take cuttings from shrubs that have flowered.
• Prune ornamental and fruiting cherry and plum trees.
• Cut beech and hornbeam hedges.

Desirable
• Eat outside at least once a day.
• Sow lettuce every two weeks to get a steady supply of young plants.
• Lift and divide June-flowering irises that have been in the same site for three years or more.
• Sow biennials for next year in seedbed.
• Lift and store tulip bulbs.
• Plant autumn crocus.

Optional
• Eat every meal outside.
• Layer strawberries.
• Sow Japanese leaf greens.
• Take stock of the garden and note holes, weaknesses and successes. Plan for this time next year.

CUTTINGS

The average uninitiated gardener is scared of taking cuttings, as though it involved a sacrament to which they were not privy. Well it doesn't. You cut a bit of plant off, stick it in some soil and watch it grow roots and become a new plant. There are some tricks and tips to make the process more likely to succeed, but the essence of the operation remains as simple as that.

A cutting is an extremely useful way of making new plants because it is quick, easy, cheap and guarantees an exact replica of the parent plant – something that propagation from seed cannot do.

The development of any cutting is a race between the growth of new roots – which will supply the plant with water and nutrients – and the loss of water from the cutting through evaporation with a resulting collapse of cells and wilting. Heat – particularly under-soil heat – will speed up the root development enormously. Moisture will delay the wilting of the plant. The more moisture the cutting has, the less likely it is to wilt before new roots can form with which to replace evaporated water. Therefore cuttings taken from fresh growth are best put in a warm place and a polythene bag placed over the top of them, tied with an elastic band around the top of the pot, which will maintain the moisture around the leaves.

Stem cuttings are by far the commonest and easiest, although some plants can be propagated from leaf and root cuttings. There are three types of stem cutting: softwood, semi-ripe and hardwood.

Strip off the bottom leaves to reduce respiration.

Dip the end in water and then into fresh rooting powder (chuck last year's supply).

Slip a polythene bag over the top of the pot to prevent moisture being lost from the cuttings.

You can fit a number of cuttings in the same pot – place them at 2.5cm (1in) intervals.

SOFTWOOD CUTTINGS

These are taken in May / June from new shoots. The advantage of these is that they are far more likely to root than older shoots. The disadvantage is that they are likely to wilt and die before these roots can get established. Therefore all softwood cuttings should be given a warm, moist environment. A propagator is ideal, but failing that put the cuttings under a bag.

Plants suitable for softwood cuttings include fuchsias, philadelphus, hebes, vines, pelargoniums, chrysanthemums, hydrangeas, ceanothus and lupins.

Before you cut your material, prepare potting compost for the cuttings. They must have a really loose root-run with good drainage. At this stage nutri-tion is not an issue, so either use special cutting compost (and I always mix this with vermiculite and sharp sand) or mix an ordinary general purpose compost half and half with sharp sand or vermiculite. Vermiculite is excellent because it provides a good root-run and drainage and yet holds sufficient moisture at the same time. Square pots are ideal for cuttings, but any container will do as long as it has drainage holes and room for roots to develop.

It is best to take softwood cuttings in the morning, when the plants are turgid. Cut a dozen or so healthy growing tips about 15cm (6in) long and put them straight into a polythene bag. This minimises water loss. Remember, it is a race from the moment that the plant is cut to when it can support itself from new roots, so anything that you can do to stop wilt will increase the chances of the cutting 'striking'. Obviously the length of the cutting will depend on the size of the plant, but always cut more off than you will eventually need.

Trim each cutting so that the bottom is just below a leaf node. I always cut them at an angle to increase the exposed area that roots will grow from. Strip off the bottom leaves so that it has just one group of leaves at the top. Dip the stem in water and then into hormone rooting powder, which you can buy by the pot in any garden store. Poke the cuttings into the soil so that at least 2.5cm (1in), preferably 5cm (2in), is underground. Give each one 2.5cm (1in) or so on either side of it. Water it and put the polythene bag over the top. Put it where it will get plenty of sunlight. It should not need watering again for a few days, but keep an eye on it. Too much water will induce mould, too little cause wilting. Use your common sense.

You will know if the cutting has

Cuttings should be taken from vigorous, healthy plants.

grown roots by signs of new leaves. When these are apparent, carefully lift the plant and pot it into normal compost for it to grow on.

That all takes much longer to read than to do, but it is the basic procedure for any kind of stem cutting.

SEMI-RIPE CUTTINGS

These are taken towards the end of summer when the new growth has ripened. They need less mollycoddling than softwood cuttings, but are slower to grow roots. Cut the stems off just below the bottom of this year's growth. If you are very organised, semi-ripe cuttings strike much more easily from plants that have been pruned hard the November before so that the new growth is vigorous and more able to produce roots.

Semi-ripe cuttings can be put either into pots like softwood cuttings or in a cold frame, set about 5cm (2in) deep and 10cm (4in) apart. Deciduous plants will drop their leaves in autumn, and these should be cleared away. Leave the cuttings until spring, when new growth will show if they have rooted. Lift them and pot them on.

Almost all deciduous shrubs are best taken as semi-ripe cuttings, as are lavender, rosemary, holly, cotoneasters and choisya.

HARDWOOD CUTTINGS

These are taken in winter from mature wood. If they are from deciduous plants they are leafless, which means that they lose little moisture and can survive for a long time. On the other hand they can be slow to root.

Put hardwood cuttings straight outside. They must be some-

where where they can be left undisturbed for up to fifteen months, although they may well be ready for potting on the following autumn. Make a deep V-shape in the soil and fill it with sharp sand. There is no need to use a rooting powder. Cut the tops at an angle just above a bud. Set the cuttings about 10cm (4in) apart along the V and backfill it so that all but 2.5cm (1in) or so of the cutting is buried. This delays drying out.

Set hardwood cuttings in a narrow trench filled with sharp sand.

Suitable plants for hardwood cuttings include most deciduous trees, blackcurrant, cotoneaster, *Ribes*, *Cornus*, roses, *Spiraea* and *Viburnum*.

EVERGREEN CUTTINGS

Some evergreens, such as box, yew and holly, take very well from cuttings, and as they are such expensive plants, this is the only way to gather a large number for edging or hedging. I take these exactly like a softwood cutting, but put them in a specially prepared bed (with a lot of sharp sand for good drainage) under cloches. This stops too much water loss. They will need watering lightly once a week. Box and holly are best taken in September and yew after the first frost. They should have rooted by the following autumn.

LABOUR SAVING

You don't have to do much at this time of year to make the garden look good. Everything is rampantly lush and even weeds look rich with growth. But along with this is a sense of the garden as a runaway horse, charging through a magnificent countryside with the gardener hanging on grimly whilst ineffectively tugging at the reins. I know that the scope of my own gardening is curtailed first by lack of time and then by lack of money. The latter would buy the former in the guise of hired help, but as I garden as much for the enjoyment of doing it as for the end result, it seems a trifle perverse to pay someone to do what I would like to be doing myself. A bit like feeling hungry and paying someone else to eat the meal for you. Gardening is like delicious food, making love or being made to laugh, something you would always like more of, but there is never enough time to do what has to be done, let alone to enjoy the finer points of it. It is all relative. But in the end there is no fun to be had from constantly feeling as though you are losing the battle. The thing becomes a chore.

So what do you do? There is bound to be some boring smart-arse who will talk smugly of cutting your coat to suit your cloth and not biting off more than you can chew. What is particularly nauseating is that they are right. You have to garden within your limitations.

The secret is to curtail the essential work, but not the scope of your imagination. There are ways of being efficient with your time and energy in the garden.

If you have grass to cut, consider if you really need it. Most town gardens are too small for lawns. Paving, once laid, needs practically no maintenance and can more or less be covered with pots. If you have enough space to warrant grass, cut only paths and lawns regularly. Nothing is duller than acres of roughly mown grass. Cut lawns high and fast, just skimming the top. If you have a cylinder mower, take the back plate off in dry weather. This means that only the excessive trimmings are collected, the rest conserving moisture as a light mulch. If you have the money it pays to have a good mower too. But that is a truism about all machines.

An awful lot of time is spent watering, particularly in town gardens. Consider installing a permanent irrigation system based on the slow release of droplets rather than a spray. This saves water and time. Failing this, at least get a really efficient sprinkler.

Never have any bare soil. It will only sprout weeds. Mulch the ground with as deep a layer of organic matter as you can, but it is best to plant something everywhere so that there is no bare soil for weeds to grow in.

If you are starting from a position of a lot of bare soil and a few small plants, it is a good idea to scatter the seeds of such plants as poppies, cornflowers, *Achillea*, night-scented stock, *Hesperis* or foxgloves liberally between your perennials so that they will come up in great swathes. If you have more room and sufficient looseness of mind, try fleshier and altogether bigger stuff like borage, comfrey, buddleia or onopordums, which will self-seed like mad.

If you just want short-term cover while waiting for long-term inspiration or time to deal with an empty spot, it is a perfectly good idea to use a green manure like mustard. This looks fine for a few weeks and will nourish the soil when dug in.

If you are going to fill every inch of available ground with plants, **you will need to feed them**. The best way to do this is with a foliar feed, like liquid seaweed or a comfrey spray. You can do

Save labour by filling every inch with plants. The left-hand border will look after itself – all you have to do is trim the edge – while the right-hand one looks bare and drab and will need constant weeding.

this using your hosepipe with a spray attachment with either proprietary pellets or a liquid reservoir.

If you are really together, you can **let weeds do the mulching for you**, while you fix your eyes on higher things. I remember visiting Peter Beales's wonderful rose nursery at Attleborough in Norfolk at this time of year and noticing that beneath the voluptuous brilliance and delicacy of his roses the ground was liberally decked with weeds. When I put this to him he rightly pointed out that they were doing no harm and not in any way detracting from the beauty of the roses. If he had time to weed, he would – as it

was he didn't, so he concentrated on the roses. A wise man.

Keep the lines clean. It is astonishing how you can add crispness and focus to the entire garden by keeping edges and hedges trimmed, gravel raked or paths weeded. None of these jobs takes long, but the effect is always transforming.

Don't fight nature. It is amazing how much time some people spend trying to grow things that have no business being there. If your garden is wet and dark, celebrate the fact with hostas, ligularias, ferns and rheums; forget about sun-loving Mediterranean plants. Or move.

Investing in a permanent irrigation system or an efficient sprinkler will save hours of watering.

Do what you enjoy most and let the garden evolve around this. If mowing grass is your thing, then shamelessly put the garden down to lawn and pray for warm, wet weeks and dry weekends. If you hate digging, don't do it. The garden will do fine without it. Gardening is not work in preparation for an exam on which your moral worth will be judged; it is something you do entirely privately – for fun. There is little enough time as it is, so you might as well enjoy every minute of it.

SOFT FRUIT

Soft fruit (as far as I know there is no such thing as 'hard' fruit) can best be defined as either berry or currant. Most of these are easy enough to grow, preferring a cool climate; they taste delicious fresh from the garden, take up relatively little space and are decorative. I rest my case.

STRAWBERRIES

Modern large-fruited strawberries are a cross between the American *Fragaria virginiana,* which arrived in Europe in 1556, and *F. chiloensis,* which did not hit England until early in the eighteenth century.

There is a native wild strawberry, *F. vesca*, and the small but delicious alpine strawberry.

Modern strawberries can be divided into three groups:

Maincrop	Ripens June/July.
Alpine	Small, ripe June to October.
Perpetual	A cross between the other two, ripe between July and October.

All strawberries are herbaceous plants, dying down in the winter. They are self-fertile, propagating from runners — plantlets that grow on long, horizontal stems.

Your soil is likely to be the determining factor in the taste of your strawberries: the richer and heavier the soil, the better the flavour. Strawberries do not grow terribly well on chalk (although I was brought up in a chalky garden and we seemed to grow strawberries well enough. If you are on chalk, do not be put off.) A light, sandy soil is likely to give an earlier crop.

The best time to plant strawberries is in September. Plants should be given a sunny site with plenty of manure dug into the soil. Replace the plants every three years, growing the new ones in a fresh site, leaving the old site as a strawberry-free zone for at least three years. This avoids disease and promotes heavier cropping. Plant at 45cm (18in) spacing with the base of the central crown at soil level.

Water the plants well as they are growing, but be careful not to get the fruits wet once they start to redden. The fruits should be kept off the ground to avoid slugs and rotting, so tuck straw or a mat around each plant.

Strawberries can easily be grown in a special planter, which has cupped holes in the sides through which you plant. Alpine strawberries can also be grown in a large pot or window box.

Strawberries should be eaten warm – ideally within minutes of picking.

Grow strawberries on rich soil for best results.

Never put them in the fridge, as this destroys the flavour. Once the fruits have been collected, cut the foliage off to about 5cm (2in) above the crown and give the plants a feed of a general fertiliser like Growmore.

GOOSEBERRIES

Gooseberry fool is the food of the gods, with gooseberry jam and gooseberry tart running close behind. Gooseberries will happily grow in cool, moist conditions as long as they can get some sun to ripen the fruit.

Bushes are best grown as standards or semi-standards, which means that the thorny branches are clear of the ground, making weeding very much easier. A single standard in a pot will look good and provide enough fruit for a meal. They should be planted in November. Gooseberries need a high level of potash, so give them a feed of potassium sulphate or rock potash in early spring and mulch well with compost or manure.

Prune the bushes so that they have an open centre. This makes them much easier to pick and reduces the chance of mildew, caused by lack of ventilation.

Gooseberries grow well as cordons, which is an extremely space-saving way of producing lots of fruit. To establish a cordon from a bush, cut the leader (the main, central stem or trunk) back by a third after planting and reduce the side shoots to 2.5cm (1in). Immediately after harvest, prune the new side shoots back to four or five leaves and the leader tied to a cane. In winter cut the side shoots back again to 2.5cm (1in) and prune the leader back to just 5cm (6in) of new growth.

RASPBERRIES

The choicest strawberry is nowhere near as good as an average raspberry. A

dish of the deep pink fruits picked from the garden, sprinkled with sugar and with plenty of single cream, eaten outside on a warm evening with a cold glass of a fruity white wine is the greatest treat the garden has to offer.

Raspberries like wet, cool conditions, which is why they are grown so successfully in Scotland. There are two types, the summer-fruiting varieties that crop in midsummer and autumn-fruiting that crop from late summer until the first frosts.

The canes should be planted vertically and firmly in rich ground in late autumn and cut back to 23cm (9in). As soon as vigorous new growth appears, this original cane should be pruned to ground level. Raspberries should have a good mulch each spring and need watering if the weather is dry.

Before you plant it is a good idea to construct support for the canes by

To produce gooseberries as healthy as this, water well and feed with potash.

banging posts in every 3m (10ft) and stapling wires between them 60cm, 1.2m and 1.8m (2ft, 4ft and 6ft) above the ground. As the canes grow you weave them between the wires and tie them in with soft twine.

Summer-fruiting varieties fruit on last year's canes, so these should be pruned every other year. In practice this means cutting the fruiting canes to ground level immediately after harvest. The canes for next year's crop should be tied to the wires at 12.5cm (5in) intervals and the tops cut back to about 15cm (6in) above the top wire in spring.

Autumn-fruiting raspberries fruit on the current year's growth, so prune all canes right back to the ground in March.

GARDEN TREES

In many ways trees are the most important elements in a garden. Without them you lack height or scale. Fortunately you do not necessarily have to own a tree to gain these virtues from it: a tree in a neighbour's garden or on the street outside can be a vital component in your garden.

The golden weeping willow Salix alba *'Tristis'*.

Nevertheless, you cannot rely on others to do the job for you. Trees need to be chosen with the same care as any other plant. There is such a huge range of possibilities of size, shape, leaf colour and shape, bark, fruit and flower, that there is really no excuse for planting an ugly or inappropriate tree. By the same token there is no reason to keep an existing ugly tree. Of course the definition of what is ugly or inappropriate is subjective and should be made very carefully. Live with the tree for at least a year before taking any action. See whether it performs at a time of year when there is little else or whether its

major virtue is lost in high summer and paid for with ten months of drabness. In a small garden a tree must have at least two virtues to justify its space, be it of flower and shape, bark and autumn leaf colour, or bare winter outline and nuts.

In a larger garden trees are vital as a wind break. Good shelter from wind will do more than anything else to protect your plants. If this means blotting out the view, then so be it. If a tree's primary function is as a wind break, make sure that its branches grow as low to the ground as possible, otherwise the wind hits the top of the tree, whips down and blows under the branches with redoubled force.

Gardens are essentially private spaces. Whilst hedges and fences are the first weapons of privacy, trees can do much to stop uninvited eyes peering in on you. If the garden is private you make it exactly as you want it without the sense of unwelcome judgement from over the fence.

Trees provide shade. That shade might be unwelcome, but there are few gardens that are not improved aesthetically and horticulturally by having some shaded areas at different times of day. The intensity of shade can vary enormously from the almost complete shade of a horse chestnut or beech to the very light, dappled shade of a birch or robinia.

Do not be seduced by speed of growth. Many trees have an initial spurt and then slow right down, just as others take a while to establish but then pull away after a few years. Some trees, such as eucalyptus, poplars or Leyland cypress, start growing at a sprint and speed up from there. In general the fastest growing trees have the hungriest roots and are the most difficult to plant around.

Planting a tree just because it will grow fast implies a certain amount of desperation or a substantial lack of imagination. If you must do it for short-term expediency (and I, in my new garden, have done just that to create fast structure), work out your long-term plans and plant the tree you would ideally like alongside the upstart, making allowance for the fact that you will need to cut the racer down after a few years to give the 'proper' tree light and space.

Trees demand patience. You are planting them for your dotage or for the next generation but one to enjoy their maturity. Almost all trees take about three years to get growing properly. Yet the first delicate sprouts of a 90cm (3ft) high oak can be immensely satisfying. Just as it is crazy to think of a child as an incomplete adult, so the young tree is every bit as much the real thing as the 30m (100ft) leviathan it will become.

TREES FOR SMALL GARDENS	
Upright (Fastigate)	
DECIDUOUS	EVERGREEN
Crab Apple *Malus baccata* 'Columnaris'	Atlantic Cedar *Cedrus atlantica* 'Fastigiata'
Dawyck Beech *Fagus sylvatica* 'Dawyck'	Irish Yew *Taxus baccata* 'Fastigiata'
Honey Locust *Gleditsia triacanthos* 'Columnaris'	Italian Cypress *Cupressus sempervirens*
Hornbeam *Carpinus betulus* 'Fastigiata'	Maidenhair Tree *Ginkgo biloba*
Lombardy Poplar *Populus nigra* 'Italica'	Scots Pine *Pinus sylvestris* 'Fastigiata')
Small-leafed Lime *Tilia cordata* 'Swedish Upright'	Western Red Cedar *Thuja plicata* 'Fastigiata'
Tulip Tree *Liriodendron tuluipifera* 'Fastigiatum'	Irish Juniper *Juniperus communis* 'Hibernica'

TREES FOR SMALL GARDENS

Good Autumn Colour

DECIDUOUS	EVERGREEN
Maples *Acer*	Dawn Redwood *Metasequoia glyptostroboides*
Birch *Betula*	Larch *Larix*
Beech *Fagus*	Maidenhair Tree *Ginkgo biloba*
English Elm *Ulmus procera*	Pond Cypress *Taxodium ascendens*
Mountain Ash *Sorbus*	Swamp Cypress *Taxodium distichum*
Oak *Quercus*	
Smoke Tree *Cotinus*	
Sweet Gum *Liquidambar*	

For Clay Soil

DECIDUOUS	EVERGREEN
Alder *Alnus*	Thuja
Ash *Fraxinus*	Fir *Abies*
Birch *Betula*	Larch *Larix*
Eucalypt *Eucalyptus*	Swamp Cypress *Taxodium distichum*
Hawthorn *Crataegus*	
Hazel *Corylus*	
Hornbeam *Carpinus*	
Lime *Tilia*	
Maple *Acer*	
Poplar *Populus*	
Willow *Salix*	

For Acid Soil

DECIDUOUS	EVERGREEN
Aspen *Populus tremula*	Juniper *Juniperus*
Birch *Betula*	Pine *Pinus*
Oak *Quercus robur*	Yew *Taxus*
Holly *Ilex*	

For Lime Soil

Deciduous	Evergreen
Ash *Fraxinus*	*Thuja occidentalis*
Beech *Fagus*	Austrian Pine *Pinus nigra*
Crab *Malus*	Yew *Taxus baccata*
Hawthorn *Crataegus*	Juniper
Field Maple	Western Red Cedar
Acer campestre	*Thuja plicata*
Horse Chestnut *Aesculus*	

Tolerant of Shade

DECIDUOUS	EVERGREEN
Beech	Coast Redwood *Sequoia sempirvirens*
Camellia *Camellia japonica*	Holly
Sycamore	Holm Oak
Acer pseudoplantanus	*Quercus ilex*
Elder *Sambucus nigra*	Portugese Laurel *Prunus lusitanica*
	Yew
	Juniper

PLANTING A TREE

Choose the site carefully. Think of the effect of the full-grown tree in terms of the total area it will cover – size, shade and the spread of its roots.

1. Dig a hole one spit deep of at least 60cm (2ft) radius, keeping the topsoil separate from subsoil.

2. Loosen a depth of a second spit thoroughly with a fork. Mix in garden compost or manure.

3. Hammer a short stake (90cm/3ft above ground) into the bottom of the hole on the windward side of the trunk.

4. Place the tree in the centre of the hole, carefully spreading its roots as widely as possible without damaging them. If necessary, train the roots on either side of the stake.

5. Holding the tree upright, backfill the hole with your topsoil. If your soil is very heavy, it is a good idea to mix this with 25% sharp sand or potting compost. Make sure that the soil is right round all the roots, leaving no air spaces. Firm it down well with your feet as you go so that the tree is really securely in the ground.

6. Scatter a couple of handfuls of bonemeal on to the surface and tie the stake to the trunk.

7. Water well (at least 9 litres/2 gallons) and mulch with a thick layer of organic material. In theory the mulch needs to be at least a metre (yard) across or the spread of the branches – whichever is the greater.

It is absolutely essential that you keep the area covered by mulch free of weeds, grass or any other plants. This will reduce the competition for water and nutrients and will make a radical difference to the speed at which the tree develops.

The weeping silver lime Tilia petiolaris *flourishes on clay soil.*

COMPANION PLANTING

There are plants which fare much better in the company of other specific plants, and plants which have great antipathy to each other. The clever gardener has to do a certain amount of matchmaking for health as well as for aesthetic pleasure. It can also save a great deal of work, because if your garden is healthy you can more or less leave the plants to get on with being themselves and simply enjoy their existence. This is a subtle approach and involves getting into the harmony of plants, but gardening has always had a suppressed hippy side to it.

SOME EXAMPLES OF GOOD COMPANIONS

The sort of combinations I am talking about are the planting of aromatic

Spinach likes the shade broad beans provide and discourages blackfly from attacking the beans.

plants in amongst vegetables to repel pests and the addition of flowers to the kitchen garden to attract predators that will eat the nasties that would otherwise eat the veg. The sort of things that smell sufficiently nauseating to a cabbage white butterfly to make it move elsewhere are basil, borage, hyssop, sage, rosemary or thyme. Any of the Allium family – garlic, chives, shallots, onions – will confuse the carrot fly and mask the smell of a carrot, which it finds irresistible. Nasturtiums, spearmint, stinging nettles and southernwood are all useful in the fight against aphids; nasturtiums also ward off whitefly. The poached egg plant (*Limnanthes douglasii*) may seem an unlikely partner to apple trees, but it attracts hoverflies, which feed on the poached egg plant's nectar and lay their eggs on the fruit trees. The hoverfly larvae then feed voraciously on any aphids which attack the apples. It is all a matter of harnessing nature to one's own ends.

Sometimes the relationship can be very basic indeed. For example, onions have a tendency to develop secondary growth after they have matured, which does not harm them but stops them keeping so well. To avoid this, keep them weeded as they mature and then let the weeds grow back so that the available nutrients and water for the onions are reduced by the demands of the weeds. This arrests growth and improves storage.

I suppose it is 'companion planting' for one plant to provide shade and protection from the wind for another. So you put a tough shrub upwind of a delicate flowering plant. A slightly

Asparagus is good for tomatoes, and lupins suppress weeds.

more sophisticated use of shelter is seen if you grow broad beans next to spinach: the beans provide shade for the spinach, slowing down its tendency to bolt when it gets dry, and in turn the spinach keeps the ground beneath the

GOOD COMPANIONS	BAD BEDFELLOWS
Asparagus and Tomatoes	Beans and Onions
Broad Beans and Brassicas	Runner Beans and Beetroot
Runner Beans and Sweetcorn	Marrows and Potatoes
Carrots and Onions	Peas and Onions
Chrysanthemums and Cabbages	Potatoes and Tomatoes
Fruit and Stinging Nettles	Capsicums and Brassicas
Radishes and Chervil	
Roses and Garlic	
Shrubs and Poached Egg Plant	
Turnips and Peas	

beans shaded and cool, which deters the blackfly that feed off the beans.

Sometimes the relationship is one of violent antipathy. Couchgrass – no more nor less than another plant after all – cannot live with turnips. So if you have a border infested with couch, you could try planting turnips thickly. The turnips will then be the weed that has to be eradicated, but they are a lot easier to deal with than couch.

Tomatoes are also said to be a good counter to couch, although I have not tried this myself. Asparagus is a good companion for tomatoes, as it gives off a gas that kills trichodorus, the tomato eelworm pest.

Lupins are known to suppress weeds generally and fat hen specifically. Beans do not associate well with onions, and tomatoes and potatoes should be kept well apart as they infect each other with disgusting diseases. Slightly more surprisingly, dandelions give off ethylene gas, which causes premature ripening of fruit and stunts other things.

You can use the ability of certain plants to work their roots deep into any ground to clear a pathway for other less robust rooters. So a green manure like annual rye grass or alfalfa has powerful, extensive roots which open out the soil as though it had been dug, ready for a subsequent crop.

Regular vegetable growers will know that they must rotate their crops to get maximum yields. The most obvious example of this is the ability of legumes (peas and beans) to fix nitrogen from the air into the ground via nodules on their roots. By planting a nitrogen-hungry crop such as the brassicas (cabbage, cauliflower, Brussels sprouts etc) after them, you use the full possibilities of interrelationships between quite different plants.

Marigolds planted among the onions attract pests that might otherwise eat your vegetables before you have a chance to pick them. The marigolds also make a cheerful display in their own right.

GREENHOUSE PLANTS

Even a tiny greenhouse can make an enormous difference to your garden. It can become the engine house of the whole operation, producing a stream of new plants all summer, extending the growing season in spring and autumn as well as being a specialist area of the garden in its own right. Rather than being just for the keen gardener, I would say that a greenhouse could be included in the smallest garden and for the most novice gardener.

SETTING UP YOUR GREENHOUSE

For the average gardener there are only two types of greenhouse to choose from – wooden or aluminium. In the end both do the same job. Most come as fearsomely complicated kits and the single most valuable piece of advice I have is to get the supplier to erect it for you. Whatever it costs is worth it.

There is no need to heat a greenhouse, though if you do it will hugely increase the range of things you can grow. Bubble plastic can do much to stop heat loss if taped to the framework, without diminishing the light level unacceptably.

Invest in thermostically controlled ventilation. This avoids the tyranny of having to open and close the greenhouse and keeps ventilation going. You can hardly have too much ventilation in a greenhouse as long as the temperature is right. Also beware overheating – the summer temperature can easily get very high.

After you have put a greenhouse up it is a good idea to dig out a trench 60cm (2ft) wide and two spits deep on either side of the central path. Put plenty of manure in this and backfill it so that you end up with two raised beds. This will radically improve the performance of plants like tomatoes, cucumbers and melons.

EARLY CROPS

There is always a period in May when the weather is good but no vegetable crops have matured. This gap can be filled by sowing lettuces and radishes directly in the ground or in gro-bags or pots in the greenhouse in late February/early March for early salad crops. Water them well and thin fairly ruthlessly to encourage strong individual growth. If sown directly into the ground they should be used up by the time the space is needed for later crops.

TOMATOES

I suspect that three-quarters of everything grown in greenhouses across the land are tomatoes. This makes sense, as supermarket tomatoes are red, round and utterly tasteless.

It is surprising how much can be packed into a small greenhouse.

Tomatoes are very easily grown from seed, sown in a seed tray in the greenhouse in April or May. Pot them on into individual pots as soon as they are large enough to handle. Don't be in a hurry to plant them out – wait until early June.

Plant the plants out 45cm (18in) apart with a 1.8m (6ft) cane for each one. The only real disadvantage of using gro-bags is that it is difficult to

Pinch out any growth in the angle between the stem and trusses.

secure the cane properly. Tie the tomatoes in every 15cm (6in) as they grow; otherwise the weight of the fruit is likely to break the branches. Tomatoes need a lot of water and a feed of liquid seaweed once a week. As the plant develops, pinch out the stems that appear in the crux between the stem and lateral branches as these do not bear fruit and take vigour from the developing fruits. As the fruit swells and ripens, pick off the side shoots that do not have fruiting trusses to allow air to circulate freely.

CUCUMBERS

Cucumbers need heat to develop, so must be planted out at about the same time as tomatoes. They do not germinate so easily, though. It is best to sow them in individual pots, making sure that they have as much light as possible and a minimum temperature of 21°C (70°). Cucumbers must have very good drainage but lots of water, so put extra sharp sand into the ground or container. Cucumbers put out tendrils that attach themselves to support and will climb as much as 3m (10ft) or more, so provide netting or strings for them to climb up. Pick the fruits before they get too big – they taste better small.

CAPSICUMS

The secret of growing sweet peppers is heat. In the hot summer of 1989 I grew them successfully outside, but as a rule they need a greenhouse to mature. Germinate seeds in single pots and plant out 45cm (18in) apart after ten weeks, when the plants are about 15cm (6in) tall. Stake each plant with a 1.5m (5ft) cane.

Capsicums are no trouble to grow and can to all intents and purposes be treated like tomatoes. They like a humid atmosphere, so spray the windows of the greenhouse in really hot weather to raise humidity. The greater the heat and humidity, the faster the peppers will ripen, progressing from green to red.

AUBERGINES

Aubergines are good grown along with peppers as they share the same requirements of high heat and humidity. They grow perfectly well in gro-bags, but are better in well-manured soil. Give them plenty of water and stake them, tying them in as they grow. Do not let the fruit stay on the plant too long in search of great size or you risk them turning bitter.

MELONS

Melons are similar to cucumbers in requirements, needing high heat, plenty of water to the roots, but not too much humidity. The flowers may have to be hand pollinated (some self-pollinating varieties are available), using a soft brush to spread the pollen from the male flowers to the female ones. Do this in bright sunshine to increase fertility. When the fruit start to develop they will need supporting individually with a stake or net. Gently press the tops of the melons to test when ripe, although sniffing cantaloupes is as good a test as any: they should smell attractively sweet.

After you have pulled the tomatoes, peppers, cucumbers, aubergines and melons, sow a couple of rows of over-wintering lettuce such as 'Valdor' on the site they occupied.

This picture was taken in October, with fruit still ripening in my greenhouse.

AUGUST

WEATHER REPORT: although the days are hotter than ever, the evenings are drawing in and getting noticeably cooler. This makes for heavy dewfall which is a valuable aid to watering, particularly for seed. It is the holiday season and the garden needs a rest — most gardens are looking distinctly tired by now. If it is dry the ground will be bone hard, yet the weeds continue to grow unabated. There are invariably thunderstorms to deal with and this means keeping a constant eye on plants that might need staking and tying in climbers to avoid storm damage.

A hot, wet August can encourage fungal infections and moulds and a hot, dry August a plague of wasps and other insects. (Wasps are bad for people but good for gardens as they eat more harmful insects.)

PLANTS IN THEIR PRIME

Bulbs: *Crocosmia*: gladioli; lilies.

Annuals/biennials: *Ageratum*; marigolds (*Calendula*); *Cosmos*; pinks (*Dianthus*); foxgloves (*Digitalis*); Californian poppy (*Eschscholzia*); sunflowers (*Helianthus*); *Helichrysum verbascum*; *Lavatera trimestris*; nasturtiums; tobacco plant (*Nicotiana*); pelargoniums; *Scabiosa atropurpurea*; *Tropaeolum*.

Perennials: *Acanthus*; hollyhocks (*Althaea*); asters; *Astilbe*; *Astrantia major*; chrysanthemums; dahlias; *Echinops*; *Eupatorium*; *Filipendula*; *Gypsophila paniculata*; daylilies (*Hemerocallis*); hostas; *Inula*; *Lavatera*; *Ligularia*; *Lychnis coronaria*; *Macleaya*; *Monarda*; evening primrose (*Oenothera*); *Phlox paniculata*; *Rudbeckia*; *Solidago*; verbascums.

Trees: rowan (*Sorbus aucuparia*).

Shrubs: *Buddleia*; deciduous *Ceanothus*; *Cistus*; *Clerodendron*; *Cotinus*; *Escallonia*; hebes; hydrangeas, especially *H. paniculata*; *Hypericum*; lavender; *Magnolia grandiflora*; *Potentilla fruticosa*; Bourbon and Hybrid Perpetual roses; vincas.

Climbers: *Clematis jackmanii* group; honeysuckle; *Hydrangea petiolaris*; climbing roses; *Solanum crispum*; *Tropaeolum speciosum*.

Vegetables: the vegetable garden is in its prime. If you have maintained successional sowings of lettuces, carrots and onions, almost all vegetables are available, particularly: artichokes; French and runner beans; sweet corn; courgettes; cucumbers; marrows; onions; potatoes; rocket; perpetual spinach; tomatoes.

Fruit: apples; figs; melons; pears; plums; raspberries.

Herbs: all herbs. Sow angelica.

Houseplants: pot bulbs for forcing for Christmas. At the end of the month start putting poinsettias into a dark place at six each evening.

WEED CONTROL

August is a month when weeds can get seriously out of hand whilst one is away on holiday. This can have long-term effects as the weeds will be spreading seed now. Have a blitz on weeds, hoeing, pulling and spraying with Glysophate.

LAWNS

The grass-cutting routine continues, as it will do for another month. New lawns can be made this month, as the dew will provide much of the moisture needed for germination, but be sure to assist this with plentiful watering.

Opposite: Spiky blue delphiniums and the unmistakable bold leaves of the hostas are the features of this lavish display. The yellow shrub rose is R. 'Graham Thomas'.

Below: The contrasting yellows of Ligularia (left) and Inula brighten this summer border.

JOBS:

Essential
- Clip hedges and topiary.
- Prune new wisteria growth back to 15cm (6in).
- Cut back flower stems (but not leaves) of delphiniums, poppies, lupins and other herbaceous plants that have finished flowering.
- Keep picking runner beans to encourage more growth.
- Keep greenhouse ventilation high, stripping off excess leaves as tomatoes ripen.

Desirable
- Start planting spring bulbs.
- Prune rambler roses after flowering.
- Plant winter-flowering pansies.
- Take cuttings from non-flowering shoots of shrubs and perennials.
- Harvest garlic and leave to dry.
- Bend over onion tops.
- Sow lettuce and parsley for autumn/over-wintering crops.

Optional
- Sow grass seed.
- Plant strawberries (not on a site where old strawberries have been).

PREPARING FOR HOLIDAY

One of the joys of getting away from the garden at this time of year is that when you get back it is inevitably a surprise how lush it is, how much it has all grown. One returns to the fray recharged and itching to become a weekday gardener as well as a weekender, an all-day-and-every-day gardener.

Before heading off for Club 18–30 with your factor 15, things, knotted handkerchief and caravan, four children and case of baked beans in tow, it is as well to prepare the garden for your absence because the only thing you can guarantee is that there will be a heatwave at home while you are away.

It makes sense to cut the grass just before leaving. But do not shave it too short, because if there is a heatwave with no rain, the grass will burn. Just give it a normal cut and accept that it will be longer than usual when you return. Incidentally, if it is exceptionally long when you get back, don't attempt to cut it down to the normal length in one go. Set the blades higher than usual and cut it once; then lower them and cut it again. This will make a much better job of it and be better for the grass.

The greatest potential danger is to **plants in containers**, especially hanging baskets. Without regular watering they can frizzle up in your fortnight away. The best ruse is to get a friend or neighbour in to water them for you. If this is not possible, an irrigation system on a computer-controlled timer attached to an outside tap should do the trick. These devices are fairly cheap and available in most garden centres. If neither option is feasible, collect all the pots and give them a really good soaking before you go. Gather them all together (which will reduce water loss) and move them into complete shade.

Houseplants are best placed on a capillary mat, which can also be bought from a garden centre. Place the mat in a half-filled sink with the other end over the draining board. Put plant pots on this end of the mat – the moisture travels up the mat, up the pot and (hopefully) up the roots of the plant.

Borders can be watered by a sprinkler attached to a computerised timing device on an outdoor tap, but failing that (and 'that' is unlikely to cover all the bits of the garden that need watering) the best bet is to make sure that the entire garden is thoroughly soaked before you go and then mulched. This should suffice for a fortnight.

August is a month when **fruit and veg** mature and vegetables in particular quickly run to seed in periods of hot dry weather. Get a friend or neighbour to pick what they can and keep what they want. You will lose less this way than if you let everything get overripe.

Make sure that **taller plants** such as delphiniums are properly staked. August is the month of thunderstorms, and a really heavy downpour with attendant wind can cause havoc to the heavy, lush growth of high summer. Twenty minutes spent staking things properly and tying in climbers will save a lot of trouble later.

It is not a bad idea to try and get some spraying of weeds done before you go away. This is purely for psychological reasons. When you come back the Glysophate will have begun to work and the leaves shrivelled up, making you feel that forces have been quietly at work on your side while you were away. Or something like that.

Finally, go round the garden the day before you are due to leave and **cut a huge bunch of flowers** of everything that is just coming out and will be finished by the time you get back. Take this to a mother, lover, friend, stranger on the street. The flowers will then be enjoyed by someone rather than blooming unobserved.

Keep pot plants watered while you are away by placing them on a capillary mat with one end in a sink full of water.

Not all gardens are past their best by the time holidays come around. Plenty here to pick and pass on to someone who'll appeciate them while you're away!

EXOTIC PLANTS

We have all been guilty of returning from holiday clutching a bottle of retsina that tasted *so* delicious in that little bar on the edge of the Adriatic, or the plum brandy that spiced the mid-morning coffee on the slopes, as well as gaily wearing the hat or caftan that was so practical out there. You get home and feel silly. The wine is too resinous and as for the clothes – well, you look daft.

I wonder if this is true of plants as well. Not many people come back clutching a bougainvillaea (although an elderly lady of my wife's acquaintance invariably collected seeds from her travels around the world and stitched them into the hem of the dress that she would wear through customs. I only visited her garden once, just outside Cambridge, and it did not seem to be particularly exotic.) Nevertheless it would be fun enough to propagate the seeds and grow them in a conservatory, if you had such a thing.

One of our biggest limitations in Britain is the sky. It is rarely blue enough for long enough to make sense of the uninhibited gaudiness of bougainvillaea or hibiscus. Our changing sky needs subtler effects.

However, if you have a garden that is reasonably well protected from frost, there are plants that could be usefully imported into the British range. The **honeybush** (*Melianthus major*) is often grown here in sheltered corners and **Acanthus** is a staple of all our gardens. **Phormiums** always strike me as aliens, with their sword-shaped leaves and violent spiky thrust, but you see them all over the place.

For all its exotic beauty, you will have problems bringing a banana plant home to grow in the garden.

There is no reason why you could not grow **bananas** if you live in the south-west, are prepared to water them copiously and protect them like an elderly invalid over the winter. *Musa basjoo* is moderately hardy, surviving a touch of frost, and *M. ensete* is more spectacular, with great floppy leaves, but it needs to be brought indoors in winter.

You could persuade *Hibiscus moscheutos* to grow on a south-facing wall, looking like a hollyhock on hallucinogenics, although it would curl up at the thought of a frost. The **cannas** are used by Parks Departments as bedding plants, where they look strident. As individual plants, left to produce their lush, banana-like foliage, they are, well, interesting. If you like that sort of thing. The **tree ferns** (*Dicksonia*) are great in the tropics and are seen surprisingly often in Cornwall and western Scotland in the shelter of the Gulf Stream, but look downright odd in suburban Britain.

HOW EXOTIC CAN YOU GET?

I think that this is where I begin to feel uncomfortable. Is anything justifiable in the garden just because it is exotic? Should one not choose and use plants that are exact within the terms of what one is trying to achieve? Not always. If that was the case the country would be awash with private gardening theme parks from white gardens to knot gardens. A bit of anarchy overspilling from the shackles of good taste never did a garden (or gardener) any harm. But a garden where the plants are arrayed like specimens will always leave me cold.

I do not know of a garden that includes only native species, but if it were to exist it would be a dull affair. Thousands of plants that we consider to be quintessential to the Englishness of our gardens are the result of people bringing home plants that were most definitely considered exotic on their introduction. Roses, camellias, chrysanthemums, pines, weigelas, anemones, rhododendrons, fuchsias, ceanothus — these and hundreds of other common or garden plants were once exotic introductions to be marvelled at.

So where do you draw the line? To my mind, **the only rule is that the plant must look at home**. This means that not only must it be able to perform within the climatic and horticultural conditions you put it in, it must also relate well to the light and general backdrop. Occasionally a plant carries this to extremes and makes itself too much

Japanese knotweed was introduced as an exotic border plant, but is now a major pest.

at home. The **Japanese knotweed** (*Polygonum cuspidatum*) was first brought to this country in 1825. As recently as 1879 the RHS's official organ, *The Garden,* described it as 'a plant of sterling merit, now becoming quite common. . .undoubtedly one of the finest herbaceous plants in cultivation.' In the 1990s it is illegal to propagate it or plant it in your garden, so invasive a weed has it become.

Every plant in every garden ought to work in its own right. It is not enough for a plant to be rare or difficult to grow or a new variety. Does it look good in that particular garden? That has to be the first and most important criterion. Otherwise it can be like the bottles and mementoes brought back from a trip abroad — fine in its time and place, but sitting uncomfortably out of context once you get back home.

*Cranesbill geraniums,
sweet Williams and
pinks in an abundant
summer garden. Bushy,
spreading plants like
this will help keep the
weeds under control
while you are away.*

DEEP PURPLE

There is a dip in the gardening performance somewhere between the middle of July and the middle of August, depending on the weather. The spark seems to go out of things and almost overnight full, voluptuous growth becomes leggy scruffiness. Lettuce are bolting like rabbits and the early beans have collapsed under the weight of their banana-like pods. The weeds seem to be the most vigorous things growing and there is a generally dissolute air about the place.

The best way to combat this is to go for depth and intensity rather than frothiness.

PURPLE FOLIAGE

The deep richness of the purple is exactly the foil needed at this time of year against the drab deadness of leaves and grass. I usually think that purple foliage standing on its own is visually uncomfortable, too much a specimen jarring with the surroundings. But as a backdrop, purple leaves add depth, particular to strong colours. If one thinks that purple is made up of red and blue, then it is easy to see how it seems to make reds seem redder. At this time of year

Planting red flowers amongst purple leaves will make them look even redder.

it is a good idea to have plants specifically to add fire to the belly of the garden, with flaming reds, yellows and orange flowers.

Purple beech makes a much better hedge than tree, for instance, if clipped tight and used as backdrop to reds, oranges and yellows. It is not a restful, easy colour like green, and tends to absorb light, so the colours against it must be strong enough to pull forward from it. With the 'hot' colours this adds subtlety and depth, where green merely provides contrast.

Berberis thunbergii 'Atropupurea' will do the same job as a low hedge and the dwarf form *B.t.* 'Atropurpurea Nana' as an edging plant. The reddish purple becomes increasingly intense as winter approaches and, if not clipped, will have brilliant red berries. Berberis is terribly easy to grow as long as it has reasonable drainage.

Rosa glauca's purple/grey leaves float like mauve smoke a metre (yard) above the ground. The more it is in the sun, the more purple will be the leaves.

The purple-leafed versions of the **smoke bush** (*Cotinus coggygria* 'Foliis Purpureis' and 'Royal Purple') are perhaps the most familiar of purple-leafed foils in a border, with the added bonus of pinkish-purple plumes in July. The leaves turn light red in autumn.

I am not that keen on **weigela**, especially when it is allowed to sprawl into a fair-sized shrub, although it can work well in a pot where it can be tucked out of sight once it has finished flowering. *Weigela florida* 'Foliis Purpureis' has bronze-purple leaves and is richer and more interesting than its green-leafed cousin.

I can only think of one climber with purple leaves (as opposed to plants that turn purple in autumn) and that is *Vitis vinifera purpurea*. This is the purple-

leafed version of the grape vine. The leaves start out wine red, becoming deep purple as summer progresses. It is an idea to grow this through the branches of a weeping pear or a willow, or if you have it against a wall try growing *Clematis orientalis* through it, using the heavy colour of the vine to intensify the lemon flowers of the clematis.

Purple-leafed sage (*Salvia officinalis* 'Purpurescens') is vital to modify the rather samey green of the herb garden, as is **purple basil** (*Ocimum basilicum*), which has the most intense purple leaves of any plant. It is not so good for cooking as green basil, but adds to a salad exactly the same depth and richness that it does to the herb garden. I recall reading that it made horrible pesto. **Bronze fennel** (*Foeniculum vulgare* 'Purpureum') tastes identical to green fennel as far as I know, but it is extremely good grown with the more crimson **shrub roses**, such as *R*. 'Cardinal Richelieu' or 'Nuits de Young', the feathery leaves and tall stalks providing exactly the right balanced contrast.

LATE PURPLE LEAVES

TREES

Purple Beech (*Fagus sylvatica* 'Riversii')
Maple (*Acer palmatum* 'Atropurpureum')
Pissard's Plum (*Prunus cerasifera* 'Pissardii')

SHRUBS

Berberis thunbergii 'Atropurpurea'
Smoke Bush (*Cotinus coggygria* 'Royal Purple')
Weigela florida 'Foliis Purpureis'
Purple Hazel (*Corylus maxima* 'Purpurea')
Purple Elder (*Sambucus nigra* 'Guincho Purple')

PERENNIALS

Sage (*Salvia involucrata* 'Bethellii')
Bugle (*Ajuga reptans*)
Bergenia (*Bergenia cordifolia* 'Purpurea')
Clematis recta 'Purpurea'
Dahlia 'Bishop of Llandaff'
Purple Fennel (*Foeniculum vulgare* 'Purpureum')
Rheum palmatum 'Atrosanguineum'
Tellima grandiflora 'Purpurea'

CLIMBERS

Vitis vinifera purpurea

A vegetable that is best grown in the flower garden is **Swiss chard**, which has green-leafed and purple-leafed forms and can be started off in containers and then planted out to fill gaps.

PURPLE FLOWERS

There are purple flowers, too, which add the right tone of intensity to your late summer garden. Hunt out purple varieties of familiar plants, like the **purple lupin** or **hollyhock**, *Clematis* x *jackmanii* and *C. viticella*. The fuchsia *F.* 'Mrs Popple' has purple petals and scarlet sepals. You can find **lavenders** which are much darker than the usual mauve. *Lavandula angustifolia* 'Twikel Purple' is particularly dark. I love the **purple mallow** (*Malva sylvestris* var. *mauritiana*), which will pop up all over the place if allowed to seed. It should be encouraged to do so.

Viola labradorica 'Purpurea' has dark purple leaves with violet-blue flowers in early summer. By the end of the summer the leaves will have turned dark green. It spreads easily and is very

The varying purples of lavender, purple sage and Polygonum bistorta add depth to the late summer garden.

shallow-rooted, so will grow in cracks and gravel, seeding itself freely along the edge of paths. It likes hot sun.

Buddleia 'Black Knight' is the purplest of the buddleias and looks good planted in a border. The **heliotropes** come into their own at this time of year, looking splendid with silvery leafed plants such as **artemisia**. **Purple loosestrife** (*Lythrum*) is one of the easiest of all plants to grow, in sun or shade.

I have already mentioned the various purple clematis, but **morning glory** (*Ipomoea purpurea*) starts out deep purple before fading to violet in the sunlight.

TOPIARY

Nothing else in the garden has the same balance between formality and wit as topiary. It adds structure and rhythm, especially in winter, and needs nothing more than a trim once or twice a year and an annual feed.

Topiary first came to this country in Renaissance times. Henry VIII ordered his gardeners to copy the Italian style and they began clipping trees and

Box keeps its shape well in small-scale topiary.

bushes into sculptural forms. By the middle of the seventeenth century it was all the rage and the influence of William III, who came to England from Holland in 1688, intensified the use of topiary in English gardens. But in the mid-eighteenth century Capability Brown swept most of the topiary gardens away and it was not until a hundred years later, in Victorian times, that topiary came back into style.

One of the most extraordinary topiary sites in the world is at Disneyworld in Florida. There they develop topiary Mickey Mouses, Donald Ducks and the whole bestiary of Disney animals in huge crates and shift them into position by crane fully finished. It is an incredible feat demanding an equal measure of horticultural skill and stunning bad taste. But topiary does not have to be figurative. It could be a ball, cone, spiral or pompom (a lollipop shape). It could be completely abstract, like the 'cloud' topiary that the Japanese are so fond of, clipping pines into rounded cloud shapes at the end of their branches. As long as the plant is being shaped and clipped by man rather than nature, it is topiary. So what is the difference between a hedge and topiary? Not much. In fact, when you have hedges like the staggering ones at Powis Castle, I would say none at all – both are works of art.

HOW TO DO IT

The secret of clipping is to use shears that are small enough for you to have complete control and to lever only one side, holding the other blade still. This gives you much more control than if you just snip away in the same way as you trim a hedge.

If you are training a bush into a shape, use lengths of bamboo tied with wire to create a two-dimensional outline which new growth will fill out into the third dimension. Remember that the leader that seems so wispy and tenuous now will become the strong branch defining the shape in a year or two – so do not snip it off by mistake!

TOPIARY IN CONTAINERS

Topiary is very effective in a pot, giving you the flexibility to move the pieces around, and to have focal points in places where a plant would be awkward to grow.

Box is exceptionally tough and can

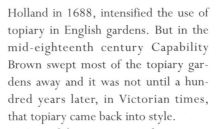

TOPIARY SHAPES

BALL

CONE

COLUMN

PEACOCK

PYRAMID

SPIRAL

'POODLE' (A BALL ON A STEM OR TRUNK)

'WEDDING CAKE'
(A SERIES OF FLAT LAYERS.)

grow very effectively in a container, whereas yew is not so happy to be transplanted and is in general a much bigger tree. (Incidentally, remember to use *Buxus sempervirens*, not *Buxus suffruticosa*. The latter is the dwarf box, is more expensive and is used for edging.)

Box is best propagated from cuttings taken in September. Dig a narrow trench in a sunny, sheltered spot and fill it back in with 50% sharp sand 50% soil. Take 10–15cm (4–6in) cuttings from this year's growth. Strip the bottom 7.5cm (3in) of leaves and stick them in the ground at 2.5cm (1in) intervals. By next spring they should have roots and be transferable to pots; you

PLANTS SUITABLE FOR TOPIARY (in order of suitability)	
Yew (*Taxus baccata*)	The best for medium or large topiary. Clip once a year in August.
Box (*Buxus sempervirens*)	Very tight. Excellent for small work. Clip once in June.
Holly (*Ilex aquifolium*)	Good for Poodles and Wedding Cakes. Clip once in August.
Lonicera nitida	Very fast growing; rather lax. Clip every eight weeks, April to October.
Portuguese Laurel (*Prunus lusitanica*)	Good for large work. Very hardy. Clip once in August.
Bay (*Laurus nobilis*)	Not hardy. Good for Poodles. Clip once in August.
Hawthorn (*Crataegus*)	Very tough. Good for Poodles. Clip twice, in May and September.
Privet	Fast growing. Lax. Clip every eight weeks.

can move them to their final site in a year's time. This is a good and cheap way of assembling enough plants for extensive box edging.

PLEACHING LIMES OR HORNBEAMS

Pleaching involves cajoling the plant to grow in a certain way more than restricting its growth by clipping. It is common to pleach lime or hornbeam to achieve a 'hedge on stilts' effect , or to make a living screen up to 4.5m (15ft) high. You do not need a large garden or a great avenue of trees to make this an extremely effective piece of garden design. A line of four trees on either side of a stretch of path perhaps 7.5m (25ft) long is a perfectly valid proposition.

It is easiest to start with standards (trees with 1.8m/6ft of clear trunk) but young trees can also be trained without too much trouble.

Lime (*Tilia*) is very good for pleaching because it is so easy to bend into shape and grows so fast from a bud. Use *Tilia platyphyllos* if possible, as it does not attract aphids and the resultant sticky goo to which other types of lime are prone. This is what you do:

1. Plant your trees 2 3m (6–10ft) apart.

2. Tie a cane between each tree at a height of 1.8m (6ft), using a measuring rod to make sure that each cane is set at the same height.

3. Tie any existing lateral growth to the cane, gently bending the branches down without breaking them. Do this over a period of years, as the branch grows in the direction you want.

4. Repeat the operation a couple more times, setting each layer about 45cm (18in) apart.

5. Prune any branches growing out to the front or back of the tree right back to the trunk.

6. If you want to create a hedge on stilts (better with hornbeam than lime), then you are merely encouraging the trees to grow together, so you can leave it at that, clipping the forward and rear branches every year but leaving the horizontal ones to form the hedge.

7. If you want an espaliered effect, with the individual branches clearly defined, prune any excess lateral branches so that you have rows that correspond to the canes.

Do not worry if you do not have a branch of any significance where the cane meets the trunk. A tiny shoot will become a branch very quickly.

Yew is the best choice for formal topiary on an imposing scale. This terrace is at Parnham House in Dorset.

PESTS AND DISEASES

It has always surprised me how obsessed many gardeners seem to be about anything that is sharing the garden with them. You cannot eliminate every creature that eats growing things, nor stop every kind of disease that plants are prone to. They happen. By far the best policy is to cool it and, with certain intelligent provisos, let the garden look after these things itself.

However, that presupposes two conditions:

1. **You look after your soil.**
2. **You refrain from using any chemical pesticides.**

The first means that each plant is getting the maximum nourishment from the soil and is therefore as healthy and strong as possible to resist any disease or insect that tries to attack it. I believe this to be the single most important factor for plant health.

The principle behind not using chemical pesticides is that by not blitz-

Gravel will deter the hungriest slug.

ing any one predator you are not upsetting the balance of the environment you are creating in your garden. This balance is a delicate affair. You have to remember that a garden is a strange and wholly artificial environment. We are cramming together plants from all over the world, from every different climate, and asking them to perform better than they ever do in the wild. In human terms, a garden is like a constant Olympic games.

If we inject a dose of powerful spray or unnatural chemicals into this strange, intense environment, we do not know how the ecosystem will respond. We can often see very specific effects initially, but the side effects and knock-on effects may take years to work through. The organic gardener opts for allowing the plants to establish their own balance and for humans to nurture them and look after them without imposing on them too much.

Chemical companies spends tens of millions of pounds each year looking for new chemicals that they can sell to

A twig of elder in each molehill is said to deter moles...

farmers to fight pests and diseases. A spin-off from this research is the garden chemical market. The companies make every effort to screen off any chemical that might possibly be harmful to anything other than the specific problem they are trying to solve. This specificity is a new trend – blanket insecticides and weed-killers are a thing of the past.

Chemical companies also spend a great deal of money researching into predator controls. This means ascertaining which insects and animals feed off particular pests and then working out a system whereby the predators can

PESTS

PEST	DAMAGE	ACTION
Ants	Protects aphids from lacewing and ladybirds.	Pour solution of pyrethrum and derris mixture into nests.
Aphids	Feed on plant sap. Encourage ladybirds and hoverflies.	Spray with soft soap, derris or or pyrethrum.
Blackfly	Particularly bad on broad beans, dahlias, nasturtiums and poppies.	As with aphids.
Carrot Fly	Larvae eat carrots, parsnips and celery.	Sow thinly, erect low screen around carrots. Avoid thinning during the day.
Earwigs	Eats dahlias and chrysanthemums	(See pages 138–139).
Greenfly	Spoils roses	Plant garlic around rose. Spray with soft soap, derris or pyrethrum. Wash with clear water soon after.
Millipedes	Eat bulbs and many plant roots.	Dig thoroughly, improve drainage.
Moles	Make hills.	Put a twig of elder in each molehill.
Scale insects	Live on fruit trees and bushes.	Paint with white spirit.
Slugs	Eat all soft and decaying leaves.	Use sharp mulches such as grit or ashes, Spray with Fertosan slug-killer.
Thrips (thunderflies)	Live on sap.	Spray with pyrethrum or derris.

easily be introduced to maintain the balance of pests. This, of course, is precisely the line of the organic gardener, so the two camps, once so hostile to each other, are meeting in the middle.

ORGANIC MEANS OF PEST CONTROL

Pyrethrum: a chemical preparation made from the ground daisy-like flower heads of the pyrethrum plant, a relative of the chrysanthemum family. It is an effective insecticide not harmful to other animals.

Derris: a plant-derived insecticide, safe for humans, birds and rodents, but lethal for fish and tortoises, so must be used with care. It is especially effective against aphids and red spider mite.

Fertosan: a mixture of aluminium sulphate and herbs, this poisons slugs but does not harm anything else. Bigger slugs will just feel a bit dodgy, but smaller ones die. Water it on to the soil, avoiding any delicate leaves.

Soft soap: this is available from a chemist and has a semi-liquid consistency. Mix 30g (1oz) of soft soap with 3.5 litres (6pt) of rainwater (or very soft tap water so that the soap dissolves properly) and spray on to aphids. It destroys the protective wax coating on their bodies, but does no harm to ladybirds or hoverflies.

Seaweed solution: the single most valuable 'chemical' aid the gardener has, and the only one I use at all. Use it as a weak spray to promote strong, healthy plants and to help against aphids, brown rot in fruit, damping off in seedlings and tomatoes, and leaf-curl virus. Magic stuff. It is better to use a weak solution every week or so than to go for a big hit every couple of months.

Biological controls: these are becoming increasingly important in the control of commercial crops and as a result are more and more available to the gardener. The principle is simply that you introduce a predator to attack the insect that is preying on your plants. This is a self-regulating system, because when all the aphids or whatever are eaten, the predator must move away or starve. In day-to-day terms the best form of biological control is to encourage ladybirds and hoverflies into the garden, as well as hedgehogs and insect-eating birds, all of which are your best allies against aphids, caterpillars, slugs, millipedes and earwigs.

DISEASES

DISEASE	EFFECT	ACTION
Botrytis	A grey mould fungus	Increase airflow and reduce moisture.
Canker	A diseased area on bark of tree.	Prune carefully, especially removing diseased branches, but don't worry too much about it.
Coral Spot	An orange or pink fungus that grows on wood of trees and shrubs.	Prune back to healthy wood.
Damping Off	A fungus that attacks seedlings, causing them to collapse. The marrow family is particularly prone to it.	Sow thinly, do not over-water and provide plenty of ventilation.
Powdery mildew	Makes white or yellow powder	Caused by dry roots. Water well and mulch to retain moisture.
Rust	Orange patches on rose leaves	Spray with seaweed solution on leaves and stem, and mulch with compost or manure.
Scab	Fungus that thrives in damp conditions and affects the surface of fruit and fruit-tree leaves – these crack, develop a brown, leathery stain, and shrivel.	Prune for good ventilation; collect all infected leaves and burn them.

WEATHER REPORT: *September is often one of the loveliest months of the year. Never unpleasantly hot, the days can become delightfully warm although the nights are rapidly cooling down. It is a bridging month, neither summer nor autumn, and carries the gardener through from one season to the other. You have to expect frost by the end of the month, although it often does not appear until well into October in the south.*

All top fruit is ripening and fine weather guarantees a successful harvest. Berries are forming on flowering shrubs, adding a new range of colour to the garden. This is all tinged with the melancholy of autumn and the knowledge that summer is slipping away. The long evenings in the garden are a thing of the past and by the end of the month it is dark by seven o'clock.

The trees still have their leaves, although they are beginning to change colour and this means that strong winds can do serious damage. However, a southerly wind on 21 September usually guarantees a fine autumn or 'Indian summer'.

PLANTS IN THEIR PRIME

Bulbs: colchicums; *Crinum* x *powellii*; *Cyclamen europaeum*, *C. neapolitanum*; *Crocosmia*; autumn-flowering crocus; gladioli; autumn snowflake (*Leucojum autumnale*); nerines; *Schizostylis coccinea*; *Sternbergia lutea*.

Annuals/biennials: whilst plenty of annuals and biennials will still be flowering, none are in their prime and all are dependent upon the vagaries of the weather as to how long they will last into autumn.

Perennials: hollyhocks (*Althaea*); Japanese anemones; Michaelmas daisies (*Aster*); chrysanthemums; dahlias; *Geum*; *Heuchera*; hostas; *Inula*; *Kniphofia*; *Lavatera*; *Ligularia*, *Macleaya*; *Penstemon*; salvias; *Sedum*; tree poppies; verbascums.

Trees: rowan (*Sorbus aucuparia*). Maples (*Acer*) are starting to turn colour.

Shrubs: *Caryopteris*; *Clerodendron*; heather (*Erica*); fuchsias; hebes; hydrangeas; *Hypericum calycinum*; tamarisk.

Climbers: *Clematis jackmanii* group, *C. viticella*, *C. florida*; honeysuckle 'Late Dutch' (*Lonicera periclymenum* 'Serotina'); *Solanum crispum*; *Tropaeolum speciosum*.

Vegetables: French and runner beans; broccoli; cabbage; carrots; cauliflower; celeriac; celery; leeks; lettuce; marrows; parsnips; potatoes; rocket; tomatoes; turnips.

Fruit: apples; apricots; blackberries; morello cherries; nectarines; peaches; pears; plums; raspberries.

Herbs: pick leaves for freezing. Collect seeds from seed heads of dill and fennel for next year's plants.

Houseplants: any houseplants put out of doors for the summer must be brought in now. Check that you are not bringing any insects or pests in with them. Reduce watering and feeding, especially for cacti.

WEED CONTROL

Weeds will be growing at a slower rate now, so it is possible to control them rather than have them run your life, as they can tend to do in the summer months. Annual weeds cleared up now are unlikely to return before next spring. Take the opportunity to start tidying the ground before winter makes conditions difficult.

LAWNS

September is the best time of the year to make new lawns and repair old ones, as the ground is still warm but the dew gives precious moisture. But water if the weather is dry. It is better to water new lawns lightly and often than to soak them. Existing grass still needs mowing, although less often and with the blades raised. Do not go into autumn with the lawn shaved short.

Long grass can have a cut now, raking up all the grass for compost. This means that any wild flowers will grow clear of the grass in early spring.

Opposite: A cluster of autumn containers — Dendranthemum 'Esther' (with the spiky-petalled orange flowers) in the centre; Spiraea 'Golden Princess', Gaultheria procumbens and Erica gracilis in the foreground.

Below: The late-flowering clematis come into their own in September. This is C. viticella 'Abundance'.

Essential
- Plant bulbs for spring.
- Clear summer bedding plants.
- Clip hedges and topiary.
- Take box cuttings.
- Clear tomatoes and other fruiting plants from greenhouses and clean soil.

Desirable
- Plant evergreens of all kinds this month.
- Keep dead-heading roses to extend the flowering season as long as possible.
- Take cuttings from geraniums and fuchsias.
- Plant biennials in their spring flowering positions.
- Plant strawberries.

Optional
- Sow grass seed.
- Plant strawberries (not on a site where old strawberries have been).
- Prune climbing roses at the end of the month.

BULBS

In order to have bulbs growing next spring, the time to put them in the ground is *now*. As ever, the secret of good gardening is to be thinking six months ahead.

Bulb-planting requires absolutely no skill and hardly any knowledge. The rule of thumb is to allow twice their own depth of soil above them and to put them pointy-end up. That's it. Everything else is fine tuning.

WHAT IS A BULB?

What differentiates a bulb from a perennial plant is that the nourishment for the flower is stored within the bulb itself. This is why a bulb will begin to shoot while still unplanted, abandoned in the corner of a shed. Not only the nourishment but all the memory needed to tell the shoot how big to grow and when to flower is stored within that little dry root.

When the flower has finished, the leaves are greedily converting sunlight and water into the nourishment for next year's flower and they – the leaves – feed from the bulb's roots. That is why you must *never* cut off the leaves from a bulb after it has flowered. Leave them until they die back of their own accord before tidying them up or else you may find that there will not be enough food stored and the plant will be 'blind' in a year's time.

We tend to call anything that is bulbous a 'bulb', but in fact there are a number of bulbous roots that have different characteristics.

Bulbs proper are made from concentric layers of fleshy leaves with a protective dry outer layer. Daffodils or tulips are typical of this. However, some lilies and fritillaries have no protective skin and the scales are separate.

Corms are replaced by new corms every year and are made from the swollen base of the stem. Crocuses, gladioli and colchicums are all corms.

Tubers are the swollen roots that are used for food storage – unlike most roots, which are solely a medium for conveying food to the plant. Tubers are found in some orchids, in *Corydalis* and in cyclamen species.

Rhizomes are swollen underground stems, usually growing horizontally. The best known examples are irises and lilies.

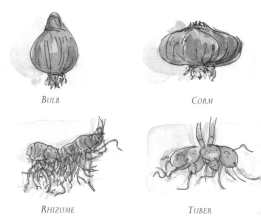

BULB   CORM

RHIZOME   TUBER

GROWING BULBS

You can force bulbs to flower earlier than usual by putting them in soil, then placing the pot in the fridge or any cool, dark place. Leave it there for a few months and the bulbs will think that it is winter. When you take them out into the light and warmth they will behave as though they have come out of a particularly hard winter and start to grow with a vengeance to make up for what they perceive to be lost time. The Dutch use this technique all the time and can predict when a bulb will flower to the nearest half a day!

If you want to create a natural effect of bulbs growing in 'drifts' in grass, the best way is to take a handful of bulbs and throw them underarm on to the ground, planting them meticulously where they land. Otherwise you are forever standing back and imagining what the grown flowers will look like and as it is striving after such artlessness is hard work enough.

Not all bulbs are pretty spring flowers. These lilies (Lilium 'Shuksan') are big and brassy.

PLANTING TULIPS

TULIPS ARE BETTER LEFT TILL NOVEMBER IN ORDER TO AVOID TULIP FIRE DISEASE, WHICH IS A TYPE OF BOTRYTIS THAT PERSISTS IN THE SOIL. BY PLANTING IN WINTER YOU REDUCE THE CHANCES OF THE FUNGUS GERMINATING. BUT DON'T PUT OFF DOING IT UNTIL THEN UNLESS YOU ARE VERY ORGANISED. THE BEST TIME TO DO ANYTHING IN THE GARDEN IS WHEN YOU ARE GEARED UP TO DO IT AND THE WEATHER AND CONDITIONS ARE SUITABLE. DOING THINGS NOW – WHENEVER THAT MIGHT BE – IS RARELY A BAD THING.

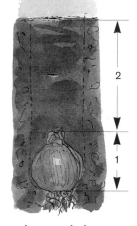

Plant bulbs so that the depth of soil above them is twice the depth of the bulb itself.

If that sounds easy, then the truth is that the ground is often like rock in early September and the dibber won't dib a proper hole. If you have a bulb planter (a contraption rather like an overgrown pastry cutter), life is made easier, but however you do it, to get the best from your bulbs you need to make your hole twice as deep as you want the bulb, put in some grit or sharp sand, followed by some compost (with bonemeal mixed up in it, three or four good fistfuls per bucket), then the bulb, then more grit, then the soil. By now the plug that you took out will be too big, so you have to break some of it off and do something else with the rest. If you have dibbed you must fill in over the bulb with compost. Multiply

that process by enough times to achieve a 'natural drift' and you have a palaver, crawling or hopping around with a bucket of compost and a bucket of grit, a bucket of bulbs, a dibber or bulb planter, a mug of tea and the radio. A couple of hours of this is quite enough for sanity. *But...* it is really worth devoting that two hours every year, gradually building up the garden's stock of bulbs.

The grit in the hole beneath each bulb is to ensure good drainage, which matters, as few spring-flowering bulbs react well to sitting in the wet. Most

Anemone nemorosa *(white flowers) and* Scilla bithynica – *plant them both now for this sort of display in spring.*

are geared up to a covering of snow in winter – which is dry until it melts, by which time they are ready for a watering as the bulbs are putting on rapid growth. If you have very light, well-drained soil, you can omit the grit.

Bonemeal is an ideal feed, because it is released slowly and therefore lasts longer, and because it provides the potash and phosphate bulbs need but not too much nitrogen. Nitrogen stimulates lush greenery, which looks encouraging, but has no influence on the flowers; in fact it is a bad thing, as lush growth is generally soft and sappy, which makes ideal conditions for botrytis.

PLANT	TYPE	SOIL PREFERENCE	PLANTING TIME	FLOWERING
Aconite (*Eranthis*)	Tuber	Rich, shaded	In flower	Late winter
Allium	Bulb	Well-drained, full sun	Autumn	Summer
Alstroemeria	Tuber	Well-drained	Spring	Summer
Amaryllis	Bulb	Well-drained	Spring	Autumn
Anemone blanda	Tuber	Well-drained	Autumn	Spring
Anemone nemorosa	Rhizome	Well-drained, part shade	Autumn	Spring
Arum	Tuber	Moist, well-drained	Autumn	Spring
Colchicum	Corm	Well-drained	Spring	Autumn
Crocosmia	Corm	Sunny, well-drained	Spring	Summer
Crocus	Corm	Well-drained	Autumn	Spring
Cyclamen	Tuber	Well-drained	Spring	Autumn
Daffodil	Bulb	Well-drained	Autumn	Spring
Dahlia	Tuber	Well-drained	Spring	Late summer
Erythronium	Tuber	Cool, well-drained	Autumn	Spring
Freesia	Corm	Well-drained	Autumn	Early spring
Fritillaria meleagris	Bulb	Damp	Autumn	Spring
Gladiolus	Corm	Well-drained	Spring	Summer
Hyacinth	Bulb	Well-drained	Autumn	Spring
Iris	Rhizome	Varied	Spring	Spring–winter
Lily	Bulb	Well-drained	Autumn	Summer
Muscari	Bulb	Well-drained	Autumn	Spring
Nerine	Bulb	Sandy soil	Autumn	Spring
Scilla	Bulb	Well-drained	Autumn	Spring
Snowdrop	Bulb	Moist	After flowering	Winter
Sternbergia	Bulb	Hot, well-drained	Spring	Autumn
Tulip	Bulb	Well-drained	November	Late spring

EVERGREENS

September is the best time to plant evergreens of all kinds. There is still a chance for the roots to become established before the really cold weather comes and the shortening days and cooler temperatures mean that there are less demands being made on them. If you cannot plant evergreens by the end of this month, it is probably best to wait until the middle of April.

An evergreen is a plant that retains its leaves for more than one growing season. Or, to put it more crudely, it looks much the same whatever the time of year. This does not mean that the plants keep the same leaves all the time – many evergreens shed old leaves as new ones grow through, but they never have a dormant period like deciduous plants. By keeping their leaves, evergreens can grow at any time of year, as long as the conditions are suitable. Deciduous trees developed the habit of shedding their leaves to protect them from cold winters. Evergreens are therefore – surprisingly – more tender than deciduous plants ,despite appear-

ing more robust in winter. Their leaves transpire constantly and are prone to damage by frost. The Ice Age killed off most North European evergreens apart from holly, ivy, yew and juniper.

It is not just cold that threatens evergreens. Too much sun and wind can be just as harmful. By planting in the shade, protected from the cold winds (invariably from either north or east), you can dramatically increase the tolerance of certain evergreens to bad weather.

THE GLORY OF GREEN

Because all evergreens retain a degree of constancy across the seasons, their primary function in a garden is to provide a structure and link, regardless of what may be going on around them. A garden without this framework would be a ghost of its summer self for half the year. Yet green is not considered a positive colour in gardening terms. It is lost in a predominance of green foliage.

Green creates an essential balance and tonal space between colours.

Even within the confines of greenery, the range of colour is huge and subtle, as anyone who has visited a pinetum will testify. In my opinion it seldom works to try and capture this range within a garden. You need a large scale with mature trees or just the arbitrary and careless profusion of green that comes naturally from any planting. The only way to tackle it in the average garden is with dwarf conifers and of these there is nothing good to say.

FLOWERING EVERGREENS

Evergreens that flower carry double value. **Camellias** would head many people's list of these (although, I admit, not mine). These evergreen shrubs carry peony-like flowers from December through to May and have the

---

NOT ALL EVERGREENS ARE GREEN

VARIEGATED PLANTS MAY BE TRULY EVERGREEN BUT ONLY HINT AT VERDANCY. THE VARIEGATED HOLLIES, 'GOLDEN KING' AND 'SILVER MILKMAID', ARE MORE YELLOW THAN GREEN. THE GOLDEN PRIVET IS JUST THAT – GOLDEN. *EUONYMUS FORTUNEI RADICANS* IS NOT ONLY NOT REALLY GREEN – MORE BUTTERY YELLOW – BUT BECOMES TINGED WITH PINK IN COLD WEATHER. AND THE MOST UNGREEN OF ALL EVERGREENS IS *PIERIS,* WITH ITS BRIGHT RED NEW SHOOTS IN SPRING.

---

virtue of performing well in shade. They need a lime-free soil, and protection from freezing winds and – even more importantly – early morning sun, which will scorch ice-covered flowers, so they are unsuitable for an east wall. **Rhododendrons** and **azaleas** are mostly evergreen and are also raised for their flowering display in spring, although as bushes they can dominate a garden. Less dominant and often more beautiful are the evergreen forms of **ceanothus**, whose blue flowers should be part of every garden's spring. Blue is a rare and precious colour in the garden and no garden can afford to be without a ceanothus. They are not hardy, and quite large specimens can succumb to a particularly cold snap, but are worth trying if you have a sunny site for one.

Melianthus major is perhaps the most exotic evergreen to grow in British gardens, although it must have a sheltered, sunny (and probably south-

Yellow 'evergreens' Euonymus fortunei *and* Hedera colchica.

ern) site. It has chalky, glaucous green leaves with serrated fingers, growing on stems to 1.8m (6ft).

Two far less exotic but very good evergreen shrubs are **Mexican orange blossom** (*Choisya ternata*) and *Osmanthus delavayi*. The choisya can flower from January onwards with powerfully sweet-smelling white blooms, and the osmanthus, whose flowers are also white and highly scented, from April. Both are as tough as old boots.

Talking tough, none come tougher than **berberis,** and the evergreen species, such as *B. calliantha*, *B.candidula*, *B.coxii* and *B. sargentii* are terribly easy to grow, flower, fruit and prickle in about equal measure.

EVERGREEN CLIMBERS

These are vital in the winter garden. **Ivy** (*Hedera*) is the easiest to grow, thriving in shade and drought — although keep it well watered until it is visibly growing strongly. The evergreen **Clematis armandii** has beautifully fresh white flowers in April, and its large, leathery leaves shine throughout the winter. It is vigorous and will cover an unsightly corner, but prefers sun.

Garrya elliptica has long silken tassels that can look wonderful in sunlight but positively dreary in the shade.

The **Japanese honeysuckle** (*Lonicera japonica* 'Halliana') is evergreen, although it might shed some leaves if feeling the cold too acutely.

EVERGREEN TREES

There are plenty to choose from, depending on the effect you want to achieve.

Conifers: cedars, cypresses, firs, junipers, pines, spruces, thujas.

Exotics: acacia, arbutus, eucalyptus, palms.

Exotic evergreens Melianthus major *(in the background) and* Phormium *'Sunrise'.*

Hedging: box, holly, holm oak, laurel, privet, Portuguese laurel, yew.

My three favourites are **holly** (*Ilex aquifolium*), **yew** (*Taxus baccata*) and **box** (*Buxus sempervirens*). They are all native plants, all easy to grow, all beautiful, all make wonderful hedges, trees, shrubs, all are easy to increase through cuttings — I have not got a bad word to say of them. **Irish yew** (*Taxus baccata* 'Fastigiata') makes a superb single specimen or a flanking pair, growing with a fastigiate or upright habit. We in Britain cannot grow the **Mediterranean cypress** (*Cupressus sempervirens*) with its marvellous slim columnar shape, and unless global warming really gets going, we never shall, but Irish yews do the same job — more clumpily,

perhaps, but with great style.

CARING FOR EVERGREENS

Whatever your choice of evergreen, remember that they go on breathing through their leaves throughout the year, and therefore need water year round. This is usually not a problem in our wet climate, but can be dangerous when it is very cold and windy. So try to protect them from freezing winds and if necessary be prepared to wrap individual evergreens in sacking or any protective material.

DID YOU KNOW?

GREENHOUSES ORIGINATED AS PLACES TO STORE EVER-'GREENS' IN WINTER.

MAKING A LAWN

We tend to take grass for granted. It is just there. But grass is a plant like any other and has many variations. So if you are going to include grass in your garden – and most of us do – it makes sense to choose the right type of grass for your own requirements.

Do you have children that need somewhere to play? Do you want a weed-free, immaculate turf? Do you enjoy cutting the grass or is it one of life's terrible chores?

Whatever your needs, the chances are that one of three types of grass will suit you.

Rye grass mix is coarse, very tough, spreads fast and grows relatively slowly. It is the grass of football pitches.

Fescues mix. Fescues are less coarse but still pretty tough and are the ideal grasses for the average lawn.

Fescue and bent mix. Bents are very refined and almost delicate. They actually like being shaved short, so are ideal for golf greens or bowling greens.

A mix of perhaps 40% dwarf rye, 30% creeping fescue and 30% red fescue is ideal for most ordinary lawns.

You don't have to go and buy the different types of seed separately and then carefully concoct the mixture. Grass comes in packets for shade, fine lawns, tough grass etc. But at least if you have an idea of what you are looking for, *you* will be making the decision and not putting yourself in the hands of a sales campaign.

When you have decided on the type of grass there is then the decision of whether to use seed or turf. Before you rush out to get turf, consider the pros and cons.

If you need to make an instant impression or you only have a very small area to grass, use turf. Otherwise go for seed every time.

GROWING FROM SEED

Either way, you must prepare the ground properly.

1. Dig the site over thoroughly. Remove all stones and weeds, and dig in plenty of manure or compost. If it is to look good a lawn must grow on rich, fertile soil.

2. Test the drainage of your soil. Dig a hole 60cm (2ft) deep and pour a bucket of water into it. Come back an hour later. If the water has all gone then your drainage is fine. Think no more about it. However, if there is still any water in the hole, then you have poor drainage and it would pay to add sand to the soil to improve it. If none of the water seems to have drained away at all then you have very poor drainage and should seriously consider laying drainage pipes.

Sharp sand is best added to the surface in a layer and either rotivated or raked into the topsoil. I have successfully sown grass straight into sand, and this is a good idea if you have very heavy soil. The roots go through the sand into the topsoil and water does not sit on the surface.

Laying drainage pipes is not a major disaster, but it is the sort of job that a professional does quicker and better than you.

3. Weeds and small stones. When you have dug and drained to your satisfaction, give the site a rough rake to take off as many small stones as you can and then leave it for a month.

The purpose of this is to let the weed seeds – which will inevitably be in the ground – germinate and come up. You can then pull them up or spray them with a Glysophate weed-killer

Seed	
PROS	CONS
Cheap.	Looks like nothing for a month.
Easy to sow.	Cannot walk on it for six weeks.
You can choose exactly the type of grass that is best for you.	Needs protecting from birds.

Turf	
PROS	CONS
Instant effect.	Expensive.
	It takes as long as seed to establish, and needs more watering to stop the edges curling up like a stale sandwich. Unless you use a reputable supplier or are an expert, it is hard to tell what sort of grass you are laying.
	Difficult to store without spoiling.
	Has to be laid correctly.
	Bulky.
	Very likely to introduce weeds.

such as Roundup or Tumbleweed, which will kill all green, non-woody plants without poisoning the soil.

You want a weed-free piece of ground so that the growing grass will not be competing for water and nutrients. All this applies to turf just as much as seed.

4. Treading. This is a good bit. When you have removed all weeds, rake the ground as smooth as you can. Then tread over the whole area, keeping your heels together, so that you are waddling rather than walking. All members of the household should be encouraged to join in.

Only waddle when the ground is dry, otherwise you will compact the soil rather than level it.

The point is to expose any dips or

The classic striped lawn – elegant, but a bit characterless for my taste.

hollows before sowing. If you omit this part of the preparation the ground will settle unevenly over the months, making cutting the grass awkward.

After you have trodden over all of it, rake it carefully again, evening the ground out.

5. Fertilising. A few days before sowing, sprinkle a granular fertiliser over the ground. This should have a balance of nitrogen (N), phosphorus (P) and potassium (K).

6. Sowing. Choose a windless, dry day.

Put the seed in an open container like a dish or bucket, and walk steadily up and down in lines about a metre (yard) apart, casting a handful in the same direction with each step. Repeat the process going across the site, at right angles to the original direction. You are after an even covering.

When you have finished, rake the ground carefully in both directions. This will cover most of the seed and ensure it is spread evenly.

If it does not rain within twelve hours, water the seed gently. It is best to water it for a longer period with a finer spray than to soak it. Keep the ground watered but not waterlogged.

7. Protection against birds and cats. Birds will eat the seeds and cats will regard the sown lawn as a huge wonderful new expanse of cat litter. Both can be deterred by pushing canes into the ground every few metres (yards) and twisting black cotton between them.

8. Mowing. The grass will initially grow in wispy clumps rather than a smooth sward. Do not be alarmed. As the roots develop, the grass will thicken out and spread evenly. If the autumn is very mild, give the grass a light trim, leaving 5cm (2in) of grass. This is much longer than its eventual length, but this will protect the new grass from frost.

By the following spring the grass will be established and can be mown normally.

LAYING TURF

Prepare the ground exactly the same as for sowing, following steps 1–4 above. Then:

1. Start at the bottom left-hand corner of the area and work across the

longest section in a straight line. Use a plank as a straight-edge and to stand on. Work back along the next line, making sure that the joins between pieces of turf are stepped, like a course of bricks. Keep long pieces at the edges, filling in small gaps nearer the middle as necessary.

2. Work up the lawn, paying great attention to getting each piece of turf tight up against its neighbour and properly tamped down. The last row may have to be trimmed to fit. This is best done with a bread knife. Fill any gaps with cut pieces.

3. Put the sprinkler on and water the turf thoroughly. Repeat this with a fine spray every day that it does not rain. It will need more water than seed as the moisture has to soak through the turf to the roots

4. Do not walk on the turf for four weeks. As with sown grass, allow it to grow rather longer than normal for its first winter. Keep an eye on the edges of the pieces of turf. If they start to curl up it means that they are too dry.

A decent mower makes the lawn less of a chore.

DAHLIAS

When dahlias were introduced to Europe from Mexico in 1789 they were regarded only as a vegetable, grown for their fleshy tuber, as one might grow a swede or potato. The flowers were a by-product. But in the early nineteenth century dahlias were brought to England as a garden flower and by the middle of the century the Victorians were growing them with fervour. They suited the 'bedding out' mentality that raised plants to put on a brief but brilliant display for a few months, regardless of the cost, skill or labour needed to produce that effect.

In the light of this, it might seem odd that I should be promoting dahlias in a book chiefly about minimising garden labour and expertise. But dahlias are a superb plant for the gardener short of time because they give such a powerful display at a time of year when the garden can look very insipid.

Dahlias do come in pretty nasty lipstick colours – fizzy oranges and pinks – but they are also available in deep reds, purples, golds and magentas, with foliage ranging from insipid green to bronze. The choice is there to be made. There are nine recognised types of dahlia, illustrated in the table opposite.

The myth that dahlias are tricky to grow is just that – a myth. They were

The neat, compact flowers of a 'pompon' dahlia.

taken up as a plant for showing, which meant that breeds with huge flowers were developed and these demanded careful and complicated maintenance, as well as being delicate out of doors. But dahlias with smaller flowers – although masses of them – are perfectly tough and easy in the garden.

You can buy either the whole plant, or tubers in spring. If the latter, ensure that you get fresh tubers from a specialist grower – these will produce far better results from exactly the same work as a shrivelled-up job from the local garden centre.

The tubers should be planted out in April at a depth of about 10cm (4in). Plants should not be exposed to any frost, so are best planted after the end of May. Dahlias need sun, so position them in a south- or west-facing spot. They will grow in almost any soil, as long as it is well drained. The more manure or compost you can dig into the soil, the better they will grow.

Stake each tuber when you plant it (so that when the stake is needed you will not damage the roots putting it in) and tie it in as it grows. It is received wisdom to disbud side buds, but take

Dahlia *'Shirley Alliance'* – one of the 'cactus' type with quill-like petals.

no notice of that nonsense. All that will do is make fewer, bigger flowers, which is fine if size is your yardstick, but hopeless if you are after a mass of slightly smaller, but just as beautiful, flowers.

The big enemies of dahlias are earwigs, which eat the flowers overnight. You may not have seen an earwig for ten years, but plant a dahlia and you will draw them from miles about.

There are a number of ways of preventing your flowers being gobbled up, including putting a few drops of paraffin inside each cane supporting the stem (the earwig hides in there during the day) or smearing vaseline on a short stretch of stem beneath the flower. Earwigs hate light, so a half-closed empty matchbox on the flower's supporting cane will provide a good hiding place for them after a hard night's dahlia chomping. You simply go out in the morning, collect the matchboxes and destroy the earwig occupants.

Frost will kill all dahlias. When this happens, you can then do one of two things. Either do as all conventional gardeners have done for the past 150 years: after the first frost blackens them, cut them down to within 15cm (6in) of the ground and dig up the tubers carefully, shaking off any excess soil sticking to them. Put them upside down in a seed tray or cardboard box for a week so that any water can drain out of the hollow stems (the stems of the largest dahlias were apparently used by the Aztecs as a means of transporting water over long distances in a sort of viaduct system). When the stems are drained, turn the tubers the right way up and stack them together in a box, with the tubers covered by slightly damp sand or peat, keeping the crowns uncovered. Store the tubers in a dark, dry, frost-free place.

1. Single
45–75cm (18–30in)
Simple flower heads with flat florets.

2. Anemone
60–105cm (24 –42in)
Fully double, often bi-coloured, internal ray of tubular florets.

3. Collarette
75–120cm (30–48in)
Inside collar of small florets.

4. Water Lily
45–115cm (18 –46in)
Full flower heads of broad, flat florets.

5. Decorative
90–150cm (36–60in)
The biggest dahlias. Fully double blooms, florets inward turning.

6. Ball
90–120cm (36–48in)
Rounded blooms with spirally arranged florets.

7. Pompon
90–120cm (36 –48in)
Globular, small heads (maximum 5cm/2in) petals rolled inwards.

8. Cactus
45–120cm (18 –48in)
Fully double, with petals like quills.

9. Semi-cactus
45–120cm (18 –8in)
Fully double, with pointed petals.

Or, just cut them off at ground level and cover them with a thick layer of straw or similar insulating material. Some will undoubtably die in the cold, but quite a few will survive. Even if you do dig them all up carefully, some are bound to rot or be eaten by mice. If you live in a very cold area then you are better digging your dahlias up and trying to store them over winter, but if you live in the south or in a protected spot, I would risk leaving them be.

SUMMER BULBS

There are an awful lot of boats to be missed in gardening. You see something good, get keen, make the ef-

The peerless madonna lily (Lilium candidum) *flourishes in full sun on chalky soil and adds a touch of class to any garden.*

fort to learn how to pronounce the Latin so you won't seem a complete idiot, buy it, then find out that the sole window of opportunity to plant it has flipped by in the great horticultural filofax and you must wait six months to plant to get the flowers you want now a further six months beyond that. It hardly seems worth the effort. But summer bulbs are mainly planted in autumn, just after spring bulbs, so now is the time to check out well-stocked gardens, see what is in flower, make a note and order the bulbs ready for planting next month.

There is a whole range of summer bulbs that get overlooked in the welter of other summer plants. Lilies, crocosmias, crinums, gladioli, alliums, nerines, agapanthus are all bulbs (or corms

or tubers or rhizomes: all bulbous in behaviour if not appearance – see pages 132–133).

There are over a thousand species of **alliums**, including onions, garlic, leeks and chives, but only a couple of dozen are properly garden plants, with their round, punk, dandelion-clock heads. *A. aflatunense* and *A. sphaerocephalum* normally flower in May/June and look great in massed ranks. (Their leaves die back as they flower, so underplant them to cover this; *Geranium endressii* would look good.) *Allium giganteum* has an enormous purple puffball, and is, as its name suggests, gigantic. Alliums form clumps which can be divided to create more clumps or left to set seed and become a fixture in their bit of the garden. I have left a batch of the previous winter's undug leeks in the ground until after flowering, and they made a stunning display of 1.8m (6ft) high stalks with lilac heads the size of a small melon.

Irises are another dramatic purple addition that look good in any June garden. Bearded irises like their rhizomes baked by hot sun and are therefore planted very shallowly, but English, Dutch and Spanish irises should be planted now, 7.5cm (3in) deep and 15cm (6in) apart.

Lilies have a reputation for petulant brilliance, but there are some that need little expertise to make them grow. Flowering in mid to late summer, they ask for simple but essential conditions.
1. They must have good drainage, yet plenty of water.
2. They want plenty of sunshine with just a little shade.

So far so manageable. If your soil is heavy, add lots of compost and grit and remember to water them regularly and plant them where there is, say, evening shade.

On the whole lilies prefer an acidic soil, but if you have a chalky garden you could still grow *Lilium henryi*, 1.8m (6ft) tall with flaming orange flowers, or *L. regale*, perhaps the easiest and most extraordinary of lilies. It was discovered in China by 'Chinese' Wilson in 1904, growing by the tens of thousands in the River Min Valley, and has

SUMMER BULBS AT A GLANCE		
	VARIETIES	MONTH OF FLOWERING
Lily	*L. regale, L. candidum*	July–September
Allium	*A. affluense, A. giganteum*	May–June
Gladiolus	Butterfly Hybrids	August–September
Crinum	*C.x powellii*	August–September
Crocosmia	*C.* 'Lucifer'	July–September
Galtonia	*G. candicans*	August–September
Schizostylis	*S. coccinea*	August–September
Sternbergia	*S. lutea*	August–September
Iris	*I. germanica*	May–August
Nerine	*N. bowdenii*	September–October
Alstroemeria	*A. aurea*	July–September
Dahlia	See pages138–139	July–October
Zantedeschia	*Z. aethiopica* 'Crowborough'	July–August

Allium flowers against a background of foxtail lilies. All alliums produce wonderful flowers — even leeks.

or Dame Edna on the rampage. They are corms and should be planted in spring about 7.5cm (3in) deep in heavy soil with a handful of sand directly under the corm and twice that depth in very light ground. They will need staking as they grow, and lifting after they have flowered, to be stored somewhere dry over winter. They are not difficult to place in a mixed border as long as you stay shy of the pinky orange colours that they are prone to. Keep to strong reds, yellows, white or the more delicate pinks. In dry weather give them lots of water.

Nerines are planted in autumn, even though they will not flower for nearly a year. The best is *N. bowdenii*, which must have as much sun as your garden can offer, ideally at the foot of a south-facing wall, and in poor, quick-draining soil. Enriching the soil will simply produce fewer flowers and more leaves. Plant nerines shallowly, just below the surface.

Crinum x *powellii* has the same need for a summer bake, but is much larger and more robust, with bright green leaves. It needs proper nourishment if it is to perform. This is the only **crinum** that is guaranteed hardy, producing pink trumpets of flowers in late summer, and if fed with a mulch of well-rotted manure it quite quickly establishes itself in substantial clumps. After the heat of summer it needs plenty of water at flowering.

Finally, a bulb worth planting and extremely easy to grow is the **summer hyacinth** (*Galtonia candicans*), which produces great spikes of white flowers at the end of July if planted in October. It looks somewhere between a lily, a hosta and a hyacinth.

never been found growing anywhere else in the wild.

L. martagon is pinky purple with the variety *album* having pure white flowers. Finally for chalk, the **madonna lily** (*L. candidum*) positively likes lime and will take a shadeless roasting. It has been grown in gardens for 3,000 years and is still without peer. Unlike most lilies, *L. candidum* should be planted very shallowly.

If you can grow ericaceous plants (rhododendrons, camellias, heathers) you are going to have a bigger choice of lilies, but I would still start with *L. re-*

gale and *L. candidum*. They are easiest and perhaps best.

Anybody living by the coast is familiar with the orange **crocosmia** or **montbretia**, which thrives in the mild climate there, but *Crocosmia* 'Lucifer' is a corm that seems impervious to any winter hardship, blazing a lick of red for weeks in summer. It is an essential plant for any late summer border. Whilst it is genuinely tough, like most bulbs, it prefers good drainage.

Gladioli have never had much glamour, too reminiscent of fifties fading allure

SITTING PRETTY

One of the more reliable laws of gardening is that just as summer is drawing to an end we start to get used to the idea of sitting outside. September is unhelpful in that respect in that the weather is often fabulous and the Indian summer seems endless. No matter. The essential task this weekend is to reassess the seating arrangements in your garden and if they are not absolutely perfect, to do something about them.

This is actually very important. The furniture in your garden deserves every bit as much consideration as the furniture in your house. It must look good in the context of its horticultural surroundings as well as being comfy to sit on or eat at.

Most gardeners realise that they need a table and at least a couple of chairs. Most gardens are improved with more seating than that. The secret is to spread it about liberally. Of course you must have your table and chairs designed primarily for eating, but you should also make sure that every vantage point and every aspect of the garden has somewhere that you can sit. This adds variety to the places to relax and contemplate the garden, and enables you to make the most of different light at different times of day and to create quite small tableaux to enjoy. Most of this is just common sense, but hardly ever done enough.

The other great virtue in having lots of seats around the garden is that you can make them into focal points and

plant around them, so that they look good when you are looking at them as well as from them and they smell especially sweet. Which is always a Good Thing.

In my 30m x 9m (100ft x 30ft) London back garden I had five separate sitting positions, two capable of seating up to eight people. While that might seem excessive, seats can be carefully blended into the scheme of things so that they seem absolutely integral to the garden.

I have a friend who has made a garden table from a massive gravestone he saved from destruction whilst driving past a graveyard. Resting on brick plinths it looks good, is utterly solid and is a constant memorial to Henry Collins Esq. RIP.

To start with patio seating. In a way this is dictated by your patio, although it should really dictate the size of the patio itself, not the other way round. You must have a table that is big enough and heavy enough to be really secure. You need enough room to move round it with others sitting eating or reading the paper without bashing into it or the surrounding plants and knocking the whole thing over. Thus you need a de-

cent patio space to operate in. An awful lot of cheapo garden tables are flimsy affairs. Try and avoid this. Go for sturdiness every time. It is very easy to make an excellent garden table from scaffolding planks. Each plank is 3cm (1 1/2in) thick and 23cm (9in) wide and you can buy these in 2.5m (8ft) lengths. Three screwed together with two by one (with a 1cm/1/2in gap between the boards to allow for drainage) make a good table. Set them on trestles made from three by two and the weight of the construction will hold it rock steady.

Benches, with or without a back, make good seating for a rectangular table like this and take up very little space.

If you have a round table, benches will not do. It has to be a really large round table to sit more than four comfortably, so bear this in mind if planning large al fresco gatherings. Chairs for a table obviously come in two guises – collapsible or solid. Solid tend to look better and be more comfortable for sitting at a table, but chairs that fold flat are easy to store. The very worst thing when you are eating at a table is a low, canvas-bottomed seat that leaves you with your backside almost on the floor and your chin at table height.

Unstained wood always looks good with bold foliage planting, where the solid form echoes the outlines of the plants. If you are using wood it must be a hardwood – preferably oak, but failing that a renewable tropical hardwood such as teak. In a small, dark garden, seats in a rich blue can look very good against the dark green background. 'Directors' (canvas-backed and seated folding wooden chairs) are

view — however small — and frondescence around them. They are for stopping at rather than relaxing on, and should take comfort as a secondary consideration after style.

If carefully chosen, a chair can be as decorative as anything else in the garden.

The author hard at work in his own garden (while small son slaves with a spade).

good, but get the sturdy variety — there are lightweight versions on the market which tend to sag alarmingly.

For the seats away from the table, it is better to use wood or to make very simple seats yourself. Don't be precious about this. A slab of wood balanced on bricks, or a piece of slate or stone, is fine. Even a square of bricks cemented together makes a perfectly good seat for perching on and admiring the view. In medieval times turf seats were common, as no doubt were wet behinds in anything but the driest weather. I have seen an old armchair, the stuffing spilling out like shaving cream, look very stylish tucked away in a corner of the garden, surrounded by honeysuckle. These sort of seats need shade, a

OCTOBER

Weather Report: although October can be a lovely month of gentle, warm days and cosy evenings, time is running out. Temperatures are falling and the soil generally becomes wetter and harder to handle. The weather is going to get worse from now on in, so it is vital to use what good weather there is to full advantage. However, there is often a period of surprisingly fine weather around 18 October, traditionally called 'St Luke's little summer' because the 18th is St Luke's Day. But the end of the month is often stormy, so if possible try and complete all your digging by then. This is also the month when the leaves fall in torrents, so you have your work cut out keeping them in some sort of order.

PLANTS IN THEIR PRIME

Bulbs: *Colchicum autumnale,*
C. speciosum; Crocus speciosus,
Saffron crocus (*C. sativus* var.
cashmirianus); *Cyclamen*
neapolitanum; Sternbergia
lutea.

Annuals/biennials: late-sown
lupins, foxgloves, verbena,
marigolds, *Moluccella laevis*
('Irish bells'); *Lavatera*
assurgentiflora and sweet peas
will still be going strong well
into October.

Herbaceous: asters; *Anemone*
japonica; sedums; *Kniphofia;*
perennial sunflowers.

Shrubs: berberis; *Ceanothus*
'Burkwoodii'; *Cotoneaster*
horizontalis; ericas; spindle
(*Euonymus europaeus*); hebes;
gorse.

Trees: the glory of October is in the
turning leaf colour on trees such as
maples (Acers); *Stewartia; Sorbus;* sweet
gum (*Liquidambar styraciflua*); scarlet
oak (*Quercus coccinea*); London plane
(*Platanus* x *acerifolia*); tulip tree
(*Liriodendron tulipifera*).

Climbers: *Clematis flammula, C.*
rehderiana, C. vitalba; Vitis coignetiae;
Parthenocissus tricupidata; Jasminum
officinale.

Herbs: parsley (June sown); sage;
rosemary; thyme; winter savory;
horseradish.

Vegetables: carrots; cauliflowers;
celery; lambs' lettuce; leeks; parsnips;
maincrop potatoes; tomatoes.

Fruit: apples; pears; plums; quinces.

Berries: cotoneaster: pyracantha;
callicarpa; berberis.

Houseplants: This is a great time for
foliage plants. Keep them away from
frosty windows, but expose to as much
light as possible. Cease feeding and
water sparingly.

WEED CONTROL

Weeds like nettles will still be growing
strongly. As you dig ground remove all
traces of weeds by hand. Be meticulous
about this – every tiny scrap of couch,
ground elder or bindweed root that
you remove now will save hours next
year. Continue hoeing where
applicable. On windless days spray
with a Glysophate weed-killer such as
Roundup or Tumbleweed.

Above: Not all
deciduous trees change
colour at exactly the
same time, so autumn
can seem like a
constant progression
from one glorious
colour combination to
another.

Opposite: Perhaps the
most brilliant autumn
colour of all is provided
by the Japanese maple
(Acer palmatum
dissectum).

JOBS

Essential
• Collect leaves
from lawns and
borders, taking
care to uncover
small plants that
would otherwise
be smothered;
save all leaves in a
heap, sprinkling
them with water to
speed up decom-
position.
• Bring in all ten-
der plants in pots
and store in a cool
but frost-free
place.
• Take hardwood
cuttings.
• Dig ground as it
becomes available.
• Harvest fruit.
• Scarify lawns.
• Lift and store
dahlias and gladi-
olli.

Desirable
• Continue bulb
planting.
• Move peonies.
• Prune climbing
roses.
• Keep ponds free
of leaves.
• Prune raspber-
ries.

Optional
• Sow grass seed
and lay turf in early
weeks of month.

PREPARING THE LAWN FOR WINTER

Continuous wear and tear on a lawn over the summer – be it by children playing or you walking up and down with a mower – causes compaction, which makes it more difficult for rainfall and soluble nutrients to penetrate through to the grass roots before they evaporate. This causes 'thatch' to build up around the roots, and it needs to be pulled out of the lawn before the next growing season. This process is known as scarifying.

The simplest way to do it – and the easiest on a small lawn – is with a wire rake. You simply rake the lawn vigorously, scratching out all the dead organic material and moss. This will also bring to the surface long stolons bare of grass leaves.

If you have a larger lawn it is possible to hire a petrol-driven electrical scarifier by the day from your garden centre; it will do the job extremely well.

AERATING THE LAWN

The lawn must then be aerated. The principle is easy: you make holes all over the lawn that let in water and fertiliser and stop compaction.

Raking up the leaves is important – a covering like this will do the lawn no good at all.

Aerate the lawn by making holes all over it with a fork. This lets in water and fertiliser, and prevents compaction.

In practice this is one of the most back-breaking jobs in the garden if you try and do it on a large area with a fork. The holes need to be at least 5cm (2in) deep, which probably requires pressure from your boot, then many soils seem to suck the tines of the fork in, meaning that you have to wrench them out again. After five minutes most people give up and go and have a cup of tea.

Thankfully there are two types of machine, both mechanical and powered, that will make light of this very important job. Again, you can hire them by the day or the weekend. One has hollow tines on a drum that takes out small plugs of soil and the other

To fill in small dips, sieve soil over the lawn so that only the tips of the grass are showing.

makes slits from triangular spikes on a drum. Both are equally effective. When you have finished, the lawn will look distinctly messy. Don't worry. It will recover quickly.

If you have very heavy soil, this is the time to brush sand into the holes you have made. Sharp sand is ideal and can be bought cheaply by the lorryload. Spread it over the surface and brush it down into the holes. The effect of this will be to improve drainage, reducing moss and winter muddiness. It does not matter if the whole lawn has a layer of sand over it – the grass will continue to grow as long as the tips of the grass are still showing through.

Excess soil brought up by aerating can be brushed across the surface in a similar way. This will help level the lawn and the soil will soon be lost in the grass.

THE JOY OF WORMS

People often complain about the worm casts that appear in great numbers from September onwards. Nine times out of ten they are to be celebrated. It means that the soil is rich and fertile and the worms are your best ally in ensuring good drainage. Brush the casts across the lawn and they too will soon be incorporated into the surface. It is very rare that a lawn is so infested that you need to consider killing the worms – perhaps soil that good should be dug up and used for vegetables or flowers!

PATCHING UP

This is a good time of year to make repairs to an established lawn. There may be dips and hollows or worn patches – all of which are easily repaired. In fact the single thing that improves the appearance of a lawn more than anything else is levelling its surface.

Hollows and dips can be dealt with in

For larger hollows, cut and lift the turf and add extra soil underneath.

two ways. For minor ones it is best to sieve soil into them so that only the tips of the grass are showing. When this has grown back the process can be repeated until the surface is level. You can sow fresh seed lightly onto this top-dressing, but if the grass below is healthy this should be unnecessary.

If the dip is bigger, the turf will have to be carefully cut and lifted, then soil put in to raise the level before replacing the turfs. If you do this now it will have regrown perfectly by next spring.

Humps and bumps are best removed by making an H-shaped cut into the lawn with a spade and rolling back the two resulting flaps of turf. Soil can then be removed from this spot, the surface raked smooth and the flaps folded back into position.

FEEDING

Lawns really benefit from an autumn feed. Proprietary feeds in powder or granule form are best and can be spread by hand or with an applicator. The autumn feed does not want to be as high in nitrogen as the spring one, but needs quite a high phosphate content, which will encourage root development.

Moss is usually a sign of poor drainage and lack of light, but close mowing and lack of feeding undoubtedly help it to establish. Proper aeration and scarification will help, and lawn sand is effective in killing the moss that is there. However, nothing will deter moss if the underlying conditions are not right. Cut the grass a little longer, feed and aerate the lawn and don't worry about a certain amount of moss. As long as the lawn is green, level, pleasant to walk and sit on and good to look at, does it really matter?

TIP
Discouraging the Worms

WORMS ARE NORMALLY A SIGN OF RICH, HEALTHY SOIL, BUT IF YOU REALLY DON'T WANT THEM IN YOUR GARDEN THE BEST COURSE IS TO MAKE YOUR SOIL A LITTLE MORE ACIDIC (EARTHWORMS DO NOT LIKE AN ACID SOIL) BY SPRINKLING SULPHATE OF AMMONIA OVER THE LAWN. THIS WILL NOT KILL THEM BUT MIGHT ENCOURAGE THEM TO MOVE TO A LESS ACIDIC SPOT – LIKE YOUR FLOWERBEDS.

AUTUMN LEAVES

For a few wonderful weeks in October the trees are ablaze with colour. This effect is dependent upon two different processes, one leading to yellows, the other to reds – all other colours such as purples and oranges are variations on these two basic colours.

All the maples are excellent value in the autumn.

The yellows are due to caratenoid pigments which are always present in leaves but usually masked by chlorophyll, the substance which makes photosynthesis possible. When the temperature begins to drop and the daylight hours get shorter the chlorophyll is not renewed and the yellow pigments become visible. In truth what you see is not so much the yellowing of the leaves but their 'degreening'.

The chemicals which produce the red pigmentation are closely related to carbohydrates and are manufactured most on warm, sunny days followed by

cool (but not frosty) nights. The cold nights confine the build-up of sugars to the leaves; hence the concentration of red pigmentation there. So the intensity of autumn colour is determined by the weather in August and September. Mild temperatures and rain lead to poor colorations. If you look at the underside of a the leaf of a copper beech (*Fagus sylvatica purpurea*) in spring or a sugar maple (*Acer saccharum*) in autumn you will see that it is green – because it has not been exposed to the carbohydrate-forming effects of sunshine.

There is nothing that we can do about our climate, but we can choose trees for the garden that will react well to the chances of autumn colouring.

THE MAPLE FAMILY

The tree family that comes into its own in autumn more than any other is the **maple** (*Acer*).

There are three sources of maples – North America, the East and Europe. The American maples are large and brilliantly coloured in autumn; the Japanese ones tend to be smaller with intricate leaves and excellent autumnal colouring; and the European maples are drabber but useful trees, like the **sycamore** (*Acer pseudoplatanus*) and the **field maple** (*A. campestre*).

THE VALUE OF LEAVES

ONE WAY OF USING LEAVES IN A NEW GARDEN IS TO SPREAD THE FALLEN LEAVES OVER THE GROUND 15CM (6IN) DEEP. THEN, USING A ROTIVATOR (WHICH CAN BE HIRED BY THE DAY), CHOP THEM INTO THE TOPSOIL. UNLIKE GREEN MATTER, LEAVES USE UP VERY LITTLE NITROGEN AS THEY ROT INTO THE SOIL, SO DO NOT ROB THE GROUND OF VALUABLE NUTRIENTS. THIS METHOD WILL CREATE USABLE TOPSOIL OUT OF THE POOREST SUBSOIL.

Perhaps the most brilliant autumn colour from an individual tree is from the **Japanese maple** (*Acer palmatum*). It has many different cultivars, of which the most famous are 'Atropurpureum' – which has deep purple leaves in summer, turning scarlet in autumn – and 'Ozakuzuki', which has olive-green leaves in summer that change to reddy-orange in autumn. *A. palmatum* 'Dissectum' has finely cut, ferny leaves which make a mound of delicate greening in summer, turning red in October. It is best grown in a mixed border, its leaves as decorative as many flowers. All the Japanese maples prefer a slightly acidic, rich, free-draining soil.

The American maples provide the most magnificent specimens. In my last garden I had a huge **sugar maple** (*A. saccharum*), which was superb in October – although an American visitor assured me that it did not begin to match up to the sugar maples in New England! The **red maple** (*A. rubrum*) is another fine autumn colourer, although it will not colour well when grown on chalky soil. The **silver maple** (*A. saccharinum*) has deeply lobed, light green leaves that turn pale yellow in October. It grows very fast into a wide-crowned tree and of all the American maples is the best adapted to our climate.

The most common European maple, the **sycamore**, is only suitable for very large gardens, growing to 30m (100ft) in sixty years. However, there is a minature variety, *Acer pseudoplatanus* 'Brilliantissimum', which has a mop head with leaves starting pink, turning greeny-gold in summer and bronze in autumn. It is best grown in partial shade. Sycamores cope very well with salt and are therefore suitable for growing near the sea.

The **field maple** is a very common tree of the countryside and can make a

very good large hedge for the boundary of a garden with a field, but is perhaps not ideal for the average garden, even though one often sees it for sale in garden centres.

The **Norway maple** (*A. platanoides*) is as tough as sycamore, withstanding urban pollution well, but is smaller and less intrusive. Its leaves turn a wonderful golden yellow for a few weeks before falling.

All three trees are fast-growing, hardy and particularly suitable for areas of 'wild' garden.

The **sweet gum** tree (*Liquidambar styraciflua*) is the most extraordinary of autumn performers. The leaves look like those of a maple, although the ridged, corky bark distinguishes it. The leaves stay shiny green well into September and then drift through the colours from orange through scarlet almost to black before falling. Sweet gum likes damp soil and must be planted

small as it dislikes being moved. The biggest example I know can be seen at Syon House in south-west London, and is nearly 30m (100ft) tall.

LEAVES FOR COMPOST

When the leaves do fall it is important to collect them regularly. There are two very good reasons for this. The first is that lawns, small plants and ponds will all suffer if damp leaves are left to rot in or over them. Paths can become slippery and dangerous. The second is that leaves rot down to make leaf-mould, the finest organic compost and mulch there is. If you walk in a beech wood you will notice that the ground is made up of a wonderfully soft, fine, black soil. This is the product of layer upon layer of fallen leaves. It is incredible in these environmentally aware days that we do not make a more concerted effort to gather leaves and compost them, especially in the streets and gardens of our towns.

The undersides of autumn leaves tend to be pale because they have not been exposed to the sun. Sunlight produces the carbohydrates responsible for the red colouring.

Traditionally leaves were raked or swept (using besoms, the traditional witch's broom made from birch twigs or ling) and collected into heaps that were allowed to rot slowly for a period of years before use. At the end of this time they had become a sweet-smelling, crumbly brown matter, looking rather like rich peat. This process can now be speeded up in two ways: firstly by blow-vacs — giant hoovers that either suck the leaves into a bag or blow them into a manageable heap — which makes collection in awkward corners and amongst plants much quicker and easier — and by watering the heap of leaves. If kept moist they will rot down within a year. A simple container for the leaves can be made from wire netting fixed to four posts at each corner.

MULCHING

Mulching: there is something squelchy and resonant about the word that is almost onomatopoeic.

What is a mulch? A layer of material spread over the surface of the soil between and around plants, not dug in but simply left like a blanket over the earth. It is the easiest and most labour-free way of fertilising the soil and keeping weeds down. It saves hours and hours of work and is one of the biggest aids to a beautiful garden.

Next question: what is a mulch made of? Nature's most natural mulch is made up of the layer of leaves that fall

A Successful Mulch will

SUPPRESS WEED GROWTH BY KEEPING OUT THE LIGHT (ALTHOUGH SOME MULCHES, SUCH AS FARMYARD MANURE OR HAY, CARRY ANNUAL WEED SEEDS IN THEM).

MAKE WEEDING EASIER BECAUSE IT PROVIDES A SOFT, FRIABLE MEDIUM.

KEEP THE SOIL WARM IN AUTUMN AND COOL IN SUMMER.

PREVENT THE SOIL FROM DRYING OUT IN SUMMER OR BECOMING TOO WATERLOGGED IN WINTER.

ROT DOWN TO IMPROVE THE TEXTURE AND NUTRITIONAL VALUE OF YOUR SOIL.

LOOK GOOD AT ALL TIMES.

at this time of year, or perhaps a thick layer of snow, but almost anything that can be spread on the soil will constitute a mulch.

Spreading a straw mulch.

Commercial growers often use black polythene, which is very effective, but has one huge drawback: it is horribly ugly. For that reason alone I would never want it in a garden of mine. So I would ignore the advice that I have seen advocated of using old carpet, newspaper or cardboard. Deliberately to make your garden ugly seems to me to be perverse.

With a few exceptions it is best to use an organic material which will rot down and improve the quality of the soil as it does so. (The main exceptions are gravel, which is very suitable for alpine plants, and stones, which are good around the base of a plant which needs cool roots, like clematis.)

THE AUTUMN MULCH

Mulching in autumn protects the soil and delicate roots from all but the hardest of frosts and stops weeds growing in the warmer periods over the winter months. It will be worked into the topsoil by earthworms dragging bits of organic mat-

ter down into their runs, improving its condition and fertility dramatically, and gently decompose ready for a topping up in spring.

It is important to lay the autumn mulch before the soil cools down. Mulch acts as insulation and will keep the cold in as effectively as it keeps it out. So get your borders weeded and mulched by the end of this month.

Weed the ground thoroughly first so that you have a clean surface. If the mulch goes down on weed-free soil it should reduce weeding to the occasional annual seedling that has to be pulled up.

We ask our garden plants to perform much more spectacularly than they are required to by nature for the continuation of the species. To carry on this Olympian performance they must

Whatever mulch you choose, spread a good, thick layer of it. Underground, the worms will be working hard on your behalf, dragging organic matter down into the soil and improving its fertility dramatically.

MULCH

WORMS

Type of Mulch		How to apply	Pros	Cons	Uses
Stones		Lay around the roots of plants.	Good for retaining moisture; long lasting.	Inorganic; do not improve soil.	Particularly suitable for clematis, which likes cool roots.
Bark		Spread in layer by shovel or hand from bag.	Can look good; slow to decompose; excellent for weed control; sterile; pleasant to handle.	Expensive; adds little nutrition to soil.	Flowerbeds and areas awkward to weed.
Garden compost		Spread in layer by shovel or hand from bag.	Free; excellent nutritional qualities; good for soil structure.	Can have weed seeds in.	Mixed borders, vegetables, entire garden.
Mushroom compost		Spread in layer by shovel or hand from bag.	Excellent nutritional qualities; good for soil structure; pleasant to handle; sterile.	Can be difficult to obtain: find a specialist mushroom grower.	Mixed borders, herbs.
Straw		Spread in loose layer from bale.	Cheap (if you can get small bales); clean; bulky.	Can have weed seeds in; can be hard to obtain.	Temporary paths, shrubs, trees, strawberries.
Hay		Spread in loose layer from bale.	Clean and pleasant to handle; easy to store; bulky.	Can have weed seeds in; can be hard to obtain; slimy when wet.	Rough areas, trees, shrubs, etc.
Grass cuttings		Spread in thick layer straight from mower.	Free; clean and abundant.	Can have weed seeds in; take nitrogen from soil as they rot down; ugly.	Shrubs, trees, hedges.
Gravel		Spread in loose layer around plants.	Easy to use; keeps slugs away; sterile.	Provides no nutrition; limited attraction.	Alpines, small areas with tender succulents.
Leaf mould		Spread in thick layer around plants.	Nutritious; good conditioner; free.	Takes at least twelve months to make.	Woodland plants (hellebores, primroses, euphorbia, etc).

be nourished in an exceptional way. Mulch is often the only practical way to do this, especially in a border of permanent plants.

Most people put mulch down too thinly. To be effective as a source of nourishment and as a weed suppressant it must be at least 5cm (2in) deep and many of the most successful gardens are mulched to a depth of twice that. This requires a great quantity of mulching material, which is another good reason to make your own compost and leaf mould – it is plentiful and free!

DIGGING

I have to confess to be being an earth-lover. The feel of warm, crumbly soil running through my fingers, the rich, brown tilth of soil that has been cultivated for years, and the scent on a summer's afternoon after a shower of rain has damped the dry earth are all exquisite to me. Digging then is an extension of this love. The more I visit gardens and the more I garden myself, the more certain I am that the one essential ingredient of a successful garden is rich soil with a good structure. Some people inherit this when they move into a new house and most are probably unaware of how incredibly lucky they are. Whatever they stick into the ground will grow like Topsy. For most of us we have to work hard to improve the soil in any way that we can.

WHY DIG?

Digging does two things:

1. It improves the structure of the soil, making it easier for roots to grow and moisture and nutrients to be retained and drained in just the right proportions.

not true

2. It mixes food and air into the earth so that the plants can gain as much sustenance as possible.

In many ways the first result – improving the soil structure – is the more important, because you can always add foliar or surface feed to a plant, but you are limited to the amount that you can change the soil without digging.

Digging is hard work. But as long as you do not strain yourself, hard work never hurt anyone. Enjoy the fresh air and the exercise and relish the undoubted fitness you will be gaining!

Of course, most people very rarely need to dig the garden. Once shrubs, trees, lawns and perennial plants of all kinds are in the ground they must not be disturbed more than is absolutely necessary, which means it is impossible to dig around them.

WHEN TO DIG

There are two occasions when digging properly is really important:

1. When you are cultivating a piece of land for the first time.

2. When you are growing vegetables.

I am going to focus on the first, the new plot, because the techniques are the same for both.

All new houses will have compacted soil. This is a fact of life. The reason for it is that the building work will have meant machines and heavy feet walking over it and compacting it down for months. This means that roots cannot easily push through the soil, water can not soak in and worms cannot move around, which is the best natural activity the soil can have.

Some builders pay contractors to rotivate the garden, giving it the appearance of being cultivated. Be careful! The chances are that the top 2.5cm (1in) is beautifully raked, but that underneath that the ground is like iron. It must be dug properly.

SINGLE DIGGING

This is the easiest – and most common – form of digging.

There is a simple series of procedures to follow to make the most of it.

1. Dig a trench one spade deep (a spit) and a spade wide, cleaning out the 'crumbs' but trying not to mix topsoil and subsoil. Put the soil in a barrow and tip it in a line along the far edge of the piece of ground you are digging.

2. Move back the width of a spade and dig the next 'trench', throwing the soil from it into the first trench. It will fall at an angle, sloping away from you at 45°.

3. Spread a good layer of whatever organic material you have over this. Well-rotted cattle manure is best, but garden compost is fine. You can buy organic manure in bags from all garden centres. Make sure that it is spread out thoroughly.

4. Repeat the process until you run out of room. At this point the soil from the first trench gets used: put it into the last trench.

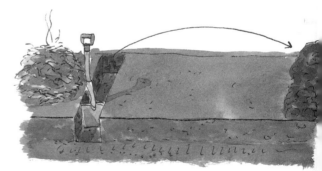

Single digging: line the soil from the first trench along the far edge of the plot you are digging.

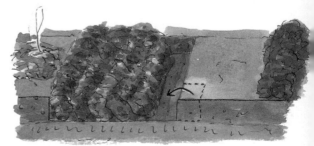

As you progress across the site, use the soil from each trench to fill in the one you have just dug.

Inevitably the soil level will have been raised above that of the surrounding area, but do not be alarmed by this. It will gently subside while retaining its new light structure.

DOUBLE DIGGING

Double digging is always cited as the most laborious of all gardening tasks. But set against the fact that it is only done once in every generation of home-owner, and the enormous difference it makes to the health of most plants, I am convinced that it is one of the most worthwhile jobs to be done, particularly if you are preparing a new border or if you are making a new garden in soil that has been compacted.

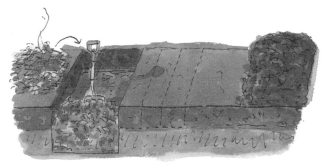

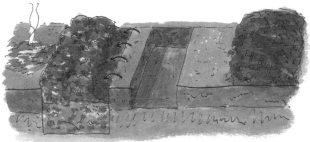

Double digging: use a fork to break up the soil at the bottom of each trench.

As with single digging, use the soil from each trench to fill in the previous one.

It differs from single digging both in procedure and in quantity of work. This is not for wimps!

1. Dig a trench one spit deep and three spade-widths wide. Move the soil, as with single digging, to the end of the plot, ready to be used to fill in the last trench. As always, try to avoid mixing topsoil and subsoil.

2. With a fork, dig over the bottom of the trench to the depth of a spit, breaking the soil up into small clods as you go. Work backwards and do not tread on the soil after you have dug it. Remember, the main reason for digging is to improve soil structure.

3. Fork plenty of manure into the newly dug bottom of the trench, mixing it into the soil.

4. Move backwards and dig the next trench, putting the soil into the trench you have just dug and manured. You will find it easiest and most logical to do this in three 'mini-trenches', starting furthest away from the already dug trench, so that the third 'mini-trench'

is like a spit of soil between two dug areas.

5. Repeat the process, moving steadily backwards until you come to the soil that you removed initially, which you will use to fill in your ast trench.

You will find that the soil is enormously raised by this process, but as with single digging, do not be alarmed. This is a sign that you are doing it properly and it will settle soon enough.

Good tools are vital for digging — invest in a stainless steel spade, and keep the wheelbarrow handy.

TIP

AN IMPORTANT TIP WHEN DOUBLE DIGGING: TAKE IT STEADILY. IT REALLY IS HARD WORK. I HAVE DONE QUITE A LOT OF IT AND RECKON MYSELF TO BE FAIRLY FIT, BUT I HAVE LEARNED TO DO SMALL AMOUNTS AT A STRETCH AND TO DO THEM PROPERLY. TWO HOURS AT A TIME IS PLENTY!

THE NO-DIG SYSTEM

The No-Dig system sounds like the ideal cultivation system for the Weekend Gardener, guaranteed to save on blood, tears, toil and sweat, but it is founded on serious principles. The idea is that digging is an entirely unnatural act and disturbs the natural structure and microlife – from the earthworm to bacterial activity – of the soil. In the unmanaged wild, plants manage to grow perfectly healthily without the ground having to be carefully dug beforehand. The argument for No-Dig gardening runs that we should learn from this and let the root systems of plants make their own natural way through the soil. Also digging often brings to the surface deeply buried weed seeds that would otherwise have failed to germinate.

All we have to do within the No-Dig principle is to mulch the surface regularly.

It is claimed that burying compost or manure in the soil removes it from the oxygen and soil bacteria which it needs in order to break down into the nutrients which the plant can use. Most of the plant's feeding roots are in the top 7.5–10cm (3–4in) of the soil and this is where 80% of the useful soil bacteria lives. Therefore simply by spreading your compost on the surface you are feeding the roots of the plant more directly than if you go to the hard work and trouble of digging it in.

The No-Dig lobby also argues that dug soil is more prone to drying out and to 'capping' – that is the process whereby the top 2.5cm (1in) of soil is compacted by the rain and then dries into a crust, stopping any other moisture penetrating to where it is needed by the roots below.

DRAWBACKS OF THE NO-DIG SYSTEM

In new gardens or anywhere that the soil has become compacted for whatever reason, it will take many years to uncompact if left to itself. It needs digging to get it back to the point at which the No-Dig system might work. Nature's laissez-faire system makes the bold assumption that man has not got there first and meddled with the natural structure of the soil. On modern building sites materials are moved by fork-lift truck and the toing and froing of these vehicles bearing pallet-loads of bricks compresses the soil structure in an entirely unnatural way. I made a garden from scratch on a new estate in Wales last year, and the ground there was packed solid down to a depth of 60cm (2ft). The water sat on it like a lake and only the strongest roots could have made any impression through it. Deep digging was the only solution.

Very heavy clay soil that has not been compacted can – so the No-Dig advocates claim – best be treated by not digging it. You simply put a layer of organic material on it every year, grad-ually building up a thin layer of rich, loose topsoil. Plants establish and feed in this and work their way into the clay, which in turn holds a rich supply of nu-trients – particularly trace minerals that quickly wash away in a lighter soil.

There is merit to this plan, although you must be confident that the soil is uncompacted, and to do that you should compare it with similar soil that you know has been left alone. Once you embark on this policy you must scrupulously avoid treading on the surface, as the structure that you are creat-ing is a very delicate affair.

PUTTING THE THEORY INTO PRACTICE

Let us assume that you have got a piece of ground that you wish to turn into a border, but you cannot face the thought of digging it or you simply wish to try the No-Dig idea out as an experiment.

First lightly hoe the surface or pull up all weeds by hand. Then cover the ground with a thick mulch. In this in-stance it could be a carpet or even black plastic, because the aim is to stop weeds more than to aid cultivation. Clear plastic will not do, as the pri-mary aim of this mulch is to block out light.

You then have a choice of action. You can leave a thick, light-excluding layer over the ground for up to a year to kill off the weeds – or even two years if you have weeds like mares' tail, horseradish or ground elder – or you can put down the initial layer of organic mulch as thickly as possible (at least 10cm/4in) and be prepared to pull up weeds as they come through. Either way, it is best not to plant or sow any-thing into the ground for at least two months, to give existing weed seeds time to germinate and be removed.

Then you plant or sow seeds on or

Nature's laissez-faire system makes the bold assumption that man has not got there first and meddled with the natural struc-ture of the soil.

within the mulch layer and mulch over the top of them as suitable. The mulch will keep the soil moist and soft and allow the roots to penetrate the earth. It will also encourage earthworms into action, who will aerate the ground for you and pull the organic matter into the ground.

If you really wish to eliminate weeds, put a light-eliminating layer over the entire plot and plant through it. Spread a thick layer of organic compost over the ground and cover it with a porous layer such as an old carpet, cardboard or newspapers. You can also buy porous black plastic that will let the rain through without letting any light in. To plant you cut slits through this layer. Underneath, the earthworms will chew away at the

compost, creating a rich growing medium.

In my opinion this is an unlovely way to garden, without any sensual awareness of the soil, but I am aware that it has its devotees who swear by it.

To make this system work two things are essential:

1. Put plenty of organic mulch on the surface, aggregating a minimum of

15cm (6in) of good quality matter every year.

2. Never tread on the surface of the No-Dig area.

This latter requirement more or less dictates that the No-Dig method of cultivation will be done in a series of small beds, so that you can reach all the growing area without treading on the soil.

Using gravel as a mulch is one way of avoiding digging and suppressing weeds. I don't think it's very attractive, but alpines and other rockery plants do well in it.

Lightly hoe the surface to remove weeds.

Mulch the soil and leave it for a couple of months; then remove any weeds that have appeared.

Cover with something porous like an old carpet and cut slits in it through which to plant.

RAISED BEDS

There are two distinct approaches to making raised beds, but the reasons are the same: to create permanent beds that are never walked upon and so never compacted, to raise the surface of the ground up to avoid bending for those with bad backs, and to reduce cultivation to light hoeing and weeding once the beds are made.

METHOD ONE

It is worth investing time in cultivating an area of ground thoroughly. In an ideal world this would mean double digging all of it, which might well take more than a couple of hours and will be impossible if you have a bad back or are disabled. If that is the case, get someone else to do it for you if you can. At the very least it must be thoroughly dug over, but manure does not need to be incorporated into the topsoil at this stage.

Then break the ground into strips 1.5m (5ft) wide with gaps of 45cm (18in) between them (just wide enough to push a single-wheeled wheelbarrow and to walk). Then cover the beds with a thick (at least 7.5cm/3in) layer of compost.

Next shovel the areas that will become the paths sideways on to the beds, making them higher and the paths lower at the same time. The beds do not want to be more than 4.5m (15ft) long, otherwise the temptation to step on or over them rather than going right round the end when you want to go to the other side becomes irresistible, and that destroys the whole point of the system. Never again will anyone stand on the beds.

The beds will look like long, low mounds. Lightly fork the topsoil from the paths and the compost together – treading only on the paths. Then either make the paths hard – with bricks, paving or whatever – or organic – by laying down clean straw, wood chips or sawdust, all of which will eventually

Shovel soil from the area that will become a path on to the bed, simultaneously raising the bed and lowering the path.

> ### TIP
>
> WHEN MAKING A RAISED BED FOR SOMEONE IN A WHEELCHAIR, BE SURE TO MAKE THE PATHS WIDE ENOUGH AND OF A LEVEL, HARD SURFACE. THE IDEAL HEIGHT FOR THE TOP OF THE RETAINING WALL WILL BE ABOUT 60CM (2FT).

rot into the ground and have to be topped up at least once a year.

METHOD TWO

The second way of making raised beds is to build a framework out of permanent materials and then infill them to make the bed. This is ideal if you are restricted to a wheelchair, have a bad back or wish to create an artificial soil environment – an acid bed for ericaceous plants in a chalky area for instance, or very rich soil in a garden with poor conditions. All the work and care can be focused precisely on the area that is going to benefit most from attention, rather than the somewhat general approach of normal borders.

To do this you need to mark out where you want the beds to be and double dig them. This ensures good drainage and a really good soil structure for the roots to grow into.

If you are building permanent raised beds *invest* in the framework. If you have the time and inclination to do it yourself, be warned that it will take more than a couple of hours!

The framework can be made of anything that will remain strong for the foreseeable future: brick, concrete blocks, boards, dry stones, railway sleepers – whatever. If you are using brick or any other solid building material, you will need to lay this on footings, which you should put into the ground before it is dug. These footings should be made of hardcore covered by at least 10cm (4in) of concrete made of a mix of 5:1 ballast and cement.

Concrete blocks will look much better if rendered with a coarse sand and

cement mix. This is probably better done professionally, but will radically improve the appearance of the beds.

If you have made the beds using mortar, either line the inside with butyl or paint it with a bitumen-based paint. This stops the lime in the mortar leaching out into the soil.

Choosing the Right Soil

Once the boundaries of the beds are made, they must be filled with soil suitable for their purposes. If this is just

general plants, a mixture of topsoil and organic matter will suffice. Make sure that the topsoil is absolutely free from weeds, as it is crazy to introduce weeds into an area that has been so carefully prepared.

If you want an acidic soil, compose t principally from peat.

If you are growing alpines or bulbs, you will have to incorporate plenty of sharp sand or grit into the soil, to make sure that it is really well drained. It may also be sensible to place a 15cm (6in)

layer of aggregate or pebbles in the bottom to increase the drainage.

Assuming that the soil has plenty of organic matter or sharp sand, raised beds will need more watering than the ordinary border. This might justify installing an irrigation system when you build the beds (see page 90 for more information on this).

Mulch the raised beds twice a year, in autumn and in spring, constantly topping up their food supply. You will also be amazed at how rapidly they compact, however scrupulously you avoid treading on them.

Vegetables in Raised Beds

If you are growing vegetables like this you need tso make three separate beds – however small each one may be – and rotate your crops around them as shown in the table below.

The reason for this is partly to prevent disease becoming established in the soil and partly to take advantage of the nitrogen-fixing qualities of legumes. (See page 113 for a fuller ex-

	Bed 1	Bed 2	Bed 3
1st year	Legumes	Root crops	Brassica
2nd year	Brassica	Legumes	Roots
3rd year	Roots	Brassica	Legumes
and then back to year one.			

planation of this.)

Sow your seeds across the width of

Well-laid bricks make the raised bed really solid; overhanging Tagetes marigolds soften the edges.

the beds in short rows or in blocks, maximising every square inch of cultivated ground.

I grew my vegetables under this system for a few years, and was amazed by how much I could produce with shorter rows than convention dictates. You can also mix crops much more, making for both a more attractive display and a more practical one – putting the things that you tend to gather at the same time all together.

NOVEMBER

WEATHER REPORT: it is rare for November to pass without a really cold snap. Frost flows downhill, so if your garden is on a slope then the bottom of it is much more susceptible to damage than the top. Frost will collect in pockets if its flow is stopped by a wall or a solid hedge, so think about 'air drainage' and make sure that any hedges are reasonably open at the bottom so that the frost can flow through it.

Cold winds can dramatically exasperate the effects of cold. Your wind breaks will be tested from now through to next summer. It is important that they are not solid and that the air is broken up by them and not simply diverted. This is why a thick deciduous hedge makes the best wind break of all — better than a wall or a solid evergreen hedge.

If we have a wet November then it is likely to be a muddy, wet winter. There is more urgency now than ever to get the earthy jobs like digging and planting done and finished before the worst of the winter weather.

PLANTS IN THEIR PRIME:

Bulbs: *Crocus sativus*, *C. speciosa*; *Galanthus reginae-olgae*; *Cyclamen neopolitanum*; *Sternbergia lutea*.

Herbaceous and hardy plants: *Helleborus niger*; *Liriope spicata*; winter-flowering pansies.

Trees: holly; common oak (*Quercus robur*); strawberry tree (*Arbutus unedo*).

Shrubs: *Fatsia japonica*; *Viburnum arreri*; *Cornus alba* 'Sibirica'.

Climbers: *Clematis tangutica*, ivy.

Vegetables: Jerusalem artichokes; cabbages; cauliflowers; celeriac; celery; chicory; leeks, parsnips; perpetual spinach; swedes; turnips.

Fruit: apples.

Berries: *Berberis thunbergii*; *Callicarpa bodinieri giraldii*; *Cotoneaster rugosa* 'Henryi'; *Crataegus*: hollies; all varieties of *Rosa rugosa*, *Rosa Glauca*; skimmias.

Houseplants: *Cyclamen persicum* miniature cultivars; the mistletoe fig (*Ficus deltoidea diversifolia*).

WEED CONTROL

Weeds will stop growing when the weather gets colder and the tops of many weeds will die back, although their roots remain fully alive below ground. As you dig and plant ,remove all traces of roots, especially of weeds such as ground elder, couch grass and bindweed – all of which can grow from a tiny fragment of root.

LAWNS

Unless the weather is unseasonably warm, they will not need cutting. If you do mow, keep the blade on the highest setting. Avoid walking on grass in frosty weather. Collect any leaves that fall on the lawn.

Opposite: The delicate fronds of pampas grass (Cortaderia selloana) contrast with the rich autumn reds of dogwood (Cornus alba 'Westonbirt') and Sorbus commixta.

Below: The rich red berries are the best reason for growing cotoneaster.

JOBS

Essential
• Plant roses and deciduous shrubs, all deciduous hedges and trees, including fruit trees, all herbaceous plants and all climbers.
• Dig vegetable garden and new borders. Leave as rough clods.
• Protect all tender plants from frost by covering with straw, bracken or leaves. Wrap clay pots to stop them cracking in frost.

Desirable
• Divide herbaceous plants. Either use a spade and chop cleanly through them or put two forks back to back and gently lever the plant apart.
• Give the greenhouse a thorough clean early in the month.
• Plant tulips in the second half of the month.
• Collect all leaves as they fall and store to make leaf-mould.

Optional
• Sow broad beans for an early crop next spring.
• Cut back all herbaceous plants to the ground, removing all dead foliage.

HEDGES

Every garden must have hedges. They are probably the most important component in garden design – they divide the garden into people-sized spaces, they give us privacy, they are a backdrop against which flowers may look their best and, perhaps most important of all, they are the best possible shelter from the wind.

What is a hedge ? A row (not necessarily straight) of plants that grow into a permanent barrier and are maintained as a solid shape. A huge variety

If you have limy soil, beech is ideal for a formal hedge. The copper and green varieties can be mingled to good effect.

of plants can achieve this effect, from trees such as **beech**, **yew** and **holly** to shrubs such as **roses**, **lavender** or **gorse**.

Hedges fulfil both a practical and an aesthetic function. This second role is

frequently undervalued. A well-kept yew hedge gives any garden a sense of solidity and stature that nothing else can achieve, and if you analyse all the great gardens in Britain, you will see that the majority feature really good hedges – very often of yew.

CHOOSING A HEDGE

First you must decide what type of hedge you want. The table opposite gives a selection, with their attributes.

Whatever you do, never be tempted to plant a **Leyland cypress**. They are wholly unsuitable for English hedges, being vast trees and in fifty years' time will all be 30m (100ft) tall and still growing. They need constant cutting to make a tight hedge and there are always better alternatives. Planting evergreen hedges at this point in the year can be a bit dodgy. The leaves are constantly making demands on their root system and any kind of transplanting is a shock to it. If you do plant evergreens now, make sure they are protected from wind, and water them well in. In very dry weather give them a spray from the hose.

Yew is expensive, but worth every penny if you can afford it. A way of reducing the initial outlay is to buy small plants – no more than 45cm (18in) tall. These will 'take' much quicker than larger ones and will soon catch them up. The same is true of all hedge plants – 45–60cm (18–24in) high is plenty. Another common mistake is to buy too

many plants for the hedge. Yew will make an absolutely solid hedge if planted at 90cm (3ft) spacing. Each plant will receive more nutrients and grow bigger as a result. The common belief that yew is very slow-growing is untrue. It will average 15cm (6in) a year if properly looked after.

Hornbeam is a much underplanted hedge. It is as tough as old boots, does not mind an exposed site and positively relishes heavy, wet soils. It looks very similar to beech but has slightly serrated leaves.

Beech prefers a limy soil and is never happy on heavy clay. Both beech and hornbeam will keep their autumnal leaves until the early spring if not too exposed, thereby providing a more permanent visual barrier and a rich russet colour all winter. Both trees should be planted in a single row at 45cm (18) spacing.

Hawthorn is another tree that is too little used in gardens. This could be because we see it so much as a farm hedge, whereas it makes an excellent horticultural barrier. It is very cheap – if you order them by the hundred plants from a nursery, as little as 50p per plant – and will grow under most conditions. Clip it twice a year, in spring and late summer, for a very neat, dense hedge. And perhaps no other hedge produces such a beautiful new green leaf in spring.

Never plant **holly** behind or against a

Evergreen Hedges.

English Name	Latin Name	Growth	Features
Yew	*Taxus baccata*	Slow	The king of hedges. Only needs clipping once a year.
Box	*Buxus sempervirens*	Slow	Good for a low hedge.
Dwarf Box	*B.s. 'Suffruticosa'*	Very slow	Excellent for edging borders and paths.
Holly	*Ilex aquifolia*	Slow	Prickly. Berries. Good for tolerating dry shade.
Privet	*Ligustrum*	Fast	Needs clipping at least twice a year if it is not to be straggly.
	Lonicera nitida	Very fast	Needs frequent clipping (3 or 4 times a year) to keep it compact.
Cherry Laurel	*Prunus laurocerasus*	Fast	Very tolerant of shade. Dislikes shallow chalk.
Portuguese Laurel	*Prunus lusitanica*	Medium	Hardy, will grow on chalk. Except in deep shade, in every way better than cherry laurel.
Holm Oak.	*Quercus ilex*	Very slow	Very handsome, tough, rigid windbreak. Prefers sun.
Lavender	*Lavandula*	Medium	Makes low hedge. Needs sun and good drainage.
Leyland Cypress	*Cupressocyparis*	Very fast	Monstrous. Never plant.

Deciduous Hedges

English Name	Latin name	Growth	Features
Beech	*Fagus sylvatica*	Medium	Prefers light soils. Flourishes on chalk. Holds leaves over winter. Good for formal hedge.
Hornbeam	*Carpinus betulus*	Medium	Likes heavy soils. Holds winter leaves. Ideal substitute for beech on clay soil.
Hawthorn	*Crataegus monogyna*	Medium	Easy to grow. Prickly.
Rose	*Rosa rugosa*	Fast	A tough, loose hedge. Flowers.
Berberis	*Berberis thunbergii*	Medium	Prickly.
Hazel	*Corylus avellana*	Medium	Good in a mixed hedge.
Blackthorn	*Prunus spinosa*	Medium	Extremely vicious thorns.

border, as the fallen leaves stay prickly for ages and you will constantly be pricking yourself when weeding. But holly makes an excellent hedge and is particularly suitable for a dry, shaded spot.

Planting a Hedge

When planting a hedge, dig a trench at least 38cm (15in) deep and put in plenty of manure or compost. Do not be tempted to put your plants too close together – remember that you are planting trees and the more space they have for their roots the faster and bigger they will grow.

Caring for your Hedge

For evergreen hedges (yew, box, holly) trim the sides from the second year, but leave the leader (the tip) until it reaches its desired height.

Deciduous hedges (beech, hornbeam, hawthorn) must be cut back by a third after planting to encourage them to form bushy growth at the base. This process should be repeated in the second winter. Thereafter they can be trimmed to shape. If you do not do this you will have a hedge with holes along the bottom.

Most hedges that fail to grow do so through lack of water. A hedge planted before Christmas has a much greater chance of survival than one planted later, because its roots will be formed and ready to take up available water when the leaves start to grow. The best thing that you can do for a young hedge, especially during the first three years, is to make sure it is clear of weeds between the plants and for a distance of at least 30cm (1ft) on either side, and to mulch this weed-free area thickly with good compost. With that sort of treatment it will reward you by shooting up into a thick barrier that needs no more care than a trim every now and then.

PUTTING THE HERBACEOUS BORDER TO BED

The true herbaceous plant dies down completely in the winter, although the roots remain alive and healthy, throwing up new, non-woody growth in the spring. This is a device that the plant has evolved to protect itself in its natural habitat, which, in the main, has hot summers and cold winters. The dead growth from the summer acts as insulation against the cold, as well as rotting down to provide nourishment. Below the ground the plant goes into a dormant state until the winter is past; then it pokes its nose over the parapet, so to speak, and gets on with growing. Because its season is so short, the plant has to grow with tremendous vigour in order to flower and set seed before autumn – hence the dramatic transformation in the herbaceous border in the months from April to the end of June.

SPLITTING HERBACEOUS PLANTS

Because herbaceous plants steadily get bigger they need splitting from time to time. November is the best month to do this. Cut off the dying top of the plant. Then carefully dig the roots up, gently levering them out of the ground. Sit the plant on top of the soil and either chop the roots into two or three equal parts with a sharp spade or prise them apart by sticking two forks back to back through the middle of the roots and levering them apart. It sounds odd, but works very well. Plant the smaller sections carefully, giving each a handful of bonemeal. The new sections will grow with increased vigour. This is the best – and cheapest – way of increasing your stock of herbaceous plants.

You may have found that some plants grew too big too near the front of the border, hiding others behind them. Now is the time to move them.

These summer-flowering plants will have died back by November. If you want to split and move herbaceous plants, this is a good time to do it.

Dig a generous hole where you wish to reposition the plant first, and then carefully dig it up, leaving plenty of soil on its roots. Check for any weeds growing in the roots and carefully pull them out. This is the moment to divide them if you are going to do it at all. As long as you leave plenty of earth on the roots and replant them fairly quickly, the plants will come to no harm, and you can dramatically rearrange the border in this way.

CUTTING BACK – OR NOT

You may wish – as I do – to leave as much growth as possible uncut

You can also cut back any unwanted growth in the herbaceous border now, though I prefer to leave as much as possible uncut throughout the winter.

throughout the winter. There are a number of advantages in this. It creates some protection from cold and wind; it retains an impression of the maturity of the border which is only too easily forgotten the next spring as everything is growing; it provides seeds for the birds to feed on in the winter; and – most importantly – the dead vegetation can look exquisite when rimed by frost or snow. Phlomis, sedums, aster, grasses – all are beautiful skeletons on a clear midwinter's day. The disadvantage is that the border will look scruffy until it is tidied in spring. There is also the good point that there are not so many competing jobs at this time of year: if you do the cutting back now, it can be done slowly and carefully, whereas next March there will be a mass of garden tasks all crying out to be done at once.

If you do decide to get on and do the work now, choose a dry, mild day. Start by cutting off all the top growth and removing it. Then weed the border thoroughly by hand, followed by a gentle fork over between the plants so that they are surrounded by clean, fresh soil. Next lift and divide the plants you wish to move. Water them in. Finally put a layer of organic mulch over all bare soil, keeping it clear of the crowns of the plants so that they do not collect water and rot. At the end of this you will have a border that is neat and tidy and in the best possible shape to overwinter before bursting into life next spring.

DEALING WITH INVASIVE WEEDS

OCCASIONALLY A BORDER WILL GET BADLY INFESTED WITH COUCHGRASS, BINDWEED OR GROUND ELDER – ALL WEEDS THAT SPREAD FROM THE SMALLEST SECTION OF ROOT. THE ONLY WAY TO DEAL WITH THIS IS AS FOLLOWS:

1. REMOVE ALL THE PLANTS AND PLACE THEM IN CARDBOARD BOXES.
2. DIG THE ENTIRE BORDER WITH A FORK, PICKING OUT EVERY TINY PIECE OF ROOT. IT IS VITAL TO TAKE ENORMOUS CARE OVER THIS AS EACH SNIPPET OF BRITTLE ROOT IS A WEED-BOMB, WAITING TO EXPLODE NEXT SPRING.
3. KNOCK THE EXCESS SOIL OFF THE PLANTS, TAKE THEM TO A TAP (HENCE THE NEED FOR BOXES) AND WASH THE ROOTS. THIS WILL WASH OUT ANY TRACES OF WEED THAT HAVE BECOME ENTWINED AMONGST THE ROOTS OF THE PLANT.

4. REPLACE THE PLANTS – DIVIDED WHERE APPROPRIATE – INTO THE CLEAN EARTH.

THIS MAY SOUND A HORRENDOUS JOB, BUT IT CAN BE DONE A SECTION AT A TIME AND IS THE ONLY WAY TO DEAL WITH A WEED-INFESTED HERBACEOUS BORDER.

ORNAMENTAL GRASSES

November is a good time to plant many ornamental grasses. I have to confess that I have always had a bit of a blind spot about grasses – it is only in the past couple of years that I have started to appreciate them.

First of all, what is a grass? True grasses must have hollow, round stems with regular nodes. The blades of grass grow out from a sheath and the flowers are grown on spikes, panicles or racemes. This group includes bamboos but properly excludes sedges and reeds.

On the whole, ornamental grasses are best planted as individuals or as clumps in a mixed border, using their outline against planting that contrasts with it. Grasses that look good on their own are shown in the chart below.

LOOKING AFTER GRASSES

Most grasses prefer a sunny site, with good drainage and not too much in the way of nutrients. It is not a bad idea to mulch around the crown of grasses with a layer of grit. This will drain moisture away from the crown, which, when combined with frost, may well kill the plants, although the huge (3m/10ft) *Miscanthus sacchiflorus* likes a damp site to flourish properly.

Not all grasses are perennials. Delicate and pretty **pearl grass** (*Briza maxima*) is an annual, as is **old witch grass** (*Panicum capillare*), which is much tougher and coarser looking. Growing another annual grass, **squirreltail barley** (*Hordeum jubatum*) is like having a miniature barley field in a border with its swaying ripple of hanging heads. These all spread by seed and you have to be careful that they do not become invasive, although they are much easier to deal with than the ones that spread by underground runners. Simply dead-head them after flowering so that the seeds do not have a chance to develop.

The perennial grasses do not want to be dead-headed because the dead flower heads are an important part of their charm. As the grasses begin to wither, cut back with shears, leaving as much as still looks good. Do not be tempted to burn pampas grass, whatever you have read – nature does not mind losing the odd plant here and there in a fire, but you would be thoroughly miffed if the damage was too great. It is much better to wait until spring and cut the clump back as far as you can without attacking the visible new growth.

BAMBOOS

It is odd to think of bamboo as a woody form of grass, but that is exactly what it is, a grass wanting to become a tree. **Timber bamboos** (*Phyllostachys bambusoides*) can grow to a height of 12m (40ft) tall in just a few months and other types will reach over 20m (70ft). Unfortunately we are very restricted in

I remember being enthralled as a child by my father telling me how he had made a chair from bamboo in Borneo and the chair, all nailed and screwed into shape, then sprouted from legs, back and seat.'

Britain as to the bamboos that will grow successfully; some do well enough, although none will grow beyond about 8m (25ft) tall and they have very thin stems compared to their tropical cousins. The average fully hardy bamboo will stop at 3.5m (12ft), but nothing else provides such a dense and exotic screen.

English Name	Latin Name	Height	Description
Pampas Grass	*Cortaderia selloana*	1.5m (5ft)	Plume-like panicles.
Golden Oats	*Stipa gigantea*	2.5m (8ft)	Delicate, hanging golden anthers.
	Miscanthus sinensis	1.2m (4ft)	Herbaceous perennial grass.
	Molinia caerulea	2.5m (8ft)	Purple spikelets on stiff stems.
	Phalaris arundinaceae	1m (3ft)	Very vigorous creeping grass.
Blue Oat Grass	*Helictotrichon sempervirens*	Leaves 30cm (1ft), spikes 1m (3ft)	
Giant Reed	*Arundo donax*	2.5m (8ft)	Strong, variegated leaves.

The feathery panicles of pampas grass make a cheerful autumnal feature in a large garden.

Bamboos have an incredible ability to go on growing long after being cut down – it's a trait that the willow family shares. I remember being enthralled as a child by my father telling me how he had made a chair from bamboo in Borneo and the chair, all nailed and screwed into shape, then sprouted from legs, back and seat.

Any grass with running roots – that grow sideways underground and send up shoots in every direction – is a potential invasive hazard and bamboos are no exception. The common hardy bamboo or **metake** (*Arundinaria japonica*) spreads like anything, as does the shorter, broad-leafed *Sasa palmata* and the **hedge bamboo** (*Bambusa glaucescens*). There are two ways of dealing with this threat. The first is to mow regularly around the clump, cutting the new shoots as if they were a lawn. Where this is not practical, dig a trench right round the plant about 30cm (1ft) from its base, making sure

that the trench is deeper than the roots. Put a barrier such as concrete, thick polythene or sheet metal in the trench. This simply and permanently contains the roots as effectively as if they were in a pot. It is exactly the same principle as growing mint.

The dark purple stalks and green leaves of *Arundinaria nitida* will stay in a controlled clump, as will the similar but much more striking *Phyllostachys nigra*, which has ebony canes.

Bamboos like plenty of moisture at their roots but do not actually want to be standing in water. This makes them ideal for the edge of a (large) pond. One of the smaller bamboos and therefore more practical for most gardens is *Shibatea kumasasa*. It makes a modest clump about 1m (3ft) high and 30cm (1ft)

across. The **Chilean bamboo** (*Chusquea culeou*) can make a very dramatic clump but it is much slower growing than many, so does not rampage across a garden so much as creep up on it by stealth.

The real problem in choosing a bamboo is that there are so many – all with unpronounceable names – and so few garden centres that sell anything like a decent selection. You have to find specialist nurseries to discover the range of what is available, and there are few enough of these. The National Reference Collection of Bamboo is at Drysdale Nursery, Fordingbridge, Hants. If you live in the south-east there is the Bamboo Nursery, Wittersham, Tenterden, Kent and in East Anglia there is Fulbrooke Nursery, 43 Fulbrooke Road, Cambs., and P.W. Plants, Sunnyside Nurseries, Kenninghall, Norfolk. All these will supply a catalogue if you send an SAE.

One way of preventing bamboo from spreading too madly is to dig a trench round it and wrap a layer of thick polythene round the roots.

APPLES

Ever since Adam and Eve went scrumping, mankind has always valued apples above all other fruit. No other fruit comes in such variety. There are over 2,500 varieties of English apple. The average supermarket will sell no more than half a dozen at most. It is tragic that most people are unaware of the possible range.

All commercial apples are picked before they ripen, so that they will store better. The trouble is that most go into the shops, are bought and eaten before they ripen. Consequently they are nothing like as good as they can be. However, you can grow your own at home, enabling you to enjoy that rare thing, a truly ripe apple.

GROWING APPLES

There are two ways to grow apples in the garden, for two distinct purposes. The first is to produce apples as the main priority, and the second is to grow an apple tree, with the fruit a pleasant by-product.

Either way, apple trees, like all trees and shrubs, are best bought bare-rooted from a specialist grower. If you

. . . and Allington Pippin.

Three of the vast range of apples we are lucky enough to be able to grow in Britain: Norfolk Royal . . .

buy a potted tree from a garden centre, the chances are you will have a limited choice and I see no point in growing apples in the garden unless you grow an apple that is delicious and special: after all, a nasty apple takes just as much work and attention as a nice one!

When planting a bare-root tree it is vital *never* to let its roots dry out, even for five minutes. Keep the roots in a sack or covered with a damp cloth until the actual moment of planting. Mulch the surface of the hole with 2.5–5cm (1–2in) of compost or manure, but not right up against the trunk, as this may cause rot.

Do not put in too much manure, just a couple of handfuls of bonemeal in the soil before you plant and a couple of handfuls on the surface after the tree is in the ground. Feed apple trees too much nitrogen and they will develop leaves at the expense of fruit. Apples need potash if they are to do well.

Planting an apple tree can be done in an hour and will transform the rest of your life. That seems a fair return on effort. November and December are the ideal months for this task.

WHICH APPLE?

There are 'family' trees that have three or more types of apples which pollinate each other, grafted on to the same rootstock, but I feel that this is a bit of a gimmick. The best apples need another apple from the same group (or an adjacent one) to pollinate them. The groups are numbered 1 to 7, with Group 1 being the earliest to flower and Group 7 the last. Examples are given in the table opposite.

If apples are to cross-pollinate, the pollen must be carried by a bee from flower to flower, so the two trees must be flowering simultaneously.

Ideally pollination should come from trees within the same group, but if that is not possible, they must at least

. . . Cox's Orange Pippin. . .

be from adjacent groups.

As a rule of thumb any suitable apple tree within 18m (60ft) of another will pollinate it. So if there is not another apple tree in sight, always plant more than one in your own garden.

Some apples will set a crop without a pollinator – but not nearly so reliably. The following come into that category:

Beauty of Bath	Worcester
Emneth Early	Pearmain
Keswick Codlin	Chiver's Delight
Charles Ross	Ellison's Orange
Greensleeves	Lord Derby
James Grieve	Newton Wonder
Sunset	Crawley Beauty

POLLINATION TABLE

GROUP 1	GROUP 2	GROUP 3	GROUP 4	GROUP 5	GROUP 6	GROUP 7
Gravenstein	Adam's Pearmain	Blenheim Orange	Ashmead's Kernal	King of the	Bess Pool	Crawley Beauty
Stark's Earliest	Beauty of Bath	Bramley's	Cornish	Pippins	Court Pendu Plat	
	Egremont Russet	Seedling	Gilliflower	Merton Beauty	Edward VII	
	Laxton's Early	Charles Ross	Duke of	Newton Wonder		
	Crimson	Cox's Orange	Devonshire	Norfolk Royal		
	Lord Lambourne	Pippin	Gala	William Crump		
	Rev. Wilkes	Discovery	Golden Delicious			
	Ribston Pippin	Granny Smith	HBowgate			
		James Grieve	Wonder			
		Laxton's Epicure	Monarch			
		Merton	Tydeman's Late			
		Worcester	Orange			
		Tom Putt				
		Worcester				
		Pearmain				

Apples are grown to predetermined sizes that are exact in definition. So:

A **Standard** has a trunk of at least 2m (6ft 6in).

A **Half-standard** has a trunk of at least 1.5m (4ft 6in).

A **Bush** has a stem of 60 or 90cm (2 or 3ft).

A **Dwarf bush** has a stem of 45cm (18in) ft.

To achieve this degree of predictable growth the apple variety is grafted on to a rootstock, which is always a type of crab apple. This is categorised according to its vigour by a number with an 'M' prefix. Apples do not grow true from seed, and do not take readily from cuttings. So grafting is the easiest way to propagate them. By grafting the bud of a variety onto the rootstock of a tree with a measured vigour you can achieve the type of fruit you want on the size of tree you want. When the graft has taken, the crab apple above the graft is cut off to leave the apple tree growing on crab apple roots. Apples are universally grown this way.

The smaller the tree the sooner it fruits. This is a great incentive for most people. But no gardener nowadays grows an apple tree for the fruit alone. You grow apples to enjoy the appleness of the thing, for the blossom and the leaves, the colour and texture of the bark and the sense of an orchard in one's garden. The fact that the fruit might be small and a bit scabby doesn't seem to me to lessen any of this. In a small garden the apples from an apple tree are a welcome by-product, whereas the tree is the thing itself.

But the gardening books almost all exhort you against growing a standard or even half-standard apple (or pear) tree, declaring them unsuitable for most gardens because they are too big, have too much fruit, are difficult to spray, difficult to pick from and so on. Almost all fruit trees sold in garden centres are dwarf trees or bushes.

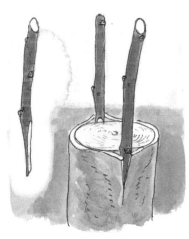

Grafting a known variety on to a crab apple is the most reliable way of propagating apples.

With the exception of a handful of good nurseries, it is almost impossible to get a standard apple tree.

The best way to grow a standard apple is to buy a 1st Maiden Whip on M25 rootstock. This sounds as though it might be an outer-London treat peculiar to Tory back-benchers, but translates as an un-pruned two-year-old tree, about 1.8m (6ft) tall. If the leader – the topmost upward-growing branch – is left unpruned and the lateral branches cut off until a sufficient trunk has established, a beautiful, large, sexy apple tree will grow itself. All you have to do is to plant it, watch it grow and be patient. Remember the old farming adage, 'Live as though you die tomorrow and farm as though you live for ever.'

BERRIES

One of the easiest ways to get colour into the winter garden is to have plants that produce colourful berries. Such plants have real importance to the gardener without much time to spare because they work twice as hard for you and give twice as much return on your invest... Oh God, I'm sounding like an accountant. Suffice to say that they are a Good Idea. Of course to get fruit – which is all a berry is – you must leave the flower to develop and for many gardeners that goes against the puritanical grain of tidiness as well as the more reasonable practice, of cutting back faded flower heads to stimulate more to follow. It is a pay-off between fewer, bedraggled flowers followed by berries or more flowers but no fruits in this season. Summer has plenty of flowers, but December needs all the colour it can get, so I plump for the berries every time.

ROSES FOR BERRIES

The most obvious candidates for this harvest of neglect are **roses**.

Not all roses produce hips (a berry by another name), but most do, and some almost more spectacularly than the flowers that form them. In the main the species roses are more prolific and interesting hip-bearers than hybrid roses. Not the least of these is the **dog rose** (*R. canina*). Amongst the richest source of Vitamin C there is, the hedgerow rose is strikingly dotted with hips until they are eaten by the birds.

Some roses are worth growing for their hips alone, but the Weekend Gardener will want to get double value from his plants, so enjoy the flowers first, leave them to form fruits and then relish the hips.

The table below gives a small selection of roses worth planting now for their hips next winter.

OTHER BERRY PLANTS

Hips have an unbreakable link for me with haws, the fruit of the **hawthorn** (*Crataegus*). Town-dwellers miss the beauty of haws, but I love them, turning a dark red as they ripen and become irresistibly delicious to birds. Of course a hedge that is neatly trimmed before it can flower will pay for its crispness both in flower and fruit.

Hips and haws framed against bare twigs or yellowing leaves are part of the pleasant melancholy of the season, but the bright red of a berry against an evergreen leaf is a laugh in the teeth of the encroaching gloom.

Like holly, **Skimmia japonica** is a red berry/green leaf number that needs male and female plants to bear fruit (with the exception of the subspecies *reevesiana*). Unlike holly, it needs rich, moist soil and a bit of shade to perform well. The leaves are smooth and aromatic.

I have to admit that until recently I have had a problem with **pyracantha** and **cotoneaster**, regarding them as uninspired and dreary. I have now seen the light. I like pyracantha's common name, firethorn, as it perfectly describes the way the berries blaze out from the unexceptional matt leaves. I feel that with pyracantha one should be as brash as possible, and although no

Viburnum betulifolium has clusters of lush red berries from late autumn.

variety is particularly coy, 'Orange Glow' is as brash as they come.

Cotoneaster is slightly more subtle and slightly less dramatic, but still jolly. There are far too many different cotoneasters to get to grips with unless you have a particular bent that way: suffice to say that there is a species for every part of every garden. Although most are completely unfussy about where you put them as long as it is not boggy, it is usual to use their adaptability for a very dry spot. I like *C. microphyllus* because the berries are as big as the leaves, and the **fishbone cotoneaster** (*C. horizontalis*) because it is

SOME GOOD 'BERRY' ROSES

NAME	HIPS
R. californica	Small red jewels.
R. moyessii	Orange-red flagons.
R. moyessii 'Geranium'	Fatter, orange flagons.
R. pimpinefolia (Burnet Rose)	Chocolate brown.
R. rugosa 'Alba'	Large, round, tomato-red fruit.
R. sericea	Bright red, slightly pear-shaped.
R. macrophylla	Large orange fruits like bristly pears.
R. villosa	Prickly, like a red gooseberry.
R. filipes 'Kiftsgate'	Masses of small clusters.
R. 'Rambling Rector'	As 'Kiftsgate'.
R. glauca	Tight clusters of round orange berries.

This striking contrast of berries and foliage is provided by Sorbus 'Joseph Rock'.

neat and can be tucked under a window; it loses its leaves in winter, leaving the red berries to take centre stage.

The oddest of berries out now are those of **Callicarpa bodinieri giraldii**, which have an almost metallic sheen to their purple shanks. This plant looks better on its own in a pot; it can then be exhibited at berry time but stashed away out of the limelight for the rest of the year.

Euonymus likes chalk, but will grow anywhere and the distinctive heart-shaped berries are part of a much older England. The **spindle** (*Euonymus europaeus*) is found growing naturally, but only in hedges and woods that are at least a hundred years old, and is often an indicator for semi-natural ancient woodland.

A tip: do not grow a spindle near your vegetables: it is irresistible to aphids and they use the spindle as a launching pad to strip your veg.

The **purple-leafed barberry** (*Berberis thunbergii atropurpurea*) is an excellent border plant in summer because of the depth and contrast that its purple leaves give to surrounding colours, but in autumn it is decorated with red berries which are rather more striking than the small yellow flowers that made them in spring. It is a really good example of choosing a plant that will work hard for you without you having to do any work for it.

The **viburnums** as a group are superb winter value in every respect and the **guelder rose** (*Viburnum opulus*) can have appropriately opulent clusters of berries. I have mentioned the yellow version 'Xanthocarpum' (see box), but the red version with its great bunches of translucent berries is more usual. *V. tinus* has midnight-blue berries against its evergreen leaves, making an intensely rich, if sombre, combination.

Just stretching this far into autumn (before the birds gobble them all up) are the exuberant berries of the **mountain ash** (*Sorbus*). The **whitebeam** (*S. aria*) is found all along urban streets, but is a worthy garden tree. The **American mountain ash** (*S. americana*) has the leaflets that one associates with this genus, and red fruits that are gathered for herbal remedies. The **rowan** (*S. aucuparia*) was planted in the Scottish Highlands as a protection against witchcraft. The berries taste good when made into a jelly, and do you good as well, because they have a high Vitamin C content.

A YELLOW CORNER

YOU COULD HAVE A YELLOW BERRY CORNER, WITH *COTONEASTER* 'ROTHSCHILDIANUS'; *PYRACANTHA ROGERSIANA* 'FLAVA'; THE YELLOW SPINDLE, *EUONYMUS MYRIANTHUS*; THE YELLOW GUELDER ROSE, *VIBURNUM OPULUS* 'XANTHOCARPUM'; AND THE HOLLY *ILEX AQUIFOLIUM* 'BACCIFLAVA', WHICH HAS MASSES OF YELLOW FRUITS LIKE TINY LEMONS.

WINTER WILDLIFE

As winter draws in, the going gets tough for all animal life in the garden. As the food supplies diminish, so the need for food to survive the cold increases. But there is much that you can do to help wildlife over the winter and it will repay this many times in spring by controlling the pests that plague every garden, as well as giving you much pleasure.

BIRDS

Birds are the most visible wildlife in any garden, and as the leaves fall they become even more apparent. Winter is the best time for bird watching in the garden, as they become more ardent in their hunt for food. Obviously the first thing you can do is to feed them. But if you do this you are making a winter-long commitment. This is because a bird uses a great deal of precious energy looking for food. If you start to put food out they will travel from quite a distance each day to your garden to eat there. If they turn up to find there is nothing there, they will have wasted reserves that they might not be able to replace. So **spasmodic food supplies can actually do more harm than good**, especially in very cold weather.

If you do decide to feed the birds, **give a good cross-section of food**,

Put the bird table out of reach of cats, and surround it with chicken wire to keep larger birds out.

making it strong on high-energy food such as nuts, fats, including butter, cheese and bacon rind, seeds and bread. A 'cake' can be made in an old yoghurt pot by half filling it with mixed seed and pouring melted lard over it. Let it cool and set hard before breaking open the casing.

Provide the right place for different birds to feed. Tits will need nuts suspended in a bag or wire container so that they can hold to the side

An upturned dustbin lid makes a functional bird-bath.

whilst pecking through the holes. Wrens will want food at ground level, put under bushes out of the way of dogs and cats. Treecreepers and nuthatches like nuts wedged into the bark of trees. A bird-table is obviously

a good idea, both to stop mammals nicking the food that you put out for the birds and to protect the birds as they eat. Get or make one with a sloping roof to keep the food dry and fit some 1cm (1/2in) chicken wire around the outside. This will be large enough to let the small birds in but will keep starlings, pigeons and cats out.

Do not worry if the odd sparrow-hawk appears and lunches off one of the small birds you are feeding. Feel privileged to witness it and accept that nature is red in tooth and claw.

Birds must have water, so provide a shallow dish with fresh water every day, or a permanent bird-bath. A dustbin lid supported by bricks works very well. If the weather is very cold a night-light underneath a metal dustbin lid will stop it from freezing over.

You can take a longer term position for the birds by **planting specifically for them**. Now is the best time of year to be planting any deciduous trees and shrubs and perennial plants.

The food chain is complicated, so it is important to provide not just berries but an environment for insects such as hoverflies, butterflies and bees on which the birds can then feed. Single-flowered non-hybrid plants will provide the best source of this.

Even if you do not plant with birds in mind at all, any well-stocked garden will have much food for birds. You can help them greatly by not cutting down any herbaceous plants until spring. The seed heads provide nourishment and can look very good, especially when rimed with frost.

MAMMALS

The simplest thing that you can do to encourage mammalian life in the garden is to **leave cover for them**. This means not doing your winter tidying until spring, leaving piles of leaves, wood and unpruned shrubby undergrowth so that they will feel protected and to increase the likely food sources for them. The rule of thumb is that if you look after the bottom of the food chain the top will help itself to it. So if you provide ideal conditions and food for invertebrates, then vertebrates will

A bag of nuts suspended from a convenient branch or hanging-basket bracket will keep the bluetits happy through the winter.

NECTAR SOURCES FOR INSECTS

Applemint *Mentha x rotundifolia*
Aubrieta
Blackthorn *Prunus spinosa*
Bramble *Rubus fruticosa*
Butterfly Bush *Buddleia davidii*
Devil's Bit Scabious *Succisa pratensis*
Fleabane *Pulicaria dysenterica*
Goldenrod *Solidago*
Greater Knapweed *Centaurea scabiosa*
Veronica *Hebe*
Honeysuckle *Lonicera*
Hyssop *Hyssop officinalis*
Lavender *Lavandula*
Marigolds *Tagetes*
Marjoram *Origanum vulgare*
Michaelmas Daisy *Aster*
Thyme *Thymus drucei*
Tobacco Plant *Nicotiana*

PLANTS WITH BERRIES AND SEEDS FOR BIRDS

Bird Cherry *Prunus padus*
Bramble *Rubus fruticosa*
Cotoneaster *Cotoneaster*
Crab Apple *Malus sylvestris*
Dog Rose *Rosa canina*
Elder *Sambucus nigra*
Guelder Rose *Viburnum opulus*
Hawthorn *Crataegus monogyna*
Hogweed *Heracleum sphondylium*
Holly *Ilex aquifolium*
Ivy *Hedera helix*
Plantains *Plantago*
Privet *Ligustrum vulgare*
Firethorn *Pyracantha*
Rowan *Sorbus*
Spindle *Euonymus europaeus*
Stinging Nettle *Urtica dioica*
Sunflower *Helianthus annuus*
Teasel *Dipsacus sylvestris*
Thistles *Carduus*

turn up to eat them. Some of these foods will be there in all-too present numbers, like slugs, snails, woodlice and earwigs. Others, such as worms will establish as a result of good horticultural practice.

The mammals that you are likely to get in all but the most urban of gardens include hedgehogs, voles, moles, wood mice, field mice, badgers, foxes and rats. It follows that you should keep the use of pesticides and other chemicals to an absolute minimum and that your own domestic animals will restrict the number of visitors. A cat is about the greatest destroyer of garden wildlife that there is.

PONDS

Now is not the best time to be making a pond, but if you already have one it is a vital focus of wildlife in your garden. As with the rest of the garden, **do not be too tidy round the pond over winter**. Leave hiding places for toads and frogs to sleep, such as in piles of leaves or clumps of dead herbage, and under stones. However, it is important to keep the water clear of leaves.

If you have fish, they will not need feeding over winter, but they must have oxygen. If the pond is deep enough it is unlikely to freeze solid, but the top can stay frozen for days, limiting the supply of oxygen. Do *not* break the ice by hitting it — the shock waves can kill the fish — but place a hot pan of water on the surface; this will gently thaw a hole.

DECEMBER

WEATHER REPORT: the strange thing about December is that much of it is often quite mild, despite the image on a million Christmas cards. This mildness often makes the grass grow and plants break into bud or even flower. However, it is invariably followed by the harsher realities of winter in the New Year, so do not be lulled into a false spring. Use the mildness to continue planting, trying to get all deciduous and herbaceous plants in by Christmas if possible, but refrain from cutting the grass and batten down all the horticultural hatches for the storm that is sure to come.

PLANTS IN THEIR PRIME

Bulbs: Some snowdrops (*Galanthus plicatus byzantinus, G. nivalis*): *Crocus laevigatus*; *Cyclamen coum*; *Sternbergia lutea*.

Hardy Plants: *Helleborus niger*; *Iris unguicularis*; winter pansies.

Shrubs: *Hamamelis mollis*; *Fatsia japonica*; *Mahonia lomariifolia*; *Viburnam bodnantense, V. farreri, V. grandiflorum, V. tinus*.

Trees: hollies (*Ilex*); strawberry tree (*Arbutus unedo*); rosebud cherry (*Prunus subhirtella* 'Autumnalis'); all conifers.

Climbers: winter jasmine (*Jasminum nudiflorum*).

Vegetables: Brussels sprouts; cabbage; carrots; celery; lambs lettuce; leeks; parsnips; winter purslane.

Houseplants: keep away from frosty windows but expose to as much light as possible. Cease feeding and water sparingly.

WEED CONTROL

Remove and burn roots carefully as you dig.

LAWNS

Lawns look as scruffy as they ever do in December. Keep off them as much as possible.

Opposite: The red stems of dogwood (Cornus alba 'Westonbirt') peek through the snow.

Below: Ornamental grasses at Wisley retain their delicate shapes in the frost.

JOBS

Essential
• Firm down plants lifted by frost, treading them carefully back into the ground. If there is snow, clear it from the branches of all evergreens.
• Continue planting in suitable weather.
• Continue digging vegetable garden or new borders.

Desirable
• Burn any of the woody, uncompostable material cleared from your borders and trees. Also burn any diseased leaves or plants.
• If you buy plants in conditions that are not suitable for planting or you do not have time, heel them into a clean piece of ground or store them somewhere sunny but sheltered.
• Start pruning apples
• Check ties on all climbers and make properly secure so that they are not damaged by high winds.

Optional
• Make paths and build walls and steps.
• Sort out tools and get mowers serviced and repaired.

BARK

Just as some plants are worth growing for their berries, so some trees and shrubs are worth a place in the garden for the beauty of their bark alone. This is the time of year when their value is most potent, as their colour and texture can play a major role in giving the garden life when all else around them is dank and drab. Many barks also look better for being wet and shine out from a grey background – which is handy in England in December. This is also the time of year when deciduous trees are best planted, so a couple of hours spent planting a few trees whose bark is decorative is barking up the right tree. (I'm sorry).

The best known bark tree is the **Tibetan cherry** (*Prunus serrula*), which has irregular horizontal scars striping the most gleaming, rich, mahogany reddy-brown bark.

Birch trees have perhaps the most varied and spectacular bark. The **silver birch** (*Betula pendula*) grows on poor land, seeding itself prolifically, establishing particularly well after fire. The white bark of its youth becomes marked with black inverted triangles, but it is still a strikingly beautiful tree.

A true white bark belongs to the **west Himalayan birch** (*B. utilis* var. *jaquemontii*), which looks at its best by winter moonlight, ghostly glowing. Like all birches it is constantly renewing its outer layers of bark. The birch that does this most spectacularly is the **paper birch** (*B. papyrifera*), whose bark hangs off in delicious cream rolls like shot silk. This is the bark that Native Americans used to use as paper and to make the hulls of their canoes.

Birches with white trunks are best planted in small groups, however limited your space – this accentuates their whiteness against a dark background. Birch is best planted to the north of the house, if you have that choice, because not only will it gain the sunlight shining directly on it, but also the moss that often hides the bark always grows on the north side (in the shade), which will then be out of immediate view.

To a greater or lesser extent, the leaves of all **maples** provide good autumn colour, but some score highly on the bark stakes too. The **paper bark maple (***Acer griseum***)** is quite like a

*The classic 'bark' tree – the Tibetan cherry (*Prunus serrula*).*

birch in the way that its bark peels. It is a small tree, and the bark comes away in rich brown rags. Even the twigs peel, so that the whole tree is like a gorgeously eccentric russet dress. An American maple, *A. pensylvanicum* or 'Moosewood', has a bark striped vertically. Young stems are a jade green striped with white. *A. davidii* has similar stripes, but of a darker, more intense coloration.

If you live on very acidic soil you will be able to grow **rhododendrons**, and *R. barbatum* is another of the peeling bark clan, this time with a greyish bark. It also has whopping great red flowers between April and June.

The **Japanese stewartia** (*Stewartia pseudocamellia*) is a member of the tea family, and has flowers like camellias in summer, with good autumn colouring too. Last but not least of its virtues is a rich brown bark that peels to reveal a new pale ochre skin, which in time will darken and peel again.

For those of you that have large gardens, I urge you to plant a **London plane** (*Platanus* x *acerifolia*), for the beauty of the peeling bark alone. Londoners have become blasé about these beautiful trees, but they are really special and will take any amount of lopping and pruning to make them fit within the confines of a garden.

A rarer bark-peeler is the **Persian ironwood** (*Parrotia persica*, named after a Mr Parrot, who was the first man – after Noah – to climb Mount Arafat). This can be more like a shrub than a tree, growing as far horizontally as it does vertically, from a number of stems, although it will grow to a height of 12m (40ft). It has bright red leaves in autumn and its smooth grey bark peels off in patches to expose a pale green underskin. This does very well on chalky (alkaline) soils.

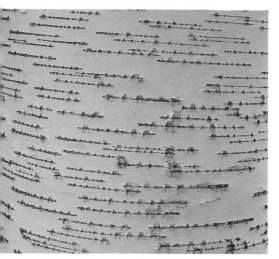

A variety of barks — the paper birch (Betula papyrifera) . . .

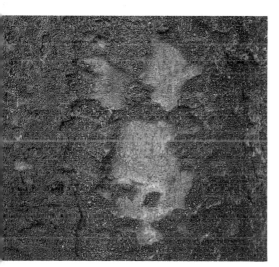

. . . *the strange, blotchy pattern of* Zelkova serrata . . .

The **pines** all have ruggedly handsome bark, but the best is the **Corsican pine** (*Pinus nigra* var. *maritima*). The deep fissures lacing the trunk are pitch black and the raised bark shades of ochre, pink and grey, giving a wonderful balance of delicate colour and rugged texture. It grows very well on sandy soils, and makes a very good windbreak.

The **stone pine** (*Pinus pinea*) tends to be associated with the Mediterranean, but it will grow in northern gardens. Its bark is less delicate than that of the Corsican pine, but has great character and it is an excellent tree.

SHRUBS FOR BARK

I have concentrated on the bark of trees, but there are shrubs whose bark shouts out from the garden once the leaves have all fallen. The first of these is the **Westonbirt dogwood** (*Cornus alba* 'Sibirica'). This has brilliant crimson stems which maintain their intensity until dressed with leaves in spring. It will grow with equal ease on dry or wet soil.

C. alba 'Kesselringii' has very dramatic — one might say melodramatic — purple-black stems. If you have more space, *C. amomum* is a more vigorous shrub and has purple shoots. Both are striking but perhaps not quite as cheery as Westonbirt dogwood.

COPPICING

The secret of *Cornus* is to coppice it every other March. This means pruning the entire shrub hard — right to the base of each shoot — so that it has to start again. This it does, with renewed vigour each time, and the new growth, one and two years old, has a much brighter colour than older stems.

Willows respond well to coppicing, also throwing up brightly coloured shoots. *Salix alba* var. *vitellina* is perhaps the best, with bright orange-yellow shoots. *S. a.* 'Chermesina' has red shoots, and the bloom-covered shoots of *S. daphnoides* reveal purple stems when rubbed. The **golden weeping willow** (*S.* 'Chrysocoma') has a magnificent curtain of yellow-green branches, especially in late winter.

Willows need a fair amount of wet to get the best out of them, but they will grow in ordinary garden soil. In fact it is almost impossible to stop any cutting from any willow growing into a tree if it is merely pushed idly into the ground. Hammer a 1.8m (6ft) willow branch into the ground in the New Year and it will be in leaf by summer as a tree.

There are two **ornamental brambles**, *Rubus biflorus* and *R. thibetanus*, whose shoots are green but covered in a white, waxy bloom. *R. biflorus* has the brighter white, but *R. thibetanus* has purplish stems which show smudgingly through their white make-up. They look startlingly vivid in winter, except in snow, when you can't see them. Like *Cornus*, they need coppicing to get the brightest winter colour and you do this immediately after they have finished flowering.

. . . *and the flaky paperbark maple (*Acer griseum*).*

MAZES, KNOTS AND PARTERRES

It may seem strange to include the rather esoteric world of mazes, knots and parterres in a book like this, but there is nothing remotely difficult about them and they are ideal in a small garden, particularly in winter.

What are they?

MAZES

These can be as simple or as complex as you will, but on the whole a very simple maze will provide plenty of diversion.

A maze can be made out of more or less any material – it has come to be synonymous with hedging, but it can be made of stones laid on the ground or even just cut into grass. Mazes are very ancient things, loaded with all kinds of symbolism, but the important point to remember with a garden maze is that it is primarily a visual element of the garden. So it does not matter at all if you can see every twist and turn or if these are severely limited.

KNOT GARDENS

Knots became a common feature of gardens in the sixteenth century. The English Renaissance loved the intricacy and harmony of knots and used them everywhere, in plasterwork and embroidery as well as gardens. In simple terms they are interwoven, symmetric geometric patterns. The 'lines' are 'drawn' with appropriate plants, and the spaces between them filled with gravel, bark or sand.

There is no need to develop a historical fetish about knots – although like any fetish, that can be fun. But all you really need to know is that they can make a fascinating, stylish and practically maintenance-free addition to the garden.

PARTERRE

Just as knots belong historically to the sixteenth century, so parterres were at their peak in the seventeenth. They were developed to their fullest grandeur in baroque gardens like Versailles in France and Het Loo in Holland, where vast areas

Symmetry is the key to the knot garden, with the 'lines' drawn with appropriate plants.

were ornamented with scrolls of low hedges, often in box, punctuated by yew, cypress, holly or box trees, which were always clipped, often into elaborate topiary designs. The best place to see an original parterre in Britain is at Levens Hall in Cumbria, with its fantastical topiary.

To make these historical elements of garden design practical to the Weekend Gardener, we must draw on the essence of them and apply that to our limited space and even more limited time.

The important thing to remember about these three elements is that they are all designed to be viewed from above and from the comfort of the house – so they are ideal for our English winter and especially for a house that has a living room looking down on to the garden.

A SIMPLE MAZE

The essential principle of a maze is that your path ahead is blocked, forcing you to make a turning. You do not need a labyrinthine layout to use that principle in the garden.

If you are planning on a large scale, yew is ideal. (Do not be tempted to use

An Elizabethan knot garden at Cranborne Manor, Dorset. Note the variety of geometrical shapes.

A typical parterre, with scrolls of low hedges arranged symmetrically around an elegant focal point.

Leyland or Lawson's cypress. It will be cheaper and will grow faster but will look horrible and be twice as much work to upkeep.) You could use a deciduous plant like hornbeam, beech or even   and this would be very economical – hawthorn. But that slightly misses the point of a maze, which is to create a solid series of barriers, and only evergreen plants will achieve that in winter.

The barriers want to be solid, but only blocking your way, not the eye line. So keep the hedges low – no more than 90cm (3ft) high. Even though they are low, do not be tempted to plant too close together. Follow the basic guideline given on pages 160–161 for the planting of hedges.

If you were prepared to experiment more it might be extremely interesting to make the barriers from stone – dry stone walls could look good in this context. Whatever you use, it must have a really solid appearance in winter.

The maze then provides visual appeal, shelter for plants and a series of enclosed spaces to give you variety in the garden. Like all hedges, it will need clipping, but if you use yew or box, this will only need to be done once a year.

A Knot in your Garden

Elizabethan knots were enormously complex with designs as elaborate as those shown opposite. Whilst that degree of entanglement is not necessary to get the effect of a knot, it is important to make it look well and truly knotted.

Whatever design you choose – and half the fun is in the choosing – use the following method to get it from paper to garden.

1. Choose a flat piece of ground near the house. This may be as small as a metre (yard) square or as large as an average back garden. It is easiest to make a knot in a square. Dig this over and weed it thoroughly, taking every care to pick out weeds like couchgrass, bindweed or ground elder, as once the knot is planted it will be almost impossible to get these out. Make sure that it is absolutely level.

2. Mark the centre point of each side with a cane.

3. Establish the centre of the square by stretching string from corner to corner. Where the two diagonals cross will be the centre. Mark this with a cane.

4. Mark the lines on to the soil with sand. The best way to do this is to cut the bottom off a large washing up liquid bottle and fill it with dry sand. Tape a temporary piece of card over the bottom and take the lid off the top. This will act as a sand-pen.

You now have all the measurements that you need to create the design.

Do not try to be overelaborate. Keep to a simple pattern with interlacing lines. The one unbreakable rule is that it must be symmetrical. Use the markers either as the corners of squares or the centre of circles.

Plant the lines with box, rosemary, thyme, lavender, santolina and germander. The box should be dwarf box (*Buxus suffruticosa*) for the lines unless your knot is very large, and *Buxus sempervirens* for marking the corners or interces with other lines. You can use different types of the same plant to achieve your effect – for instance golden thyme and ordinary thyme or silver-leafed box and the dark green leaves of *Buxus suffruticosa*.

Once you have planted the intertwining mini-hedges, you can either use the spaces for herbs or annuals, or simply mulch the ground with a thick layer of gravel or bark. This will suppress the weeds and will not stop you from planting there at a later date if you wish.

Designing a Parterre

In a way any organisation of beds with flowers is a parterre, although originally it referred to a separate piece of enclosed garden with ornate designs of hedges uninterrupted by tall plants. The difference between a parterre and a knot is that the design of a parterre does not intertwine, and the scrolls make it flow, inviting movement rather than contemplation. But the means of preparing them are identical. A parterre lends itself to a larger space and can successfully be broken with rather larger uprights than a knot. The illustration at the top of this page gives one possible design.

TIP

The great advantages of mazes, knots and parterres are that they take effect from the moment that they are planted, they look good in every season and they take very little effort to keep them looking at their best.

GARLIC THE WONDERPLANT

Garlic was first cultivated in the mountainous region between Afghanistan and Mongolia, where it is still found growing wild, but probably as an escapee from cultivation.

The ancient Egyptians loved garlic, so much that the first recorded strike in history was settled only when the 300,000 slaves building the Great Pyramid of Cheops were granted an increase in their daily ration of garlic.

Garlic immediately evokes the baked heat of the Mediterranean, so it might seem odd to be dealing with it in the middle of winter, but now is the time to plant your garlic for next summer.

GROWING AND HARVESTING

Garlic (*Allium sativum*) needs a long growing season to mature and a couple of months of cold weather to instigate the correct growing pattern. Traditionally it is planted on the shortest day, 21 December, and harvested after the longest, 24 June.

Whenever you plant it, garlic matures in July, so the earlier it is planted the more likely you are to get plump bulbs. You can plant as early as November in the warm south of England and certainly no later than March in the north.

You can use normal, shop-bought garlic for the seed, breaking the individual cloves from the parent bulb and planting them at 12.5cm (5in) intervals in rows 30cm

(1ft) apart. The cloves must be pushed into the ground, pointed end up, so that the tip is just below with the surface.

Choose the sunniest site in the garden. The soil needs to be well drained and rich, so plant on a piece of ground that is well dug and manured. If you have very heavy soil it is a good idea to mix in a generous amount of sharp sand or horticultural grit before planting to aid drainage. And that is it. Keep the growing plants free of weeds and let the garlic get on with it on its own.

When it is ripe the tops of the leaves first turn yellow and then shrivel

Hang garlic bulbs somewhere dry and they will keep all winter.

right up. At this point you carefully lift the bulbs with a fork, shaking all dirt from the roots, and let them dry for a few days on the ground. Then gather them by the dead tops and hang them somewhere dry – indoors or out. They must be completely dried if they are to keep all winter and not go mouldy. Keep the fattest bulbs to start next year's crop.

If the plant fails to make a multi-cloved head, keep the large single bulbs and use them for next year's crop – they will invariably make a large head.

Fresh garlic is incomparably good to eat, improving almost all meats and vegetables by its presence. The difference between a clove a month or so old harvested from one's garden and a dried-up piece that has been around for months is huge. Garlic is also a medicinal miracle, known to have antiseptic properties; it aids digestion and is perhaps the best antidote to respiratory infections.

STORING

Although garlic is best stored in a string bag somewhere cool, you can also make a braid and hang it in the kitchen. This is not difficult – you use the same technique as you would for making a string of onions.

1. Cut the hairy roots off the bottom of each head of garlic, but leave the dried top attached.

2. Take a piece of rope as long as you want the final braid (about 60cm/2ft) and, laying the dried top of the garlic against the rope, tie it to the rope with thin string.

3. Work from the bottom up, turning the rope so that you work right around it. As you tie more heads of garlic on to the rope, they will hide the stalks of the ones below them.

4. When the rope is covered or you run out of garlic, tie the top off so that it is neat and attach a loop of string to hang it from.

THE REST OF THE FAMILY

Garlic is a close cousin of onions, leeks, chives and shallots.

Onions are grown from seed or from 'sets'. When grown from seed there are two ways to raise them. The first is to sow them in trays or a seedbed and transplant them into their final position about 10cm (4in) apart when they are the thickness of a drinking straw. The second is to sow the seeds in their final position and thin the seedlings twice, firstly to spacings of 2.5cm (1in) and then of 10cm (4in). The advantage of the first method is that you can select the healthiest plants

and nurture them more carefully, but the second method is less trouble and does not disturb the growing plants, providing a quicker maturing crop.

'Sets' are bulbs specially grown for planting and are ideal for conditions that are not particularly conducive to onion cultivation or where pests are a problem. Do not be tempted to pick out the largest bulbs: smaller sets are less likely to bolt (that is run to seed). Push the sets into the ground in March. Birds have a habit of pulling them up (but not eating them) before the roots have had a chance to establish – but they can be replanted without coming to any harm.

Shallots are like a bunch of small onions – almost like the cloves of a head of garlic, in fact. They are used whole and are ideal for stews.

Leeks are harvested over winter and will withstand almost anything the weather throws at them, although the varieties with blue or purplish-green leaves are hardiest. Leeks differ from garlic, onions and shallots in that they are grown from seed and transplanted when about the thickness of a pencil into holes 'dibbed' for them.

Chives are perennials (and plural: there is no

singular 'chive'), dying down each winter and growing back in spring. You eat the hollow, slender leaves, which will regrow indefinitely when cut. Unlike garlic, chives like cool, damp sites.

Chinese chives have flat leaves and are used like normal chives. They are grown from seed and mature fast. Like chives, the leaves die down in winter.

GARLIC THE GOOD COMPANION

A CLOVE OF GARLIC PLANTED BY THE BASE OF A ROSE BUSH WILL GUARANTEE FREEDOM FROM GREENFLY. IT ACTS AS AN ORGANIC SYSTEMIC INSECTICIDE, THE ROSE TAKING UP THE QUALITIES FROM THE GARLIC VIA ITS ROOTS AND ABSORBING THEM WITHIN ITS OWN SYSTEM. TRY IT. IT WORKS!

CHRISTMAS DECORATION

You do not need to buy dried Christmas decorations specially. The garden has its own supply that can be plundered. Here is a list of potential dried flowers.

PERENNIAL PLANTS FOR DRYING
Acanthus spinosus
Achillea (Yarrow)
Alchemilla mollis (Ladies' Mantle)
Allium (Onion flower heads)
Anaphalis margaritacea (Daisy)
Artichoke
Aruncus dioicus
Astilbe (Goatsbeard)
Catananche
Cynara
Dahlia
Echinops bannaticus; E. ritro (Globe Thistle)
Eryngium (Sea Holly)
Gypsophilia paniculata (Baby's Breath)
Hydrangea
Lavandula (Lavender)
Phlomis russeliana
Physalis alkekengi (Chinese lantern)
Rodgersia
Roses
Sedum spectabile; S. telephium
Solidago (Goldenrod)

CUTTING FLOWERS FOR DRYING

Flowers that you intend to dry should be cut at the right moment. Unlike cut flowers that you place in water, they will not develop after picking, so they should be cut at the peak of flowering. If you leave them too late, they will drop petals or seeds as they dry. This is a tricky business — only a combination of common sense and trial and error will get it right — but forewarned is forearmed.

METHODS OF DRYING

The easiest method of drying flowers is to hang them upside down in bunches and let the water drain and evaporate from them. Water will pass from cell to cell until it reaches the atmosphere outside. When the atmosphere and the plant reach a balance of humidity, the plant has dried as much as it can in that atmosphere. It follows that the drying flowers must be hung in as dry a place

ANNUALS PLANTS FOR DRYING
Ageratum
Amaranthus caudatus (Love-Lies-Bleeding)
Anethum graveolens (Dill)
Avena sterilis
Briza maxima; B. minor
Calendula (Common Marigold)
Celosia
Centaurea cyanus (Cornflower)
Clarkia
Consolida ambigua
Delphinium ajacis (Larkspur)
Gomphrena globosa (Globe Amaranth)
Helichrysum (Strawflower)
Helipterum
Hordeum jubatum
Lagurus ovatus
Limonium sinuatum (Statice)
Lunaria annua (Honesty)
Lonas
Moluccella laevis (Bells of Ireland)
Nicandra physalodes (Shoo-Fly Plant)
Nigella damascena (Love-in-a-Mist)
Papaver (Poppy)
Xeranthemum annuum (Everlasting Flower)

as possible. If you hang them somewhere moist, fungus and infection will get in and the flowers will rot rather than dry.

An airing cupboard is good, as is a rack above a boiler or cooker, but ideally ventilation is needed. If you are drying flowers, remember that you must keep them out of the light, otherwise they will bleach.

POT-POURRI

By drying and keeping just the petals of scented flowers, you can make your own pot-pourris. These are a direct spin-off from the herbs strewn across medieval floors to keep unpleasant smells and disease at bay.

You need to start collecting flowers and herbs for this in the spring. Always gather flowers in the morning, before the sun has evaporated any moisture off the flower heads. Reject any flowers that are not in perfect condition. Remove the petals and lay them out on trays or sheets of newspaper. Place these somewhere dark and well ventilated, pulling them out to turn them from time to time until they are thoroughly dried.

Then take them out and blend the petals together, using roses, honeysuckle, jasmine, lavender, philadelphus, carnations and pinks, woodruff leaves, lemon verbena, sweetbriar, southernwood and the various mints.

Do not mix too many scents of different types together, but let one predominate. You can have a number of different mixes for different rooms.

You will need a fixative to ensure the scent lasts. Ground orris root is the traditional one, or you can buy gum benzoin or coumarin. Add orange or lemon peel.

When your pot-pourri is thoroughly mixed, store it in a sealed jar in the dark for at least a month, before putting it out in shallow bowls. The idea is that you dabble your fingers in the petals as you pass by, raising a scent powerfully evocative of summer.

Flowers are not the only dried things that look well for Christmas or any other winter decoration. Leaves, nuts, oranges, bark, fir cones, acorns and moss are all useful tools in this armoury. Slits cut in the rind of citrus

Why buy expensive Christmas decorations when there is a wealth of free material in the garden? Drying flowers is easy once you have mastered the art of picking them at the right time.

fruits will make them dry much quicker.

TABLETOP TOPIARY

Making 40cm (16in) cones.

These can look stunning either side of a fireplace or on a large table.

You will need:

Newspaper, pencil, 60cm (24in) piece of string, scissors, tape, florists' wire, snips, sphagnum moss, 2 x 45cm x 90cm (18in x 36in) squares of 2.5cm (1in) chicken wire, 4 x 18cm x 18cm (7in x 7in) squares of chicken wire.

1. Make a 90cm (36in) square from the newspaper. Tie the string to the pencil and use this as a compass to draw the largest circle that will fit on the paper. Fold the paper into equal quarters, unfold and cut along the fold lines and circle. These pieces are your patterns.

2. Cut out the chicken wire, using the newspaper patterns.

3. Roll each of the quarter circles into cones, joining them with the cut ends. Fill them with the moss.

4. Fold the bottom 5cm (2in) of each cone inwards to form a shelf as a base. Reinforce the bottom of each cone with an 18cm x 18cm (7in x 7in) square of chicken wire, securing it with the cut ends.

That alone looks great, mimicking the conventional yew topiary cone. You can embellish this by poking flowers or any other kind of decoration into it.

An alternative is to pin sheet moss over the outside of the chicken wire, securing it with florists' wire.

I have used this cone a number of times and nothing could be easier for making a dramatic, stylish decoration.

Oasis can be the ground for further embellishment – try pinning fir cones, acorns, cinnamon sticks or dried oranges to it. Play! This is all an aspect of gardening and if you can use garden materials in this way indoors, it helps the way you use the garden in the larger sense out of doors.

Tabletop topiary can made from living plants. **Rosemary** is particularly well suited to this. The variety *R. offinicalis* 'Miss Jessopp's Upright' can be made into a standard, and I have seen rosemary trained as an espalier and around wire frames. It should be potted in normal potting compost mixed 50/50 with sharp sand and with plenty of crocks or stones at the bottom of the pot. This is to ensure fast drainage, as rosemary hates sitting in water.

Thyme and **sage** are also fun to experiment with, clipping them and training to shape. The great advantage of using small plants like this is that it only takes a year or so to get the end result. They also smell good.

Cut a large circle out of newspaper, then cut it in four.

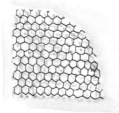

Use the newspaper patterns to cut out chicken wire and roll into cone shapes.

Fill with sphagnum moss and decorate with flowers.

HOLLY ETC

When we bring holly indoors around the time of the shortest day (21 December) to decorate the house or make wreaths of it, we are responding to an ancient pagan instinct to gather signs of permanence and vitality as charms against the encircling gloom and darkness of winter. Holly, with its bright red berries against rich green

brighter than those of any other plant. Of course by no means all hollies have berries. Only female plants bear berries and they must have a male plant reasonably nearby to fertilise them. Unfortunately you cannot always tell if a plant is male or female from its name: for example, 'Golden King' is a female and 'Golden Queen' a male. 'Silver Queen' is also a male. Very confusing.

If you do have a female plant, with a male to hand to provide pollination, you may still not have red berries. *Ilex*

lies is staggering, from the weird *I. a.* 'Crispa', whose whole being, trunk, branches and smooth leaves twist crazily, to the **hedgehog holly** (*I. a.* 'Ferox'), which has not only prickly edges to its leaves, but spikes all over each surface. The **'Highclere' hybrids** (*I.* x *alterclerensis*) are on the whole unprickly and more vigorous than *I. aquifolium* and its hybrids. You can get hollies that are practically all yellow with a touch of green, or hollies that are almost blue; milky hollies, hollies in every shade of green under the sun.

LOOKING AFTER YOUR HOLLY

Did you know that…

Despite being such a feature of the English landscape, holly is not fully hardy in this country. In a very cold winter it will lose all its leaves and every now and then a really cold spell will kill it.

Holly leaves are very inflammable and burn furiously when lit.

Holly will grow happily in the shade, although variegated types produce their best colours when grown in the sun. Once established, holly will itself cast such a deep shade that nothing will grow beneath it. It is very drought-resistant, and, once established, will not need watering. By the same token it is never very comfortable on wet, ill-drained soil.

Despite the risk of an icy wind causing leaf drop, most species of holly make an excellent protective barrier for other, more fragile plants. The wind has a natural pruning effect on holly, restricting growth and causing a denser formation that a tree growing in the middle of a wood. Clipping a holly hedge has much the same effect, and a really thick holly hedge is well nigh impenetrable. I love the story of Peter the Great, later seventeenth-century Czar

Variegated holly topiary at Barnsley House, Gloucestershire.

leaves is as vital a symbol of life as anything else.

Holly is one of my favourite trees. In spring its new leaves look almost wet in their glistening newness and in winter the berries last longer and shine

aquifolium 'Bacciflava' has yellow berries, like clusters of tiny lemons.

There are over 400 different species of holly and another 400 different cultivars and hybrids. **Common English holly** (*Ilex aquifolium*) is instantly recognisable by its deep green, prickly leaves in hedgerows and gardens across the country. But the range of different hol-

MISTLETOE

THE TRUTH IS THAT NO ONE REALLY KNOWS HOW TO GROW MISTLETOE. IT MUST HAVE CLEAN AIR – WHICH CUTS OUT MOST OF THE COUNTRY ANYWAY – AND THE SEED MIGHT WELL HAVE TO PASS THROUGH THE INTESTINES OF A BIRD TO GERMINATE SUCCESSFULLY. THE BEST WAY TO GROW YOUR OWN MISTLETOE IS TO SQUIDGE THE FRUIT – THE MILKY WHITE BERRIES – INTO THE CRACK OF A SUITABLE TREE, OR IN A FLAP MADE WITH YOUR KNIFE, BETWEEN MARCH AND MAY. MISTLETOE IS A PARASITE AND IS PICKY ABOUT ITS HOST. IT LOVES APPLE, LIKES POPLAR AND HAWTHORN, AND WILL GROW ON OAK. IT IS MORE LIKELY TO GROW ON ROUGH BARK THAN SMOOTH, WHERE THE BERRIES CAN GET WEDGED INTO A CREVICE. ITS NORMAL PROCESS OF GERMINATION IS FOR THE BERRY TO BE EATEN BY A BIRD (INCLUDING THE MISTLE THRUSH – HENCE THE NAME), WHICH WILL THEN FLY OFF TO A BRANCH NEARBY AND EITHER WIPE ITS BEAK CLEAN OF THE STICKY FLESH, ACCIDENTALLY DEPOSITING THE LITTLE BLACK SEED, OR IN SOME DIGESTIONARY FUTURE EXCRETE THE SEED. THIS WILL BE PARCELLED IN ITS OWN MANURE HEAP. THE RAIN WILL WASH THE SEED DOWN THE BARK UNTIL IT IS CAUGHT IN A CRACK, STILL WITH AN AMOUNT OF NOURISHMENT TO SEE IT ON ITS WAY. THE ROOTS OF THE SEEDLING GROW INWARDS TO THE HEARTWOOD OF THE BRANCH, EVENTUALLY REACHING RIGHT ROUND IT, THE ROOTS RADIATING INWARDS LIKE THE SPOKES OF A BICYCLE WHEEL. AS LONG AS THE TREE REMAINS HEALTHY THE MISTLETOE WILL FLOURISH, BUT IF THE TREE DIES, THEN SO MUST THE MISTLETOE. DID YOU KNOW... THE PRACTICE OF HANGING MISTLETOE AND KISSING BENEATH IT STEMS FROM THE TIME WHEN IT WAS HUNG ABOVE A DOOR AS A SIGN OF PEACE AND ANY VISITOR WAS GREETED WITH A KISS OF WELCOME. BUT EACH KISS SHOULD PROPERLY BE PAID FOR – WITH A BERRY PLUCKED FROM THE SPRIG. WHEN THE BERRIES ARE ALL GONE, THE KISSING HAS TO STOP.

of Russia, creating an afternoon's entertainment by ordering his servants to push him in a wheelbarrow through the middle of a vast holly hedge nearly 3m (9ft) high and 120m (400ft) long. They certainly knew how to enjoy themselves in those days.

But if you do have a holly hedge, think twice before planting it at the back of a flower border, because the leaves fall and remain prickly for years, spiking you every time you weed. If you clip holly regularly – whether in a hedge or single specimens – it will produce very few berries.

HOLLY TOPIARY

If you have a straggly holly tree or bush, there is a two-hour job that will transform both it and your garden.

Holly is ideal for abstract topiary (see pages 126 and 127). Hard clipping makes it produce leaves, so an empty, straggly area can become dense if it is clipped back. The three shapes best suited to Holly are 'Standards', 'Wedding Cakes' and 'Poodles'.

Because the trunk of holly is so smooth, it should be used as part of the

If you use holly as a barrier in your garden, it will keep almost anything out.

composition. Using shears, secateurs and a saw, attack the straggly holly to form it into a rough outline of the shape you want. Do not worry at this stage if it is not crisp and clean-looking. If need be, tie branches down or up with string to encourage them to grow horizontally. A standard keeps to the same shape, but poodles and wedding cakes can have tiers added as the tree grows if the fancy takes you. Either way, it will only need clipping once a year and will get better and better each time you do it.

TIP

SPRING IS THE BEST TIME TO PLANT HOLLY, OR, FAILING THAT, EARLY AUTUMN. BUT ONCE ESTABLISHED, IT HATES TO BE MOVED – SO THINK CAREFULLY BEFORE PLANTING! DO NOT WORRY IF SOME OF THE OLDER LEAVES FALL IN THE SPRING OR SUMMER AFTER PLANTING: IT IS OFTEN A SIGN THAT THE PLANT IS ROOTING HEALTHILY.

CHRISTMAS DAY FLOWERS

The Christmas garden is inevitably short on flowers. So it is terribly important to make the most of what will flower at this time of year and to plan ahead so that you can go into the garden on Christmas morning and collect a posy, however small, for the table.

The first flower for Christmas must be the **Christmas rose**. This, of course, is not a rose at all, but a hellebore, *Helleborus niger*. All the hellebores are superb winter flowerers, but the white petals of the Christmas rose with its yellow starburst of stamens inside are the most precious. Plant it in light shade with plenty of manure and leave it be: it resents being moved or mucked about.

You can never have too many hellebores at Christmas, if for no other reason than they make the most beautiful cut flower and they are also prone to damage by the rain, so may be ruined by the weather. But hellebores are expensive to buy as plants, so it makes sense to propagate from your initial stock. This is surprisingly easy for a plant that has a repuation for being a bit of a prima donna. All you do is this:

1. About the beginning of March, weed and prepare the soil around the base of each hellebore. Be careful not to damage the roots of the plant.

2. Do nothing.

3. The plant will drop seeds on to this immaculately prepared seedbed. These seeds will germinate into dozens of baby hellebores.

4. Very carefully lift the seedlings when they are large enough to handle – about Mayish.

5. Pot them up in potting compost and put them in light shade, protected from the extremes of weather.

6. Plant them out in their final position in early autumn.

Iris unguicularis is another Christmas stunner. It is curiously out of place in the drab pearly light of a northern midwinter, with its bluey violet flowers bravely anticipating the bulbs of spring and the irises of a hot June border. It is actually the heat of the previous summer that will dictate whether this flowers for Christmas — the hotter July and August are, the sooner the subsequent flowering will come. But it should, and usually does, provide rare colour for Christmas Day. Once cut the flowers only last a couple of days, so consider them a treat and enjoy them for the rest of their flowering days *in situ*.

They like a dry, sunny site, sheltered from cold winds. Keep them free from dead leaves, as this will encourage slugs: a good way to stop them chewing the plant is to give it a good mulch of grit. Slugs and snails hate this.

Like hellebores, this is a plant that dislikes being moved, but if you must, do it in August.

By the way – make sure that you buy the species and not one of the many forms. These can be perfectly nice, but all tend to flower later, in early spring.

For Christmas it must be *Iris unguicularis* pure and simple.

I am very fond of **winter pansies**, although many would think them a vulgar cliche. Well, I am all for a bit of vulgarity, especially at Christmas. Winter pansies are really a type of viola, *V. wittrockiana*. The 'Floral Dance', 'Ice Queen' and 'Universal' series are all winter-flowering, having been specially bred to tolerate low

Iris unguicularis: *plant in spring for flowers on Christmas Day.*

temperatures and poor light. Plant them with plenty of manure and with as much sun as possible. The secret of pansies is to pinch off the flowers after planting. This gives them a chance to develop strong roots and the subsequent flowers will be all the better for this initial decapitation.

SEASONAL SHRUBS

If you are to have a reasonable variety in your Christmas bunch of flowers, you will need to grow some shrubs that come into their own at this time of year. **Viburnums** top this list. *Viburnum bodnantense* 'Dawn' is the best known, with its fragrant pink flowers that seem impervious to ice or snow. *V. farreri* is another with highly scented flowers, this time white. *V.*

tinus is a compact shrub with evergreen leaves and a sprinkling of white flowers from December into spring.

Viburnums are pretty undistinguished for most of the year and should not be allowed to become too sprawly, otherwise their drab leaves and sparse habit outweigh the virtues of their winter flowers. Prune after flowering.

The **winter-flowering honeysuckle** (*Lonicera fragrantissima*) – which is distinctly a shrub and not a climber – has deliciously scented white flowers.

It has almost no other virtues, so celebrate these little bursts of exquisite scent by cutting them and bringing them into the house. It will grow very happily in shade, so another idea is to grow the bushes in pots which can be brought indoors or left just outside the back door while they are flowering, and then put out of the way for the rest of the year.

Wintersweet (*Chimonanthus praecox*) needs a sheltered, sunny spot and good soil and will train as a climber up a south wall, but is really a sprawly shrub with scruffy leaves. When the leaves drop, yellow flowers with purple centres appear, smelling as sweetly as any. This is a truism of most winter-flowering shrubs: their flowers perform on leafless branches. A

word of warning about wintersweet, though: it takes at least six years before flowering. Given that the plant you buy is likely to be three years old, that means putting up with its dullness for up to five years before being rewarded with its especially fragrant harvest. But it is worth the wait.

An evergreen shrub that will provide flowers now is **mahonia**. Not every type, but *M. media*, *M. acanthifolia* and *M. lomariifolia* can be depended upon. Their leaves are prickly and hostile, but the flowers richly yellow and fragrant. They prefer shade to sun, so are useful for the odd dark corner.

CHRISTMAS CLIMBERS

There are a few climbers that will do their thing for you on Christmas Day and which are an essential element of any garden in midwinter. **Winter jasmine**

The Christmas rose (Helleborus niger) *makes the most beautiful cut flower for the Christmas table. Grow lots, as they are wonderful in the garden, too.*

(*Jasminum nudiflorum*) is easy to grow, but is often a green squiggle with only a few dots of yellow flower. To get it to flower as fully as it can, you need to prune it each year. It is not self-supporting, so must have a basic framework of stems which are tied to trellis or some pretty firm support. Cut everything else hard back to this framework after flowering. Also, a third of the main stems should be cut to the ground each year. Complicated? Not really, and it does transform an untidy straggle to a beautiful mass of yellow flowers in midwinter.

Each Christmas posy will be different, depending on the season – some years you will have primroses, snowdrops and even rosemary flowering, other years you will be scratching around for just the odd bloom. But it is worth planning your spring planting to provide something for a floral Christmas present to yourself.

One of the best winter-flowering shrubs: Viburnum tinus.

FINALLY,
A WORD OF CAUTION

DON'T TAKE THE GARDEN TOO SERIOUSLY…
IF YOU ARE NOT HAVING FUN, THEN YOU ARE
DOING IT WRONG. TAKE IT EASY, TAKE YOUR TIME
AND DO IT YOUR OWN WAY. FIND OUT WHAT YOU
LIKE ABOUT GARDENING AND KEEP DOING IT. IT IS
BOUND TO BE THE RIGHT THING FOR BOTH YOU
AND YOUR GARDEN.

APPENDIX

A GUIDE TO THE SEASONS

Many gardening books refer to the seasons as though that were explanation enough for when to do various jobs in the garden. I know that I have often been confused by this. In practice – allowing for regional variations – the following is a reasonable rule of thumb:

SPRING   March, April, May
SUMMER   June, July. August
AUTUMN   September, October, November
WINTER   December, January, February

FERTILISERS AND FEEDS

The three main ingredients of garden fertiliser are nitrogen, potash and phosphates. It might be helpful to know what each contributes to the welfare of your plants.

Nitrogen (N): makes things grow more vigorously, especially foliage and green matter. Works as an activator in the compost heap. Can be detrimental to flowering and fruiting if provided in excess; too vigorous growth makes for weak, sappy plants more prone to pests, diseases and wind damage.
Evidence of nitrogen deficiency: leaves appear pale green or even yellowish; plant looks spindly and undernourished.
Cause of deficiency: poor light, very lightweight soils in which nitrogen is leached away, or containers.
Remedial action: feed with: dried blood, sulphate of ammonia, manure, leguminous green manures such as annual lupins, bonemeal, fish blood and bone, seaweed, cocoa shells.

Potash (K20): potash or potassium (K) is used by the plant to develop flowers and fruit.
Evidence of potash deficiency: the peformance of the plant suffers: fruiting is lessened and flowering is not up to scratch. The leaves become brown around the edges and foliage turns blue, yellow or purple. Sometimes leaves roll inwards.
Cause of deficiency: growing in very chalky or very peaty soils, or very sandy, light soils where all nutrients are quickly washed away.
Remedial action: improving the soil texture by digging and adding plenty of organic matter will improve potash retention in light soils. Feed with a fertiliser that contains potash, such as sulphate of potash, seaweed, rock phosphate, wood ash, cocoa shells, potassium chloride and potassium sulphate.

Phosphate (P205): phosphates – compounds of phosphorus (P) – develop strong root growth, so are essential for all plants.
Evidence of phosphate deficiency: the plant does not thrive and the leaves look dull and yellowish.
Causes of deficiency: very waterlogged soil or very acid (peat) soils.
Remedial action: dig as deeply as possible, mixing in plenty of organic matter and horticultural grit. Used raised beds in very bad areas. Feed with bonemeal, superphosphate, fish blood and bone.

Bonemeal is very slow-acting, but particularly useful for shrubs and trees. A sprinkled handful should be applied every time you plant anything. A dressing of bonemeal in early spring, after weeding and before mulching, will help spring growth.
Fish blood and bone is another excellent general organic fertiliser, as is **Growmore**, which is generally used as a dressing on soil a few weeks before planting or sowing vegetables.

RECOMMENDED BOOKS

I referred to a great many books while writing this book, some of them very specialist indeed. I am an avid collector of garden books, but there are a few that I return to time and time again. They are:

The RHS Gardeners' Encyclopedia of Plants and Flowers (Dorling Kindersley, 1989)
The RHS Gardeners' Encyclopedia of Gardening (Dorling Kindersley, 1992)
Hilliers Manual of Trees and Shrubs (David & Charles, 1991)
Peter Beales *Classic Roses* (Collins Harvill, 1985)
A.M. Clevely *Topiary* (Collins, 1988)
Margaret Elphinstone and Julia Langley *The Green Gardener's Handbook* (Thorsons, 1990, new edition as *The Organic Gardeners' Handbook*, 1995)
Hugh Johnson *The Principles of Gardening* (Mitchell Beazley, 1979)
Tony Lord *Best Borders* (Frances Lincoln, 1994)
Christopher Lloyd *The Well-Tempered Garden* (Penguin, 1987)
Christopher Lloyd *In My Garden* (Bloomsbury, 1993)
Eleanor Perenyi *Green Thoughts* (Pimlico, 1994)
Roger Phillips and Martyn Rix *The Pan Garden Plants Series* ((Pan, 5 volumes, new editions 1993–95)
Rosemary Verey *The Garden in Winter* (Windward, 1988)

INDEX

INDEX